RESERVATION : A QUEST FOR JUSTICE

Dedicated To

Those Who followed the footsteps of their emancipator and the architect of the Constitution Dr. Babasaheb Ambedkar, and who secured the utmost benefit of the costitutional safeguards and developed their personality and family and achieved their moral and material well-being; and who helped their brethren in their development and who were amidst them with mind and body in their struggle for human rights and who served the nation in different capacities and with full devotion.

Contents

Preface

It gives me a great pleasure to bring out the book, "Reservation : A Quest for Justice."

Indian Society is, obviously based on caste system, graded inequality and untouchabiity. The invidious discriminations based on untouchability caused a great harm to the so called untouchables and ultimately to the nation as a whole. We had to wage a war against the British imperialism at the one hand and to other against the Brahmanic Traditionalism during the pre-independence period. Ultimately, we became free and formed our own Constitution.

We have pledged to reconstruct the Indian Society on the sublime values of Justice, liberty, equality and fraternity. We have to protect and respect the fundamental rights of each and every citizen and sincerely apply the directive principles of state policy in governance of the country so that everybody would be able to secure justice, social, economic and political. This fundamental objective prevails over and reflects virtually in various provisions of the Constitution. All the laws in force are expected to be in conformity with the Constitutional philosophy and various provisions.

We have adopted several means and methods to combat inequality, untouchability, illiteracy and all sorts of injustice. Reservation in education, employment and political field is one of the means to achieve our Constitutional objective of social justice. We are, undoubtedly marching ahead towards the goal, but very steadily. There are certain impediments in our way. Unless we discern them we cannot obliterate them.

It is only the caste prejudice against the so called Depressed Classes which is the biggest obstacle in the way to social justice. Caste, is, of course, a notional phenomenon; based on Traditional Hindu religious mythology. Now, we have adopted a new philosophy of liberty, equality and fraternity with full deliberation, consideration and determination. We can remove the caste prejudice with this philosophy but still it is in vogue. Some times the caste prejudice takes the form of hatred towards the Depressed Classes, some times it takes the form of caste violence and atrocities. They are deprived of all the benefits of economic development. This leads to chaos and crisis in the society. It is said very loudly that, the weaker sections of the society have got abundant, but it is much ado for nothing. Still the oppressed classes are suffering to a great extent.

In order to combat with such an oppressive situation it is necessary to implement the policy of reservation in all the fields under relevant articles of the Constitution, with all sincerity and honesty. The policy of reservation is one of the means "to preserve and promote the essence of equality." Persons of reserved category may be able to remove the inferiority complex from the minds of their own brethren by their own example and do the needful with the help of power and authority. This way we may be able to bring about necessary change in the society. Education and employment would certainly be helpful and efficacious to the underprivileged people in achieving progress. Thus, They would be uplifted to the higher level and joined with the main stream of society. This will certainly strengthen the nation as a whole.

While entering the new age of global society we have to honestly develop a new social order envisaged under the Constitution of India. As an active member of UNO and other Peace organizations, we have to adhere and conform to the developing concept of human rights in the world scenario.

Thus, the main purpose of this book is to take into account some of the important arguments raised against the policy of reservation meant for the socio-economic development of the weaker sections of the Indian society and to reveal the foulness in those arguments, in the light of constitutional provisions and judicial pronouncements to that effect. I hope that every person having interest in this area of study would appreciate my endeavour in writing this book.

I am grateful to Dr. S.N. Busi, IRES (Rtd.) Hyderabad A.P. for his help and advice. I am thankful to Prof. Ajmer Sinh Kajal, Rohatak (Harayana), P.K. Manokaran Vellore (T.N.) Ayu. Yogesh Varhade (Nagpur), M. Sayalu (Brainsa, A.P.), and Dr. G.R. Gajbhiye (Aurangabad).

I am thankful to Shri Dhage, Librarian, Dr. Ambedkar College of Law, Aurangabad, Shri D.K. Kale, Librarian M.P. Law College, Aurangabad and Shri Bhimrao Chavan, Asst.Librarian, Dr. Babasaheb Ambedkar Marathwada University, Aurangabad for their valuable co-operation.

I acknowledge the help and assistance of my son Deepak Kshirsagar, Asst. Professor, Maniyar Law College, Jalgaon.

I am thankful to Kotgire Brothers for preparing typescript of the book.

I am really indebted to all the authors and authorities who have graciously enlightened and enriched this study. I am thankful to the Publisher of the bock for having published it in a short duration.

Date : 26th November 2012 **Dr. R.K. Kshirsagar**
Place : Aurangabad

1

Introduction

The unique feature of the Hindu Society is its base in the divisive caste system and dehumanizing untouchability. It has, obviously ruined the nation as a whole in general and the so called untouchables in particular. Therefore, the struggle for the annihilation of caste and abolition of untouchability was launched quite a long back. It could not be, however, successful because of increasing adverse religious rules and custom, political indifference and grinding poverty.

However because of the compelling strategic political situation emerged during the British rule, the Indian Society had to accept certain reforms. Ultimately, under the able leadership of Dr. Babasaheb Ambedkar, the chief architect of the Constitution of India, it became possible to legally take out the vicious vigour of the caste system and abolish untouchability. Moreover, the Constitution has pledged to uplift the weaker sections of the society to the higher level by providing certain protective safeguards. Thus, the quest for justice is in vogue with the help of constitutional safeguards.

1.1 Background of Constitutional Safeguards

(a) Untouchability has been a distinguiushing feature of Hindu social system. The people subjected to untouchability were called "untouchables". The so called untouchables were lowest of the low in the hierarchy of Hindu Caste System, and they were subjected to invidious discriminations on the ground of untouchability.

In the opinion of Dr. Babasaheb Ambedkar, untouchability was developed from 400 AD to 600 AD and it was deliberately imposed by the Brahmanic forces on the so called "Broken Men", who were adherents of rational and egalitarian Buddhism as they were unwilling to accept the supremacy of Brahmanism, discard Buddism and abandon beef-eating[1]. Thus untouchability came into existence merely out of hatred and jeolousy of Buddhism. Of course, "untouchability is the notion of defilement, pollution, contamination and the ways and means of getting rid of that defilement."[2]

It was, however not acceptable to the so called untouchables. It is but natural that no society would willingly accept the system of its own subjugation. Consequently, with the origin and development of untouchability the movement of its opposition also came into existence. But, due to adverse socio-political situation, limited resources and stringent religious rules contained in the Manusmriti, the so called untouchables could not get success in their struggle for emancipation. As a protest against Hinduism, some of the victims who were subjected to virulent form of untouchability were converted to Islam and Christianity and Sikhism. Some of the saints among the touchables and untouchables also tried to remove untouchability from the Hindu Social System; but in vain.

Later on, the untouchables liberation movement got an impetus during the British rule. Knowing the martial qualities and honesty of the untouchables and their strategic role in the Indian history, the British authorities gave opportunity to the untouchables to enter the British Army. The untouchable soldiers also fought alongwith the British Army against the forces of the native princes and feudal lords with a determination to defeat the high caste autocratic rulers. The role of the untouchables in the war of Bhima-Koregaon in 1818 and the mutiny of 1857 was decisive and historic. Due to military service, the untouchables got livelihood, opportunity to exemplify their valour and earned confidence, but there was no significant change in their untouchable status.

However, with the emergence of democratic institutions, spread of education, means of communication and independence movement in India in the British rule the untouchable's liberation movement gathered some momentum. The christian missionaries and Islamic revivalists also were active in bringing awareness to the masses. The liberal and humanist Hindu reformers and their organizations like Brahmo Samaj, Arya Samaj, Tattvabodhini Sabha, Manava Dharma Sabha and many other organizations worked for bringing about social change. Even Dalit organisations like South India Buddhist Association (1890), Adi-Dravid Mahajan Sabha (1891)

Sanmargbodhak Nirashrit Samaj (1903) Ramnami Mahasabha (1901) Somavanshiya Mitra Samaj (1904) Sadhujan Paripalan Yogam (1905) Antyaj Samaj (1906) Jagan Mitra Mandal (1906) Pratyaksha Raksha Deva Sabha (1908) Walmiki Sabha (1910) Hindu Social Service League (1911) Akhil Bengal Ṇamshudra Sangh (1912) Bharatiya Dusadh Maha Sabha (1914) Jatav Veer Mahasabha (1917) etc. were actively working for their untouchable brethren.[3]

The Indian National Congress (1885) and The Muslim League (1906) were active in the political field The leaders like W.C. Banerji, Gopal Krishna Gokhale, Dadabhai Naoroji, Feroz, Shah Mehta, Surendra Nath Banerji were leading the national independence movement under the banner of Indian National Congress. The leaders like Aga Khan, Muhammed Ali, and others led the Muslim League in those days. In view of the advent of democratic process, the Muslims were under the apprehension that the Hindu majority would dominate and overpower the Muslim minority. Therefore, the Muslim league demanded separate electorate for Muslims. The British Government passed the Act of 1909 and provided among others, for separate electorate to the Muslims. Even then, the Muslims felt that they would not be benefitted in the politics of number in the legislature. In order to thwart the dominance of majority Hindus, the Muslim League demanded that the untouchables ought not to be included in Hindu Population in the ensuing census of 1910. The census commissioner for the first time divided the Hindus under three separate categories (1) Hindus, (2) Animist or Tribals, and (3) the Untouchables or Depressed Classes. This was a great jolt to the Hindus, who were already disturbed because of untouchables' conversions. Consequently, they started a campaign to retain the untouchables in their own fold.

In the mean time Bengal, which was partitioned, was reunited in 1911. The Hindus met in a conference held at Haridwar in 1915 where they formed an organization of the Hindus called "Sarvadeshik Sabha", to unite Hindus, avert conversions and eradicate untouchability. Lucknow Pact was made in 1916, with the initiative of Hindus and Muslims, but the British Government put a pre-condition that all the communities including the Depressed Classes must approve it. The Depressed Classes, however accepted to approve the Lucknow Pact provided the Indian National Congress resolves to remove untouchability. This was decided in the conference of the Depressed Classes held under the presidentship of Sir Narayan Chandavarkar under the aegis of Depressed Classes Mission Society in November 1917.[4] In the mean time Shri M.B. Dadabhoy moved a resolution in the Imperial Legislative Council on 16th March 1916 for the upliftment of the Depressed Classes. However, the said resolution was withdrawn on the positive assurance of the Congress to that effect. In this backdrop, the Indian National Congress in its annual session held in December 1917 at Calcutta under the presidentship of Ani Beasant passed the resolution against the practice of untouchability.[5]

(b) Dr. Babasaheb Ambedkar just entered the arena of Socio-Political reforms in India. He viewed the problem of Depressed Classes from political point of view. He thought, the problem of Depressed Class was "eminently political and must be treated as such."[6] This unique approach led him to think that, "the problem of the Depressed Classes will never be solved unless they get political power in their own hands."[7] Therefore, he demanded separate electorate for the Depressed Classes at first on 27th January 1919 while giving evidence before the South-borough franchise Committee. He considered that, "Untouchability constitutes a definite set of interests which the untouchables alone can speak for. Hence it is evident that we must find the untouchables to represent their grievances which are their interests and secondly, we must find them in such numbers as will constitute a force sufficient to claim redress."[8]

Thus, the year 1919 marked an era of emergence of Down-Trodden Communities as a "Separate Element" in the Politics of India under the able and dynamic leadership of Dr. Babasaheb Ambedkar. However, in his report submitted to the Simon Commission in 1929, he demanded adult franchise and joint-electorates with reserved seats. While giving evidence before the Simon Commission in 1928, he replied to a question, "if there is no adult franchise?" saying that "then we would ask for separate electorate."[9] Thus, in the wake of non-acceptance of adult franchise, he was constrained to demand for separate electorate.

In order to decide the nature of future constitution and settle the growing communal problems amicably; the British Govt. convened Three Round Table Conferences in London during 1930-32 consisting of the representatives of all the political parties and various interests. The Depressed Classes were represented by Dr.Babasaheb Ambedkar and Rao Bahadur R. Srinivasan. The memorandum submitted to the Round Table Conference by them bears, inter alia, the following demand.

"The Depressed Classes must be given sufficient political power to influence legislative and executive action for the purpose of securing their welfare. In view of this they demand that the following provisions shall be made in the electoral law so as to give them, (1) Right to adequate representation in the Legislatures of the country, provincial and central, (2) Right to elect their own men as their representatives, (a) by adult suffrage; and (b) by separate electorates for the first ten years and thereafter by joint electorates and reserved seats."[10]

Dr. Babasaheb Ambedkar could ably convince all the delegates to the Round Table Conference about the judiciousness of his demand. However, Mahatma Gandhi strongly opposed the demand of separate electorate to the Depressed Classes. He was of the view that the Depressed Classes do not need political rights at all. He said very categorically before the R.T.C. that, "what these people need more than election to the legislatures is protection from social and religious persecution."[10(a)] He thought that the Depressed Classes were an inseparable part of Hindu Society and separate electorate would creat "a division in Hinduism", which he was not ready to tolerate at any cost.

However, the British Government fully convinced with the merit of the demand made by Dr. Babasaheb Ambedkar declared the Communal Award on 16th August 1932. The Communal Award inter alia envisaged separate electorate for the Depressed Classes.

The Scheduled Castes, however got 71 seats out of 1463 Legislative Assembly Seats in the eight (seven) British Provinces, including Madras (18), Bombay (10), Bengal (10), United Provinces (12), Bihar and Orissa (7), Central Provinces (10), and Assam (4), these seats were to be filled by election, "from special constituencies in which only members of the "depressed classes" electorally qualified will be entitled to vote."[11]

Mahatma Gandhi who was in Yerwada Jail in those days started his epic fast on 20th Sept.1932. Althogh he previously signed the pledge to be bound by the verdict of the Prime Minister on the issue of communal problem, he could not stick up to his own words.

Dr. Babasaheb Ambedkar was caught in a dilemma either to save the life of the leader of the nation or to safeguard the interests of approximately five crores of his brethren. Ultimately both the parties came to an agreement known in history as "Poona-Pact", on 24th September 1932.

TEXT OF THE POONA PACT

(1) There shall be seats reserved for the Depressed Classes out of the general electorate seats in the Provincial Legislatures as follows :

Madras	30
Bombay with Sind	15
Punjab	8
Bihar and Orissa	18
Central Provinces	20
Assam	7
Bengal	30
United Provinces	20
Total :	**148**

These figures are based on total strength of the Provincial councils announced in the Prime Minister's decision.

(2) Election to these seats shall be by joint electorates, subject however, to the following procedure :

All the members of the Depressed Classes registered in the general electoral roll in a constituency will form an electoral college, which will elect a panel of four candidates belonging to the Depressed Classes for each of such reserved seats, by the method of the single vote; the four getting the highest number of votes in such Primary election, shall be candidates for election by the general electorate.

(3) Representation of the Depressed Classes in the Central Legislature shall likewise be on the principle of joint electorates and reserved seats by the method of Primary election in the manner provided for in clause (2) above, for their representation in the Provincial Legislatures.

(4) In the Central Legislature, eighteen per cent of seats allotted to the general electorate for British India in the said Legislature shall be reserved for the Depressed Classes.

(5) The system of Primary election to a panel of Candidates for election to the Central and Provincial Legislature, as hereinbefore mentioned, shall come to an end after the first ten years, unless terminated sooner by mutual agreement under the provision of clause (6) below.

(6) The system of representation of the Depressed Classes by reserved seats in the Provincial and Central Legislatures as provided for in clauses (1) and (4) shall continue until determined by mutual agreement between the communities concerned in the settlement.

(7) Franchise for the Central and Provincial Legislatures for the Depressed Classes shall be as indicated in the Lothian Committee Report.

(8) There shall be no disabilities attaching to anyone on the ground of his being a member of the Depressed Class in regard to any elections to local bodies or appointment to the Public Services.

Every endeavour shall be made to secure fair representation of the Depressed Classes in these respects, subject to such educational qualifications as may be laid down for appointment to the Public Services.

(9) In every Province out of the educational grant, an adequate sum shall be earmarked for providing educational facilities to the Members of the Depressed Classes.[12]

Thus, according to Poona-Pact the Depressed Classes were to get 148 reserved seats in the British Provincial Assemblies 12(a) and 18 per cent of the seats from British India in the Central Legislative Assembly. They were to be elected by "joint-electorate" with reserved seats. They were also to get fair representation in Public Services and they would be entitled to educational facilities.

Although Dr. Babasaheb Ambedkar was reluctant to accept the Poona-Pact, he accepted it under the unique situation. It would not be appropriate to assess its merit in the background of present situation. There must be some covert and concrete reason in conceding to give more seats to the scheduled castes than they were to get under the Communal Award. This speaks a volume as to why Gandhiji accepted the Poona-Pact. It was however an agreement between the two parties for sharing power on the agreed formula. It is, undoubtedly one of the basic and historical documents on which our present polity is based. Its spirit is lying in the present constitution.

c) In keeping with the promise, the British Govt. passed the Government of India Act, 1935 in August 1935. The Act provided for representation to the Scheduled Castes in the Federal Assembly as well as in the Provincial Legislative Assemblies as settled under the Poona-Pact. Accordingly, the Scheduled Castes got 19 seats from the quota of 105 General Seats in the Federal Assembly and 151 seats in the Provincial Legislative Assemblies of various states.[13] There were 6 seats in upper chamber of the Federal Assembly, but no seats were alloted for upper chambers of the State Assemblies for the scheduled castes. Table 1:1, Table 1:2 and Table 1:3.

There was, however no allocation of seats under the Act of 1935 for the Scheduled Castes in the upper chamber of The Provincial Legislature.

Under the Government of India Act, 1935 elections to the Provincial Assemblies were held in the beginning of 1937. The Congress formed ministries in 7 Provinces and the Muslim League formed its ministries in 4 provinces. The League was in favour of coalition ministries in all the Provinces, but the Congress did not

TABLE 1.1

Allocation of Seats Under the Government of India act, 1935, for the Lower House of the Federal Legislature for British India

Province	*Total Seats*	*General Seats*		*Sikh Seats*	*Mahomedan Seats*	*Anglo Indian Seats*	*European Seats*	*Indian Christian Seats*	*Seats for Representatives of Commerce and Industry*	*Land holders Seats*	*Seats for Representatives of Labour*	*Women's Seats*
		Total of General Seats	*General Seats reserved for Scheduled Castes*									
1	**2**	**3**	**4**	**5**	**6**	**7**	**8**	**9**	**10**	**11**	**12**	**13**
Madras	37	19	4	--	8	1	1	2	2	1	1	2
Bombay	30	13	2	--	6	1	1	1	3	1	2	2
Bengal	37	10	3	--	17	1	1	1	3	1	2	1
United Provinces	37	19	3	--	12	1	1	1	--	1	--	1
The Punjab	30	6	1	6	14	--	1	1	--	1	--	1
Bihar	30	16	2	--	9	--	1	1	--	1	1	1

(Table Contd.)

(Contd. Table 1.1)

Province	Total Seats	General Seats		Sikh Seats	Mahomedan Seats	Anglo Indian Seats	European Seats	Indian Christian Seats	Seats for Representatives of Commerce and Industry	Land holders Seats	Seats for Representatives of Labour	Women's Seats
		Total of General Seats	General Seats reserved for Scheduled Castes									
Central Provinces and Berer	15	9	2	--	3	--	--	--	--	--	1	--
Assam	10	4	1	--	3	--	1	1	--	--	1	--
North-West Frontier Province	5	1	--	--	4	--	--	--	--	--	--	--
Orissa	5	4	1	--	1	--	--	--	--	--	--	--
Sind	5	1	--	--	3	--	1	--	--	--	--	--
British Baluchistan	1	--	--	--	1	--	--	--	--	--	--	--

(Table Contd.)

(Contd. Table 1.1)

Province	*Total Seats*	*General Seats*		*Sikh Seats*	*Mahomedan Seats*	*Anglo Indian Seats*	*European Seats*	*Indian Christian Seats*	*Seats for Representatives of Commerce and Industry*	*Land holders Seats*	*Seats for Representatives of Labour*	*Women's Seats*
		Total of General Seats	*General Seats reserved for Scheduled Castes*									
Delhi	2	1	--	--	1	--	--	--	--	--	--	--
Ajmer-Merwara	1	1	--	--	--	--	--	--	--	--	--	--
Coorg	1	1	--	--	--	--	--	--	--	--	--	--
Non-Provincial Seats	4	--	--	--	--	--	--	--	3	--	1	--
Total :	**250**	**105**	**19**	**6**	**82**	**4**	**8**	**8**	**11**	**7**	**10**	**9**

Source : DBAWS(8) p. 448.

TABLE 1.2

Allocation of Seats Under The Government of India Act, 1935, for the Upper Chamber of the Federal Legislature for British India

Province or Community	*Total Seats*	*General Seats*	*Seats for Scheduled Castes*	*Sikh Seats*	*Mahomedan Seats*	*Women's Seats*
1	**2**	**3**	**4**	**5**	**6**	**7**
Madras	20	14	1	--	4	1
Bombay	16	10	1	--	4	1
Bengal	20	8	1	--	10	1
United Provinces	20	11	1	--	7	1
The Punjab	16	3	--	4	8	1
Bihar	16	10	1	--	4	1
Central Provinced and Berar	8	6	1	--	1	--
Assam	5	3	--	--	2	--

(Table Contd.)

(Contd. Table 1.2)

Province or Community	Total Seats	General Seats	Seats for Scheduled Castes	Sikh Seats	Mahomedan Seats	Women's Seats
North-West Frontier Province	5	1	--	--	4	--
Orissa	5	4	--	--	1	--
Sind	5	2	--	--	3	--
British Baluchistan	1	--	--	--	1	--
Delhi	1	1	--	--	--	--
Ajmer-Merwara	1	1	--	--	--	--
Coorg	1	1	--	--	--	--
Anglo-Indians	1	--	--	--	--	--
Europeans	7	--	--	--	--	--
Indian Christians	2	--	--	--	--	--
Total :	**150**	**75**	**6**	**4**	**49**	**6**

Source : DBAWS(8) p. 449.

TABLE 1.3

Allocation of Seats Under The Government of India Act, 1935, for the Lower House in Each Provincial Legislature

Province	Total Seats	General Seats		Seats for representatives of backward areas and areas	Sikh Seats	Mahomedan Seats	Anglo-Indian Seats	European Seats	Indian Christian Seats	Seats for Representatives of commerce, industry, mining and planting	Land-holders Seats	University Seats	Seats for representatives of labour	Seats for Women				
		Total of General Seats	General Seats reserved for Schedule Castes											General	Sikh	Mahomedan	Anglo-Indian	Indian Christian
1	2	3	4	5	6	7	8	9	10	11	12	13	14	15	16	17	18	19
Madras	215	146	30	1	--	28	2	3	8	6	6	1	6	6	--	1	--	1
Bombay	175	114	15	1	--	29	2	3	3	7	2	1	7	5	--	1	--	--
Bengal	250	78	30	--	--	117	3	11	2	19	5	2	8	2	--	2	1	--

(Table Contd.)

(Contd. Table 1.3)

Province	Total Seats	General Seats		Seats for representatives of backward areas and	Sikh Seats	Mahomedan Seats	Anglo-Indian Seats	European Seats	Indian Christian	Seats for Representatives of commerce. industry.	Land-holders Seats	University Seats	Seats for representatives of labour	Seats for Women				
		Total of General Seats	General Seats reserved for Schedule Castes											General	Sikh	Mahomedan	Anglo-Indian	Indian Christian
United Provinces	228	140	20	--	--	64	1	2	2	3	6	1	3	4	--	2	--	--
The Punjab	175	42	8	--	31	84	1	1	2	1	5	1	3	1	1	2	--	--
Bihar	152	86	15	7	--	39	1	2	1	4	4	1	3	3	--	1	--	--
Central Provinces and Berar	112	84	20	1	--	14	1	1	--	2	3	1	2	3	--	--	--	--
Assam	108	47	7	9		34	--	1	1	11	--	--	4	1	--	--	--	--
North-West Frontier Province	50	9	--	--	3	36	--	--	--	--	2	--	--	--	--	--	--	--
Orissa	60	44	6	5	--	4	--	--	1	1	2	--	1	2	--	--	--	--
Sind	60	18	--	--	--	33	--	2	--	2	2	--	1	1	--	1	--	--

Source : DBAWS(8) p. 446.

concede the said proposal. This gave rise to Communal tension in the Country.

When the Second World War was started in 1939, the British Government declared India to be a belligerent country without consulting Indian Leaders. As a protest against the said decision, the congress ministers in all the provinces resigned and the governors suspended the constitution in those provinces. However, the Muslim League continued to be in government. This gave rise to communal controversy and crisis.[14] Ultimately, the Muslim League at its Lahore convention of 1940, held under the leadership of Barrister M.A. Jinnah resolved to have a separate Muslim state for them, to be called Pakistan.[15]

In order to solve this communal deadlock the viceroy reorganized the executive council in 1941. His Majesty's Government sent Sir Stafford Cripps to India in 1942 to make a definite offer of dominion status to India after the end of war. This offer also could not satisfy the Indian Leaders. The Congress raised the solgan of "Quit India" calling upon the British to withdraw from India. The agitation was however forcibly suppressed by the British Government.

When the second world war was at its height, the viceroy had set up a Defence Advisory Committee in July 1941. Dr. Babasaheb Ambedkar was nominated as a member on the said committee. Making the best use of this opportunity, Dr. Babasaheb Ambedkar appealed to the Government to restart the recruitment of the untouchables in British military. His demand was conceded favourably. The First Mahar Battalion was raised in September 1941.[16] The Mazhabis and Ramdasi Sikhs also were recruited in the British Army.

In the mean time Dr. Babasaheb Ambedkar became the Labour member in the Viceroy's Executive Council in July 1942. In August 1943 he could secure 8.33 per cent reservation in Government Services for the Scheduled Castes. He could secure the approval of the Government to the Post-Matric Scholarship Scheme for the Scheduled Castes in 1944. This facility was extended to the Scheduled Tribes in 1948.

(d) By that time the Indian National movement under the aegis of Congress and other organizations became very strong and widespread. Mahatma Gandhi made it more popular. Subhash Chandra Bose and his Azad Hind Sena gave a heroic fight against the colonial power in the second world war. Even the Indian Navy revolted against the British imperialism in Feb.1946. All these events led the British Government to annoance that soon they would accord political freedom to India.

The British Government under the Primeministership of Mr. Clement Attlee decided to accelerate the process of giving self-government to India. It sent out a Cabinet Mission consisting of three cabinet ministers to settle rising unrest in India. The cabinet mission declared its plan amidst chaos on 16th May 1946. The provisions of the plan were as under.

(1) There should be a Union of India consisting of British India and the Indian states. The union would deal with foreign affairs, defence and communications.

(2) All subjects other than the union subjects and all residuary subjects should vest in the provinces.

(3) The states would retain all subjects other than those ceded to the union.

(4) The Constitution of Union of India would be framed by the constitution making body. The Legislative Assemblies of the Provinces would elect the members of that body on the basis of one representative for one million of the population. Thus, elections to the Constituent Assembly was held indirectly.

The Sikh and Muslim legislators would elect the quota of their communities as determined on the basis of population.

The representatives of the provinces were to divide themselves into three sections A, B and C. They would have the strength as under :

TABLE 1.4

SECTION – A

S.No.	*Province*	*General*	*Muslim*	*Total*
1.	Madras	45	4	49
2.	Bombay	19	2	21
3.	United Provinces	47	8	55
4.	Bihar	31	5	36
5.	Central Provinces	16	1	17
6.	Orissa	9	0	9
Total		**167**	**20**	**187**

SECTION – B

S.No.	*Province*	*General*	*Muslim*	*Sikh*	*Total*
7.	Punjab	8	16	4	28
8.	N.W.F.P.	0	3	0	3
9.	Sind	1	3	0	4
Total		**9**	**22**	**4**	**35**

SECTION - C

	Province	*General*	*Muslim*	*Total*
10.	Bengal	27	33	60
11.	Assam	7	3	10
Total :		**34**	**36**	**70**
Total :		**210**	**784**	**292**

Total for British India	**292**
Total for Indian States	**93**
Total :	**385**[17]

However, in the meantime due to partition of India, some parts of Indian Territory merged with Pakistan and nearabout 600 Indian states were merged with India. Therefore, the Constituent Assembly had undergone some changes in its strength. Eventually, there were 235 representatives of the provinces and 72 representatives of the Princely States in the Constituent Assembly. The statewise strength of the Constituent Assembly on 23rd Aug. 1949 was as under : Table 1:5 and Table 1:6.

1.2 Framing of the Constitution of India

According to Cabinet Mission Plan the elections to the Constituent Assembly were held in July 1946. The Muslim League, however decided to boycott the Constituent Assembly. The Sikh members decided to participate in the constitution making. The Constituent Assembly was firstly convened on 9th December 1946. Dr. Sachhitanand Sinha being the senior most person among the members, got the privilege of presiding over the first session of the Constituent Assembly. However, Dr. Rajendra Prasad was elected President of the Constituent Assembly. Dr. H.C. Mukherjee was elected Vice-President of the Constituent Assembly.

Dr. Babasaheb Ambedkar, who was very keen to safeguard the interests of the Scheduled Castes in the now constitution of India, got elected from Bengal on the Constituent Assembly. Later, he submitted a Memorandum, "States and Minorities", on 15th March 1947 to the Constituent Assembly on behalf of the working committee of the All India Scheduled Castes ferderation and demanded, inter alia, for separate electorate, adequate reservations in the government services and educational facilities for the scheduled castes in the United States of India."[19]

Lord Wavell invited Pandit Nehru to form Interim Government on Sept.12, 1946. Muslim League joined the Interim

TABLE 1.5
Party / Communitywise Break Up of Seats (For British India) was as follows :

S.No.	*Party*	*Hindus*	*SC*	*Muslim*	*Anglo Indians*	*Indian Christians*	*Parsee*	*Backward Tribes*	*Total*
1	2	3	4	5	6	7	8	9	10
1.	Congress	156	29	4	3	6	3	4	205
2.	Muslim League	-	-	73	-	-	-	-	73
3.	Unionist Krishak	1	1	1	-	-	-	-	3
	Praja Muslims	–	–	1	-	-	-	-	-
4.	Shahid Jirga	-	-	1	-	-	-	-	1
5.	SCF	-	1	-	-	-	-	-	1
6.	Independents	-	-	-	-	-	-	2	2
7.	Sikhs	-	-	-	-	-	-	-	-
8.	Communists	1	-	-	-	-	-	-	1
9.	Landlords	3	-	-	-	-	-	-	3
10.	Commerce and Industry	2	-	-	-	-	-	-	2
	Total :								292
								Sikhs	+ 4
								Total :	**296**[18]

Source : (B.Shiva Rao, p. 393, Vol. I).

TABLE 1.6
Statewise Membership of the Constituent Assembly of India (As on 23rd August, 1949)
Provinces - 235

Sr.No.	*Provinces*	*Members*
1.	Madras	49
2.	Bombay	21
3.	West Bengal	21
4.	United Provinces	55
5.	East Punjab	16
6.	Bihar	36
7.	C.P. and Berar	17
8.	Assam	8
9.	Orissa	9
10.	Delhi	1
11.	Ajmer – Merwara	1
12.	Coorg.	1
	Total	**235**

Indian States 72

Sr.No	*States*	*Members*
1.	Mysore	7
2.	Kashmir	4
3.	Baroda	3
4.	Jodhpur	2
5.	Jaipur	3
6.	Bikaner	1
7.	Kolhapur	1
8.	Mayurbhanj	1
9.	Sikkim Coach Bihar	1
10.	Tripura, Manipur, Khasi States	1
11.	Rampur – Banaras	1
12.	Orissa States	4
13.	CP and Borar States	3
14.	Madras States	1
15.	Bombay States	4
16.	Himachal Pradesh	1
17.	United State of Kathiawar (Saurashtra)	4
18.	United State of Matsya	2
19.	United Stae of Rajasthan	4
20.	United State of Vindhya Pradesh	4
21.	United States of Gwalior – Indore – Malawa (Madhya Bharat)	7
22.	Patiala and East Punjab States Union	3

(Table Contd.)

(Contd. Table 1.6)

Sr.No	States	Members
23.	United State of Travancore amd Cochin	7
24.	Cutch	1
25.	Junagadh	1
26.	Residuary States	1
	Total :	**72**
	Total :	**307**

Source : CAD, Vol. I (2009).

Government on October 13, 1946. Congress inducted Jagjivan Ram in the Ministry. Whereas league inducted Jogendra Nath Mandal in the ministry from the Scheduled Castes. This Government remained in office till the partition of India. During this period there was unrest in India due to independence struggle and communal riots.

In view of partition of India under the Mountbatten Plan of June 3, 1947, a separate Constituent Assembly was set up for Pakistan consisting of the representatives of the provinces which formed the part of Pakistan, including, the provinces of Sind, Baluchistan, West Punjab, East Bengal and the North Western Frontier province and the district of Sylhet in Assam. India got rest of Indian territory. There were fresh elections in the provinces of West - Bengal and East - Punjab. In the reshuffling process, Dr. Babasaheb Ambedkar lost the seat from Bengal wherefrom he firstly got elected to the Constituent Assembly. Therefore at the initiative and support of Congress he got elected from Bombay Legislative Assembly.

In keeping with the promise, the British Parliament passed the Indian Independence Act, 1947 on 18th July 1947. Accordingly, there would be two separate and independent dominions, to be known as India and Pakistan from 15th August 1947. In the first ministry constituted by Pandit Nehru after indepence, Dr. Babasaheb Ambedkar was included in the cabinet as Law minister. The Constituent Assembly constituted on 9th December 1946 was in work. It had 299 members on 31st October 1947.[20] Later on, with the merger of nearabout 600 princely states in India, the strength of the members of the Constituent Assembly rose to (235 + 72) 307 on 23rd August 1949.

It was consisted of representation of almost all the interests. The minorities including Nepali (1), Sikhs (5), Parsi (3), Christians (7), Anglo-Indians (3), Backward Tribes (5), Muslims (31) and the

Scheduled Castes (33) were duly represented on the Constituent Assembly.

For the purpose of framing the constitution, the Constituent Asssembly appointed thirteen important committees. They were : 1. Advisory Committee, 2. Steering Committee, 3. Rules Committee, 4. States Committee, 5. Union subjects Committee, 6. Union Powers Committee, 7. Union Constitution Committee, 8. Provincial Constitution Committee, 9. Order of business committee, 10. Adhoc Committee on Supreme Court. 11. Fundamental Rights Sub-Committee. 12. Minorities Sub-Committee and 13. Drafting Committee. These committees after due deliberations submitted their reports between April-August 1947 to the Constituent Assembly. On the basis of those reports, Dr. B.N. Rao, the Constitutional Advisor prepared the Draft of the Constitution. He took three months to complete his work. This Draft contained 240 Articles and 13 Schedules.

The Constituent Asssembly constituted the Drafting Committee on 29 August 1947. It was consisted of :

1.	Dr. Babasaheb Ambedkar	:	the hon'ble chairman
2.	Shri Alladi Krishna swami Ayyar	:	Member
3.	Shri N. Gopalaswami Ayyangar	:	Member
4.	Shri K.M. Munshi	:	Member
5.	Saiyid Mohd. Sadulla	:	Member
6.	Sir B.L. Mitter [N. Madhav Rao]	:	Member
7.	Shri D.P. Khaitan (T.T. Krishnamachari)	:	Member

After the first meeting Shri B.L. Mitter ceased to be a member and in his place N. Madhav Rao was nominated by the President on December 5, 1947 and T.T. Krishnamachari was appointed in the vacancy caused by the death of D.P. Khaitan; Shri B.N. Rau who was previously Prime Minister of Kashmir, was appointed as Constitutional Advisor in July 1946. Mr. S.N. Mukherjee was the Chief Draftsman of the Constitution. The Drafting Committee worked for 141 days and prepared the final draft consisting of 315 Articles and 8 Schedules. The Draft of the Constitution was placed before the Constituent Assembly on Feb. 21, 1948. It was approved by 284 members out of 299 and after due deliberations it was adopted on November 26, 1949. Thus, the Constituent Assembly took 2 years, 11 months and 17 days to frame the Constitution.

In addition to the President, Vice-President and The Chairman and Members of the Drafting Committee there were several other members belonging to the different fields and representing various interests. There were several intellectual giants, like Pandit Jawaharlal Nehru, Sardar Vallabh Bhai Patel, Prof. K.T. Shah (Bihar), Pandit Lakshmi Kanta Maitra (West Bengal), Dr. P.S. Deshmukh (C.P. & Berar), S. Nagappa (Madras), Frank Anthony (C.P. & Berar), Pandit Thakur Dass Bhargava (East Punjab), Prof. Sibban Lal Saksena (U.P.), V.I. Muniswamy Pillai (Madras), Smt.Dakshayani Velayudhan (Madras), Dr.Manmohan Das (W. Bengal), Shri H.V.Kamath (C.P. & Berar), Naziruddin Ahmad (W. Bengal) Sardar Hukum Singh (East Punjab), Begum Aizaz Rasul (U.P.)], R.K. Sidhwa (C.P. & Berar), Mohd. Tahir (Bihar), Loknath Misra (Orissa), Mahavir Tyagi (U.P.), Pandit HIrday Nath Kunzaru (U.P.), Rev. J.J.M. Nicholas Roy (Assam), K. Santhanam (Madras), A.V. Thakkar (Saurashtra), Deshbandhu Gupta (Delhi), Syamanandan Sahaya (Bihar), H.J. Khandekar (C.P. & Berar), P.J. Chacko (Travancore-Cochin), Sardar Bhopender Singh Man (East Punjab), Smt. Hansa Mehta (Bombay), K.M. Jedhe (Bombay), L.S. Bhatkar (C.P. & Berar), and many others.

The committee on fundamental rights and minorities headed by Sardar Vallabha Scheduled Castes and Scheduled Tribes. It had stated in its report that these backward communities deserve such treatment due to their peculiar position arisen out of social injustice and discrimination inflicted on them for centuries together.

Thus, the Constituent Assembly representing the best brains of India, with the intention to uplift the age long suffering masses, provided special safeguards in the Constitution of "Sovereign, Socialist, Secular, Democratic, Republic of India," which came into implementation on 26th January 1950.

1.3 Philosophy of the Constitution of India

'The Objectives Resolution' moved by Pandit Jawaharlal Nehru in the Constituent Assembly on 13th December 1946 formed bedrock of the philosophy of the Constitution of India. It runs as under :-

"(1) This Constituent Assembly declares its firm and solemn resolve to Proclaim India as an Independent Sovereign Republic and to draw up for her future governance a constitution.

(2) Wherein the territories that now comprise British India, the territories that now form the Indian States and such other parts of India as are outside British India and the states as well as such other territories as are willing to be constituted into the Independent sovereign India, shall be a Union of them all; and

(3) Wherein the said territories, whether with their present boundaries or with such others as may be determined by the Constituent Assembly and thereafter according to the law of the Constitution, shall possess and retain the status of autonomous units, together with residuary powers, and exercise all powers and functions of government and administration, save and except such powers and functions as are vested in or assigned to the union, or as are inherent or implied in the union or resulting therefrom; and

(4) Wherein all power and authority of the Sovereign Independent India, its constituent parts and organs of government, are derived from the people; and

(5) Wherein shall be guaranteed and secured to all the people of India Justice, social, economic and political; equality of status, of opportunity, and before the law; freedom of thought, expression, belief, faith, worship, vocation, association and action, subject to law and public morality; and

(6) Wherein adequate safeguards shall be provided for minorities; backward and tribal areas, and depressed and other backward classes; and

(7) Whereby shall be maintained the integrity of the territory of the Republic and its sovereign rights on land, sea, and air according to justice and the law of civilized nations, and

(8) This ancient land attains its rightful and honoured place in the world and make its full and willing contribution to the promotion of world peace and the welfare of minkind."[21]

This objectives Resolution was fully discussed, critically analysed carefully interpreted, properly re-drafted and finally unanimously approved on 22nd January 1947. It formed the Preamble of the Constitution of India.

The reamble to the Constitution of India, reveals the philosophy of the constitution. It is as under -

"We, the people of India, having solemnly resolved to constitute India into a sovereign Socialist[22] Secular[23] Democratic Republic, and to secure to all its citizens :

Justice : Social, Economic and Political.

Liberty of thought, expression, belief, faith and worship;

Equality of status and of opportunity;

and to promote among them all fraternity, assuring the dignity of the individual and the unity and integrity of the nation.[24]

In our Constituent Assembly this Twenty sixth day of November, 1949, do hereby adopt, enact and give to ourselves this Constitution".

Thus, the preamble envisages, inter alia, the sublime values of justice, liberty, equality and fraternity.

(1) It starts with, "we, the people of India". This indicates the prime source of its origin. It is not ordained by the British Parliament, nor it is revealed by any divine power nor by any regal authority. It was, however enacted by "we, the people of India" or on their behalf living at that time and space and at the present time and space in India and posterity. It reveals that sovereign power is with the people in India. Thus, it is the embodiment of hopes and aspirations of the people of India.

(2) "We" have constituted India into a 'Sovereign Socialist Secular Democratic Republic'.

Every Term or Word has a definite meaning and specific connotation. India is "sovereign" means there is no internal or external authority to decide, complete, control or restrain its own affairs. We obey the rules of the UNO because it is our voluntary decision to be bound by those rules. It is socialist in a sense it is socialistic in philosophy and pattern. It would oppose capitalist system of economy. Although this principle was underlying in Directive Principles of State Policy, it was specifically enunciated in the preamble by the 42nd Amendment of the Constitution in 1976. Our country is secular, in the sense that the state has no religion of its own, nor it would be partial to any one. This principle was also reflected in the fundamental right to religion, but it was specifically added to the preamble by the 42nd Amendment, 1976. India is a democratic country. We have adopted parliamentary form of democracy. The representatives elected by adult sufferage by the people would decide the affairs of the country. Thus, every one has got equal share in the governance of the country. Even the under-privileged people of the society have got a share in the governance of the country. We have Republican form of Government. There would be no hereditary head of the state. The head of the state is indirectly elected by people after every five years and every decision and action is taken in his name. He is assisted by the council of ministers who are jointly responsible to the parliament.

(3) The primordial objective which we have resolved to secure to all the citizens of India is, 'justice'. The term 'justice' is a very comprehensive one, including 'social, economic and political justice.

According to Encyclopaedia of Social Sciences, "the term justice is currently used in two senses as representing, on the one hand, the faithful realization of existing law as against any arbitrary infraction of it; and as representing, on the other, the ideal element in all law - the "Idea" which the law tends to subserve".

Thus, justice is a generic term which includes both the procedural and substantive justice. The former being the basic procedure and the spirit what is generally known as natural justice; and latter is giving what one is due for. However, it is not mere abstract term, but it is substantive one.

(4) Preamble of our Constitution declares liberty of thought expression, belief, faith and worship. Liberty is a reasonable opportunity in which one can develop his personality without any restraints. There can not be domination of any caste or community or of the state on any individual or group of individuals, it removes bonded labour, unclean avocations, beggary and prostitution based on any ground.

(5) We have pledged to secure equality of status and opportunity. Everyone would be entitled to a fair chance to improve his personality. Thus, equality is a philosophical and humanitarian concept, it should not be taken in literal sense.

(6) We have pledged to promote among all the citizens fraternity. This concept was missing in 'objectives resolution' on which, the preamble is based. However, it was Dr.Babasaheb Ambedkar who could realize the true import of fraternity in the Indian Social Context, as such he included it in the preamble of the Constitution.[25] Fraternity means, fellow feeling. It cosists in a sentiment which leads an individual to identify himself with the good of others.[26]

Every one would be entitled to lead a life of self-respect and dignity. No one would be compelled to or unduly influenced by any one to accept a way of life which is against his will and reason. No one is required to submit before any ideology or ideologue. Everyone would be bound to the philosophy of human brotherhood.

For every citizen the unity and integrity of the nation is important than any petty regional, linguistic and communal feelings. Any communal and disruptive activity would be against the nation. Every body has to solve any problem within the constitutional frame work.

The preamble of the Constitution of India is, undoubtedly a charter of justice, liberty, equality and fraternity to one and all.

However, it is especially significant in respect of the weaker sections of the society, as it was a unique occasion in their life to witness such a charter of rights after some centuries in the past. It pledges to give them all that they had lost on the ground of ill conceived notion of caste, creed and religion.

The preamble, obviously serves as a key to interpret the Constitution as and when it is required. It is however expected to give such an interpretition to the constitutional provisions which would conform with the ideal embodied in the preamble. Of course, "where the language of the enacting sections is clear and unambiguous, the terms of the preamble cannot qualify or cut down that enactment."[27]

1.4 Nature of Special Safeguards

(1) The special safeguards meant for the Scheduled Castes, Scheduled Tribes and Other Backward Classes for their educational advancement under Article 15(4) and reservations in public employment under Article 16(4) are parts of the scheme of equality under the fundamental rights.

(2) The purpose of the special safeguards under the Fundamental Rights, Directive Principles of State Policy and other provisions of the Constitution is inter alia, to secure justice, social, economic and political to the backward classes.

(3) The special provisions struck to the root of their problems including abolition of untouchability, segregation and backwardness. The constitution primarily abolishes their tradition imposed low status stigma and legally uplifts them to the level of general people.

(4) All the provisions contemplated to safeguard the interests of the backward classes are obvilously based on the Objectives Resolutions, and Preamble to the Constitution. Even they are rooted in the history of social reforms in our country, especially from 1857 to 1947. The special rights owe much to The American Civil Rights but preceed to the Declaration of Human Rights by the UNO.

(5) The special safeguards are not meant to give something additional to the backward classes. The safeguards are to empower the backward classes so that they may be able to equally share the benefits under the Constitution as other citizens. They are meant to build the capability of the disadvantaged people to take the benefit of the fundamental rights under the Constitution on par with others.

(6) The special safeguards start with 'non-obstante clause' which means, 'a clause used in any instrument intended to preclude in advance, any interpretation contrary to certain declared object or purpose.'

Thus the Constitution removes in clear terms the obstacles if any and clears the way to social justice as pledged under the preamble and under certain articles.

(7) The special safeguards empower and authorise "the State" as defined under Article 12 of the Constitution to faithfully discharge the duties under the special provisions.

(8) The special safeguards are taking their shape and accommodating new amendments according to exigencies of time and needs of the nation. Even they are accommodating judicial interpretations time and again.

(9) The educational and economic safeguards have no time limit but they are commensurate with socio-economic condition of the backward classes of the society. However, political safeguards provided under Article 330, Article 332 and Article 243 (D) and Article 243(T) would continue for a period as provided under Article 334 of the Constitution.

(10) The special safeguards have accommodative value. It is because of the safeguards the SC, ST and OBCs feel that they have, obviously regained human identity, individual dignity and equal citizenship under the Constitution. They naturally feel that they are inseparable part of fraternity of Republic of India.

1.5 Opposition to Special Safeguards

(a) We find certain ill conceived objections and allegations against the policy of reservation and the weaker sections. They are as under :

(1) Discrimination on the ground of caste is unconstitutional.
(2) It creats vested interest in backwardness.
(3) It perpetuates casteism.
(4) It is the policy of 'Rob-Peter-to-pay-paul'.
(5) It is harmful to national unity.
(6) It is the gift of colonial power.
(7) A number of accidents in recent past can be traced to such indiscriminate promotions.
(8) Chosen few get benefits. Hence reservation should be based on economic condition rather than social status.
(9) It has created unemployment amongst the educated caste Hindus.

(10) It is against equality before Law and equal opportunity to all.

(11) This has caused loss to the hereditary occupations.

(12) Dalits became arrogant and defiant.

(b) These objections are, of course ill conceived, unsupported and baseless. No body has taken care of corroborating these statements by appropriate evidence. Therefore, it is not necessary on the part of pro-reservationists to disprove these statements. It is, however, worthwhile to state the truth in sequential order in brief.

(1) Discrimination on the ground of caste is undoubtedly unconstitutional, but protective discrimination is constitutional. Reservation is depended on social and educational backwardness and not only on the basis of one's caste. Caste is, of course, one of the criterion of deciding one's social status. It was held in -

P. Rajendran Vs. State of Madras, (1968) that, if the reservation in question had been based only on caste and had not taken into account the social and educational backwardness of the caste in question, it would be isolative of Article 15(1). But it must not be forgotten that a caste is also a class of citizens and if the caste as a whole is socially and educationally backward reservation can be made in favour of such a caste on the ground that it is a socially and educationally backward class of citizens within the meaning of Article 15(4)."[28]

(2) It can not create vested interest in backwardness. No body has any vested interest in his own low social status and grinding poverty, Reservation is a means of upliftment from backwardness. The caste Hindus have vested interest in keeping others in backwardness.

(3) The object behind reservation is not to perpetuate casteism. There are number of other factors responsible for it like our social structure, political parties, poverty, religious texts and institutions etc. Reservation is to nullify casteism.

(4) It is not rob-peter to pay paul. Peter is expected to pay very little as compensation for what he has already robed from Paul. It is a matter of legitimate share in the benefits and not any unjust adjustment.

(5) It is not harmful to the national unity. The object of reservations is to uplift the backward classes to the level

of developed classes and join with them. Probably abolition of reservation may create anti-national feeling in Dalits. Unless there is 'we' feeling, there can not be a nation. Reservation is meant for equality and 'we' feeling. Whether there would be unity and integrity in the absence of reservations ?

(6) Casteism is a gift of the Brahmanic Power. Reservation is a remedy on the ills of casteism.

(7) In majority of the cases the accidents are caused by contributory negligence. Negligence is the fault of an individual for which the entire community cannot be held accountable.

(8) The statement "chosen few get benefit" is based on "Divide and Rule Policy." Reservations are meant for all the weaker sections of citizens. Where 'caste' and not economic condition is the status deciding factor, economic criterion is meaningless. Where economic condition cannot decide the caste status, caste is the only criterion of backwardness. However, so far as OBCs are concerned 'creamy layer' criterion is applied in deciding backwardness of some individuals as per decision of the Hon'ble Supreme Court in Indra Sawhney Vs. Union of India. It has been specifically laid down that 'creamy layer' can be, and must be excluded."[29]

(9) Very few of Dalits could avail the benefit of reservations, that too very recently. For the problem of increasing unemployment the blame should be given to the national planning, economic policy, growth of population and certain other factors and not to reservation policy.

(10) The Principle of equality is applicable only among equals and not among unequals. In unequal society the principle of equality creates inequality.

(11) Due to industrial revolution, policy of the government, new avenues in the enterprising business and education, and technological advancement in the market, the hereditary occupations are at loss. However, there is no change in the occupational pattern in respect of agriculture and business.

(12) 'Dalit became defiant' is a statement based on caste prejudice and feudalist attitude and not on facts.

1.6 Objectives of the Study

In addition to above stated objections against the special safeguards, especially the policy of reservations in educational institutions and public services, some new objections and tricks are being invented to tactfully thwart the policy of reservation and to demoralise the backward classes. We have to take into account the seriousness of those objections and tactics against the special safeguards and address them in detail. Thus, the objectives of the present study are as under :-

(1) The first and foremost objection against the reservation is it is not a fundamental right of the backward classes, as such it is not obligatory on the part of the state to implement it. In this respect, it is proposed to inquire from legal point of view whether it is a fundamental right or not.

(2) Another argument is whether it is fundamental right or not, people belonging to the weaker sections have no merit and efficiency necessary for the particular post. It is necessary to inquire as to whether it is rationally correct to make such imputations only on the ground of caste ?

(3) Even after proving merit and efficiency, it is further argued that the Constitution which provides for reservations itself is subject to review and revision. Therefore, it is necessasry to know whether the Constitution is such an ordinary document which could be revised or changed abruptly without adopting any Constitutional procedure ?

(4) When the attempt to constitutional revision was failed because of strong opposition from the people committed to constitutional philosophy, the anti-reservationists resorted to the trick of sub-categorization to minimize the vigour of united strength of the weaker sections of the society. Even they are contemplating to exclude certain castes and communities from the list of the beneficiary schedules. Therefore, it is necessary to inquire into the procedure of inclusion in and exclusion from the respective schedules of any caste or tribe as the case may be, and legality of sub-categorization of castes on the basis of constitutional provisions and the judicial verdicts.

(5) The anti-reservationists found an opportunity in the new economic policy in criticising the provisions of constitutional safeguards. They argue that the concept of constitutional safeguards became irrelevant and redundant in the process of growing globalization, liberalization and privatization. It is necessary to inquire into the truth of this statement in the

light of constitutional provisions and international commitment to human rights.

6) Legal provisions are made and the machinery to implement those provisions is also present, but common people do not find justice. Is there any drawback in monitoring and supervising machinery or there is lack of substansive political will ? It is, therefore, necessary to inquire into the matter. Thus, the object of the present study is to analyse and interpret the relevant facts in their proper perspective within the parameters of constitutional provisions, judicial pronouncements and experts opinions. Thus the main thrust of the study is on the points in question. This study would be helpful in understanding the true objective of the Constitution and the special safeguards meant for the weaker section of the society.

References

1. For details, see DBAWS : Vol. 7 : Education Deptt. Govt. of Maharashtra, (1990).
2. *Ibid.*, p. 249.
3. For details, see, "Dalit Movement in India and its Leaders," by Dr. R.K. Kshirsagar. (1857-1956). M.D. Publications Pvt. Ltd. 11 Darya Gunj, New Delhi, (1994).
4. Keer Dhananjay : Dr. Ambedkar : Life and Mission. p. 35, Popular Prakashan, Bombay. (3rd 1971).
5. DBAWS : Vol. 9, p. 1, Govt. of Maharashtra (1991).
6. DBAWS : Vol. 2, p. 506, Govt. Maharashtra (1982).
7. *Ibid.*, p. 506.
8. DBAWS : Vol. 1, p. 256, Govt. of Maharashtra (1979).
9. DABWS : Vol. 2, p. 465.
10. *Ibid.*, Ed. 2, pp. 550-51.
10a. *Ibid.*, Vol. 2, p. 661.
11. *Ibid.*, Vol. 8, p. 457.
12. DBAWS : Vol. 1, p. 429.
12a. Total General Seats were 787.
13. DBAWS : Vol. 8, pp. 448, 449, 446, 447. Govt. of Maharashtra. (1990).
14. Sharma M.P. The Government of the Indian Republic p. 14. Kitab Mahal, Allahabad. (1951, 1968).
15. *Ibid.*, p. 15.
16. Longer V. Forefront for ever. p. 30. The Mahar Regimental Centre, Saugar. (1981).

17. Mahajan V.D. Constitutional History of India. p. 193. S. Chand and Co. New Delhi (1964).
18. Rao B. Shiva. The framing of India's Constitution Vol. I : p. 393. Indian Institute of Pub.Administration New Delhi (1966).
19. DBAWS. Vol. 1, p. 484.
20. Basu D.D. Introduction to the Constitution of India. p. 351. Printice Hall of India, New Delhi (1976).
21. CAD Vol. 1, 13th December 1946, p. 59.
22. Added by the Constitution (42nd) Amendment Act, 1976.
23. Added by the Constitution (42nd) Amendment Act, 1976.
24. Added by the Constitution (42nd) Amendment Act, 1976.
25. DBAWS : Vol. 13, p. 81. Govt. of Maharashtra.
26. DBAWS : Vol. 3, p. 44.
27. Basu D.D. Constitutional Law of India. p. 1. Printice-Hall of India, New Delhi (1978).
28. P. Rajendran Vs State of Madras. AIR 1968 SC 1012; 1014, 1015.
29. Indra Sawhney V. Union of India. AIR 1993 SC 477; 561, 586.

2

Provision of Reservation : A Fundamental Right

It is reasonably believed that the special safeguards provided under Article 15(4) and Article 16(4) are the fundamental rights of the Scheduled Castes and the Scheduled Tribes under the Constitution of India, as such they are mandatory, inviolable and irrevocable. However, this belief is being impaired from the very beginning by persons and organizations including the Judiciary. Hence, it is proposed to know whether those special safeguards are fundamental rights of the weaker sections of the society or mere misnomer.

2.1 Reservations and Facilities in Educational Institutions

So far as reservaton in educational institution is concerned the relevant provisions under the Constitution are as under :

Article 15 (1) : The state shall not discriminate against any citizen on grounds only of religion, race, caste, sex, place of birth or any of them.

Article 15 (4) : Nothing in this article or clause (2) of article 29 shall prevent the state from making any special provision for the advancement of any socially and educationally backward classes of citizens or for the Scheduled Castes and the Scheduled Tribes.[1]

Article 15 (5) : "Nothing in this article or in Sub-Clause (g) of Clause (1) of Article 19 shall prevent the state from making any special provision, by law, for the advancement of any socially and educationally backward classes of citizens or for the scheduled castes or The Scheduled Tribes in so far as such special provisions relate to their admission to the educational institutions including private educational institutions, whether aided or unaided by the state, other than the minority educational institutions referred to in clause (1) of Article 30."[2]

(2) The object of Article 15(4) is to make it constitutional to reserve seats for Scheduled Castes and Scheduled Tribes and Backward Classes in the educational institutions, as well as to make other special provisions as may be necessary for their advancement including the provision of payment of scholarship, hostel facilities, concession in fees, relaxation of age etc. etc. In the words of Prof. Marc Galanter, "Article 15(4) extends to all areas of governmental activity which are not controlled by a more specific provision. Thus, preferences in housing, education, welfare, government contracts and local political arrangements are authorised by and must be within the scope of Article 15 (4)."[3]

Under Article 29(2) the educational institutions are open to all the citizens irrespective of their religion, race, caste, language or any of them. Other things being equal the weaker sections cannot be disallowed for taking admissions on general seats on the basis of merit.

(3) It should be borne in mind that Article 15(4) has been included as a part of Article 15 under the chapter of Fundamental Rights in the Constitution by 1st Amendment Act, 1951. The immediate object of the first amendment was to overvide the decision in state of Madras V. Champakam Dorairajan[4] in which the Communal G.O. of the then Madras State providing caste wise or Community wise reservations in the educational institutions, was struck down by the Supreme Court. The honourable court pronounced that under Article 29(2), a citizen has a right as a citizen and "not as a member of any community or class of citizens." Therefore the first amendment as stated above has been resorted to do away with the legal difficulties in providing reservations in educational institutions.

(4) It ought to be remembered that the *Constituent Assembly* did not think it necessary to include such provision in the Constitution. In this respect Prof. K.T. Shah moved the amendment (No. 323) to provide under Article 15(2) - "or for Scheduled Castes or Backward tribes, for their advantage, safeguard or betterment." Thus the said Article had it been amended as aforesaid, would have been as under -

"Nothing in this article shall prevent the state from making any special provision for women and children, or for Scheduled Castes or Backward Tribes for their advantage, safeguard or betterment." Dr. Babasaheb Ambedkar himself rejected the proposed amendment saying that, "it may have just the opposite effect". Further he said that, "the object which all of us have in mind is that the Scheduled Castes or Backward Tribes should not be segregated from the general public."

"For instance, none of us, I think, would like that a separate school should be established for the Scheduled Castes when there is a general school in the village open to the children of the entire community. If these words are added, it will probably give a handle for a state to say, "well, we are making special provision for the Scheduled Castes. To my mind they can safely say so by taking shelter under the article if it is amended in the manner the professor wants it. I therefore think that it is not a desirable amendment."[5]

It does not mean that Dr. Babasaheb Ambedkar was against any such provision of reservation in the educational institutions for the weaker sections of the society. He possibly thought that the proposed amendment would lead to wrong interpretation and thereby wrong application of the same.

Probably he might have felt it unnecessary in the light of provision under Article 46. He must have believed that the provision under Article 46 embodied under Directive Principle of state policy would get reasonable preference over the Principle of Educational equality provided under Article 29(2).

He believed in constitutional morality, commitment to social upliftment and public welfare. He thought that the people in government would implement the Constitution in letter and spirit and respect the principles evolved during the freedom movement. Poona Pact was the inseparable part of the total freedom movement, which pledges to endeavour to secure fair representation in the public servies and adequate facilities for the educational development of the Depressed classes.

However, in order to meet the emergent situation created by the court decision in the said case, the first amendment bill was introduced on 16th May 1951 and it was passed by thumping majority. In this respect Prof. Marc Galanter states that, "The Constituent Assembly had rejected the inclusion in the original Constitution of a provision similar to Article 15(4). Now the same assembly, in its incarnation as the provisional Parliament, passed it with little opposition, on the ground that it was needed to empower the state to carryout the Directive Principle by insuring that the Fundamental Rights guarantees of equality did not obstruct substantive equalization."[6]

(5) Under clause 4 of Article 15 of the Constitution certain facilities and concessions are being given to the SC/ST students.

The scheme of awarding Post-Matric Scholarships to those students, which started in pre-independence era (1944-45) has been continued after independence also. Still the scheme is in vogue with certain modifications and amendments. Now it is being operated by the Ministry of Social Justice and Empowerment, Govt. of India through the State Governments. The scholarship rates are being raised from time to time commensurate with increase in the price level of the essential articles, but they are insufficient for maintenance of the students. The students presently having not more than annual income of Rs.Two Lakh are eligible for Post-Matric Scholarships.

(6) The scheme of awarding Post-Matric Scholarships to the students of the Scheduled Tribes was started from the year 1948-49. Presently, the tribal development division is under a separate Ministry of Tribal Affairs. The ministry operates through the State Governments. The Tribal students having not more than Rs.2 Lakh family income p.a. are entitled to get the scholarships and other benefits.

(7) The students belonging to the socially and economically backward classes, referred to as "other backward classes" are also entitled to Post-Matric Scholarships and other facilities under Article 15(4) of the Constitution. The scholarships are awarded through the respective State Governments /UT Administrations. It is in operation from the year 1949-50. Presently the students having income not more than Rs. One lakh p.a. are eligible for the same.

(8) The object of the scheme is to provide financial assistance to students of the Scheduled Castes, Scheduled Tribes and other Backward Classes; so as to enable them to pursue their post-matriculation education. It is, however subject to caste and means test. The eligible students belonging to either the Scheduled Castes including the scheduled castes converts to Buddhism, or the Scheduled Tribes or the other Backward Classes are entitled for the said scholarship. The scheme is available only to those students whose income does not exceed the prescribed upper limit.

(9) So far as reservations in admission in the educational institutions are concerned they were in vogue in some states before independence, but there was no uniformity and regularity in that respect. The scheme of reservations in admission was revived by the Ministry of Education, Govt. of India in the year 1954.

The Ministry of Education in November 1954, addressed all the state Governments suggesting to them that certain concessions may be given to students belonging to Scheduled Castes / Tribes in the matter of their admission in the educational institutions.[7]

However, the scheme of reservations was not properly formulated and implemented by the State Governments. While issuing the above said guide lines, it was proposed to review the scheme after five years of its implementation.

Eventually on the recommendations of the All India Council of Technical Education, the Ministry of Education have issued Circular No. 33-3/62 U-V (1) dated 28th September 1962 to all state Governments / Union Territory Administrations and Universities requesting them to allow the following concessions to Scheduled Caste / Scheduled Tribes students.

(a) 20 per cent of seats in all technical institutions should be reserved for Scheduled Castes / Scheduled Tribes with a distinct reservation of 15 per cent for Scheduled Castes and 5 per cent for Scheduled Tribes. However, this reservation is interchangeable between these two communities, and if candidates are not forthcoming from both the communities, these can be utilised for general.

(b) Where admissions are restricted to candidates having a minimum percentage of marks, a reduction of 5 per cent for Scheduled Castes / Scheduled Tribes may be allowed provided that the lower percentage prescribed does not fall below the minimum required to pass the qualifying examination.

(c) If there is a maximum age limit it may be raised by 3 years for Scheduled Castes / Scheduled Tribes.

(d) A minimum qualifying standard should be prescribed for admission to any technical institutions. Scheduled Castes and Scheduled Tribes students should be eligible for admission to the reserved seats, if they attain this minimum standard without any reference to the gap between their marks and the marks of the last person admitted to the open seats.[8]

(10) Both the provisions, "any special provision" under Article 15(4) and the state shall "promote with special care" the educational interests of the Scheduled Castes under Article 46 of the Constitution are comprehensive enough to include steps such as special coaching, hostels, reimbursement of fees, reservations, scholarships etc. in respect of the weaker sections of the society.

The Supreme Court held in Chitralekha V. State of Mysore [9] that, "Article 46, 341, 342 and 15(4) form a group which has relevance in making of a special provision for advancement of any socially and educationally backward classes of citizens in the matter of admissions to colleges."

However, due to mere non-appearance of the word, "reservation" in Article 15(4) unlike Article 16(4) can not be construed that the Article does not contemplate reservation. The word "any special provision is inclusive of "Reservation" as such there was no need to mention it under Article 15(4).[10]

(11) While construing Article 15(4) Marc Galanter states that, "Article 15(4) extends to all areas of government activity which are not controlled by a more specific provision. Thus, preferences in housing,education, welfare, government contracts; and local political arrangements are authorised by, and must be within the scope of Article 15(4). Unlike Article 16(4), this Article doesnot limit the state to reservations as a method of preference. Reservations may be used to implement Article 15(4), but government may also employ methods such as fee concessions, scholarships, special facilities (housing, medical etc) which do not involve reservations at all."[11]

(12) The total reservation under Article 15(4) will not exceed fifty percent of the total seats. In Balaji V. State of Mysore The Supreme Court struck down the quota of 68% fixed in educational admissions by Mysore State and stated that "speaking generally and in a broad way, a special provision should be less than 50%; how much less than 50% would depend upon the relevant prevailing circumstances in each case. Therefore, the reservation of 68% directed by the order of the Mysore Government dated 31-7-1962 in Technical Institution, is plainly inconsistent with Article 15(4)."[12]

(13) However, the honourable Supreme Court pronounced in T.M.A. Pai V. State Karnataka,[13] that there cannot be reservations in private unaided educational institutions. In this background the parliament introduced Article 15(5) by the 93rd Constitution Amendment Act, 2005 to enable the state to provide for reservations in educational institutions including private educational institutions, whether aided or unaided, with the only exception of the minority educational institutions.

(14) Recently the Parliament has passed "the Central Educational Institutions (Reservation in Admission) Act, 2006 (5 of 2007). The said Act under its Section 3, provides 15 per cent of the total seats for the Scheduled Castes, 71/2 per cent of the total seats for the Scheduled Tribes and 27 per cent of the total seats for the other Backward Classes in the Central Educational Institutions as defined under section 2(d) of the Act. The object of the Act is "to introduce reservation in only such institutions which are defined as "Central Educational Institions," and not other private unaided institutions."[14]

(15) It is worthwhile to note that, the Parliament has deliberately introduced Article 21 A, Right to Education by 86 the Constitution Amendment Act, 2002. It states that, "the state shall

provide free and compulsory education to all children of the age of six to fourteen years in such manner as the state may by law, determine." Accordingly, "The Right of Children to Free and Compulsory Education Act, 2009" was passed in 2009, with a sublime objective of providing for free and compulsory education to all the children of the age of six to fourteen years in a neighbourhood school till completion of elementary education freely without payment of any fees or capitation fees. Under the Act 2009, the education is not only free but it is compulsory also. It is a fundamental duty of every parent or guardian to send his child, or as the case may be, ward between the age of six and fourteen years to the neighbourhood school. (Article 51A(k).

Moreover, there is a provision under section 12 of the said Act for reservation for the disadvantaged children especially the Scheduled Castes, Scheduled Tribes and the socially and educationally backward classes to the extent of twenty five per cent in the government and private aided and unaided schools across the country. However, as per Article 15(5) of the Constitution the minority institutions are exempted from this provision.

The objective of providing reservation is to ensure quality education in the renowned and standard schools to those disadvantaged students who are otherwise unable to seek admission in such schools due to their inability to pay heavy fees or who are unable to seek admission in such schools due to caste prejudices. However, there remained a flaw in the said Act. The Central Institutions (Reservation in Admission) Act, 2006 provides 15%, 7 1/2% and 27% respectively to SC, ST and SEBCs; and the Hon'ble Supreme Court upheld its validity. On the ground of analogy, legal provision and confirmation of validity of the Act of 2006, there should have been provision of equal quota in the Act of 2009 also. Thus it is submitted that the reservation of seats as mentioned in the Act of 2009 is inadequate and disproportionate to the SC, ST, OBC population.

The Right of Children to Free and Compulsory Education Act, 2009 was to come into operation on 1st April 2010, but it was challenged in the Supreme Court on the ground that the Act violated the right of private educational institutions to manage their own affairs including admissions of the students without any interference, by the state which they allegedly got under Article 19(1)(g) of the Constitution. However, the hon'ble Supreme Court upheld the constitutional validity of the Act on April 12, 2012 and pronounced that the decision will have prospective effect.[14(a)]

(16) The Constitution under its Article 45, under the Directive Principles of State Policy states that, "the State shall endeavour to

TABLE 2.1
Funds Released under the Scheme of Post Matric Scholarship to the Scheduled Caste Beneficiaries during 2007-08 to 2009-10

(Rs. in Lakhs)

S.No	State / UT	2007-2008		2008-2009		2009-2010 (Upto 31.12.09)	
		Funds Released	No.of Beneficiaries	Funds Released	No.of Beneficiaries	Funds Released	No.of Beneficiaries (Anticipated)
1.	Andhra Pradesh	24048.4	382059	23978.11	479723	16623.92	608318
2.	Assam	469.82	16718	0.00	16800	0	0
3.	Bihar	0.00	50046	2692.70	53330	1000.00	70130
4.	Chhattisgarh	482.85	54927	100.00	53686	0	0
5.	Goa	0.00	138	0.00	127	0.00	0
6.	Gujarat	240.36	84379	1556.29	75449	2000.00	82859
7.	Haryana	494.93	24512	369.52	26620	2676.48	27590
8.	H.P.	78.84	7501	0.00	9305		0
9.	J & K	0.00	4670	378.47	10956	150.00	12605
10.	Jharkhand	35.32	15296	0.00	16862	514.74	18568

(Table Contd.)

(Contd. Table 2.1)

S.No.	State / UT	2007-2008		2008-2009		2009-2010 (Upto 31.12.09)	
		Funds Released	No.of Beneficiaries	Funds Released	No.of Beneficiaries	Funds Released	No.of Beneficiaries (Anticipated)
11.	Karnataka	7020.59	312556	3267.91	226970	1300.00	355549
12.	Kerala	4072.44	105728	8132.43	106836	3200.00	120062
13.	Madhya Pradesh	695.983	127225	1699.21	133610	1954.66	141367
14.	Maharashtra	15953.63	320048	1000.00	377729	13400.00	509131
15.	Manipur	139.95	2292	163.76	3276	60.00	3767
16.	Meghalaya	0.00	193	0.00	0	0.00	0
17.	Orissa	0.00	56333	500.00	63091	0.00	0
18.	Punjab	539.8	51499	200.00	60420	0.00	0
19.	Rajasthan	3204.42	221108	10340.11	195260	5397.72	214786
20.	Sikkim	0.00	218	3.44	265	1.00	301

(Table Contd.)

(Contd. Table 2.1)

S.No.	State / UT	2007-2008		2008-2009		2009-2010 (Upto 31.12.09)	
		Funds Released	No.of Beneficiaries	Funds Released	No.of Beneficiaries	Funds Released	No.of Beneficiaries (Anticipated)
21.	Tamil Nadu	6978.05	431272	500.00	425074	0.00	0
22.	Tripura	180.56	11765	410.98	21371	410.16	21887
23.	Uttar Pradesh	22313.71	628884	4916.98	680625	19967.13	713160
24.	Uttaranchal	0.00	38450	1089.36	38028	400.00	42051
25.	West Bengal	358.25	203512	3250.23	353516	3835.67	303100
26.	Daman & Diu	0.33	113	0.00	116	0.00	0
27.	D&N Haveli	0.00	0	0.00	0	0.00	0
28.	Delhi	0.00	487	0.00	0	0.00	0
29.	Pudducherry	200	6882	0.00	6976	0.00	0
	Total	87508.23	3158811	64549.49	3436021	72891.48	3245231

Source : Annual Report, 2009-10 (p. 236), Ministry of Social Justice and Empowerment, Govt. of India.

TABLE 2.2

Funds Released under the Scheme of PMS alongwith number of beneficiaries during the year 2007-2008 to 2009-2010 (S.Ts.)

(Rs. in Lakhs)

S.No.	*State / UT*	*2007-2008*		*2008-2009*		*2009-2010 (Upto 31.12.09)*	
		Amount	*Bene.*	*Amount*	*Bene.*	*Amount*	*Bene.*
1.	Andhra Pradesh	2284.39	147323	1662.13	183974	831.00	213620
2.	Arunachal Pradesh	0	0	0.00	0	0.00	0
3.	Assam	1857.1363	49919	1696.18	64952	2510.12	70149
4.	Bihar	0	1334	170.00	4550*	0.00	0
5.	Chattishgarh	130.24	65630	160.28	72160	375.95	82995
6.	Goa	13.804	583	18.96	595	54.26	654
7.	Gujarat	315.965	107895	387.36	122843	194.00	134911
8.	Himachal Pradesh	59.72	1866	10.00	2271	0.00	2600
9.	Jammu & Kashmir	43.44	6252	0.00	10077	0.00	10182
10.	Jharkhand	107.97	18470	1058.48	25163	1267.00	27712

(Table Contd.)

(Contd. Table 2.2)

S.No.	State/UT	2007-2008		2008-2009		2009-2010 (Upto 31.12.09)	
		Amount	*Bene.*	*Amount*	*Bene.*	*Amount*	*Bene.*
11.	Karnataka	456.87	62678	1053.97	69152	1863.63	76069
12.	Kerala	29.79	8472	298.03	9173	284.40	10580
13.	Madhya Pradesh	583.41	72458	1228.18	89223	3236.50	105369
14.	Maharashtra	2155.56	94629	2500.00	129384	1250.00	134875
15.	Manipur	1438.78	36297	1912.68	39123	2163.28	44996
16.	Meghalaya	2435.7199	48170	1342.12	52985	672.00	0
17.	Mizoram	1370.20	37550	1421.18	33758	1571.26	37134
18.	Nagaland	1593.495	32013	1467.27	35606	734.00	39878
19.	Orissa	95.97	44691	461.75	48802	231.00	52706
20.	Rajasthan	4616.6188	148148	4654.00	176194	1661.31	193813

(Table Contd.)

(Contd. Table 2.2)

S.No.	State / UT	2007-2008		2008-2009		2009-2010 (Upto 31.12.09)	
		Amount	Bene.	Amount	Bene.	Amount	Bene.
21.	Sikkim	25.631	1494	25.13	1819	37.88	2001
22.	Tamil Nadu	4.76	3182	2.50	4241	72.34	4580
23.	Tripura	295.89	12890	433.19	14892	538.26	17828
24.	Uttar Pradesh	7.50	5519	0.00	8144	0.00	4990
25.	Uttarakhand	32.35	15566	230.52	15127	188.98	16639
26.	West Bengal	44.79	17537	389.28	42524	195.00	33425
27.	A & N Islands	4.447	430	3.00	441	0.00	559
28.	Damand & Diu	0	127	0.14	164	1.73	197
	Total :	20003.447	1041123	22586.31	1257337	19933.90	1318462

* *Anticipated Beneficiaries*

Source : Annual Report, 2009-10 (p. 112), Ministry of Tribal Welfare, Government of India.

provide early childhood care and education for all children until they complete the age of six years." However, no law at the union level has been made so far. There is, however need of providing nutritional, medical and educational care during the early childhood especially for the students belonging to the Scheduled Castes, Scheduled Tribes and OBCs.

(17) The matter of education is under the concurrent list, at Item No.25; as such both, the Union Government as well as State Governments are competent to make appropriate legislation in that respect. However, while passing the Right of Children to free and compulsory Education Act, 2009 the Union Government is silent on the education of the students after the end of fourteenth year. Now-a-days education upto eighth class carries very little value. However they get through the matriculation with a great difficulty. It has been recently reported that, "India is failing to properly educate its work force especially beyond the high school level." Accordingly India's gross enrolment ratio (GER - the number of students enrolled versus the number of eligible students - for higher education) in 2003 was merely 13.2 per cent; it is now projected to rise to 15.7 per cent still it would be lower than the global average.[14(b)] The GER in respect of the weaker sections of the society certainly might be lower than the general GER. It is, of course a matter of great concern to us.

(18) The rules and regulations in respect of reservations and grant of scholarships and matters relating to educational empowerment of the SC/ST and OBCs are being made from time to time; by the Union Government and they are being executed by the State Government / Union Territories Administration.

In addition to these facilities some other facilities, like, grant of additional scholarship amount, providing hostel facilities, supply of books, reimbursement of tuition fees, pre-matric scholarships etc. are given by the State Governments / Union Territories Administration from their own funds. These facilities are operated through the Department of Social Welfare / Tribal Welfare Department / Backward Classes Welfare Department in the states.

Although the efforts of the state are not fully commensurate with the educational and economic needs of the disadvantaged groups, we cannot ignore the progress, what so ever they achieved so far.

The following tables indicate the amount released under the Post-Matric Scholarships to the SC / STs during 2007-08 to 2009-10. See Table 2:1 and Table 2: 2.

2:2 Reservations in Public Services

1*(a)* In order to secure social and economic justice to the Scheduled Castes and Scheduled Tribes, the Constitution provides as under :

16(1) : There shall be equality of opportunity for all citizens in matters relating to employment or appointment to any office under the state.

.......(4) "Nothing in this article shall prevent the State from making any provision for the reservation of appointments of posts in favour of any backward class of citizens which, in the opinion of the State, is not adequately represented in the services under the State."

.......(4A) "Nothing in this article shall prevent the state from making any provision for reservation in matters of promotion, with consequential seniority to any class or classes of posts in the services under the state in favour of the Scheduled Castes and the Scheduled Tribes which in the opinion of the state are not adequately represented in the services under the state."[15]

.......(4B) "Nothing in this article shall prevent the state from considering any unfilled vacancies of a year which are reserved for being filled up in that year in accordance with any provision for reservation made under clause (4) or clause (4-A) as a separate class of vacancies to be filled up in any succeeding year or years and such class of vacancies shall not be considered together with the vacancies of the year in which they are being filled up for determining the ceiling of fifty percent reservation on total number of vacancies of that year."[16]

.......(46) "The State shall promote with special care the educational and economic interests of the weaker sections of the people, and in particular, of the Scheduled Castes and the Scheduled Tribes, and shall protect them from social injustice and all forms of exploitation."

(b) 320 (3) : The Union Public Service Commission or the State Public Service Commission, as the case may be, shall be consulted [a] on all matters relating to methods of recruitment to civil services and for civil posts;

(4) Nothng in Clause (3) shall require a Public Service Commission to be consulted as respects the manner in which any provision referred to in clause (4) of article 16 may be made or as respects the manner in which effect may be given to the provisions of article 335."

(c) 335 : "The claims of the members of the Scheduled Castes and the Scheduled Tribes shall be taken into consideration, consistently with the maintenance of efficiency of administration, in the making of appointments to services and posts in connection with the affairs of the Union or of a State.

Provided that nothing in this article shall prevent in making of any provision in favour of the members of the Scheduled Castes and the Scheduled Tribes for relaxation in qualifying marks in any examination or lowering the standards of evaluation, for reservation in matters of promotion to any class or classes of services or posts in connection with the affairs of the Union or of a State."[17]

(2) The said provision under 16(4) is expected to be in operation till the backward classes are not adequately represented in the services under the state. Thus the reservations under this clause have no time limit. The clause removes the obstacle in the way of the state in making any provision in this respect.

However, this provision has to be read alongwith Article 335 which states that, "The claims of the members of the Scheduled Castes and the Scheduled Tribes shall be taken into consideration, consistently with the maintenance of efficiency of administration, in the making of appointments to services and posts in connection with the affiars of the union or of a state."

(3) In accordance with the provision under Article 16 (4) of the Constitution, the Govt. of India, vide its Resolution MHA No. 42/21/49 NGS dated 13th September 1950 decided to continue the then existing reservation for the scheduled castes to the extent of 12 1/2% of total vacancies filled by direct recruitment by open competition, and to the extent of 16 2/3% where recruitment is made otherwise than by open competition. In respect of the Scheduled Tribes the reservation was provided to the extent of 5 per cent of the toal vacancies filled by open competition or otherwise by open competition.[18]

(4) The percentages of reservation for the SCs and STs were increased from 12 1/2 per cent and 5 per cent to 15 per cent and 7 1/2 per cent respectively, vide 27/25/68/EST(SCT) dated 25th March 1970 for any type of recruitment (for direct recruitment otherwise than by open competition, it is 16 1/2% for the SCs) and promotions.[19] The State Governments also adopted more or less the same reservation policy as adopted by the Union Government. The inrease in reservations was commensurate with the increase in population as per 1961 census.

(5) The policy of reservation in the public sector undertakings was accepted in principle in 1954 and various ministries were accordingly requested to issue suitable instructions to the undertakings under their control to make reservation for the SC/ST in their services.[20] Vide O.M. No. 5/1/63 SCT (1) dated 4th March 1964. Accordingly, the Bureau of Public Undertakings, Ministry of Finance in its D.O.Letter No. 2(115)/68-BPE (GM) dated 18th

September 1969 communicated to the ministries a draft directive to be issued to the public undertakings on the subject.[21] As a result of these instructions most of the Public Sector Undertakings have now agreed to provide reservations for SC/ST in their services on the lines of reservations in the Central Government Services.

(6) There was no reservation in posts filled by promotion by selection or on the basis of Seniority-Cum-Fitness in any appointment initially in 1950. However in cases of promotion in posts filled on the basis of departmental examination, the reservation was 12 1/2 per cent for the Scheduled Castes and 5 per cent for the Scheduled Tribes, vide MHA O.M. No. 5/4/55-SCT (1) dated 4th January 1957.[22] In General Manager V. Rangachari.[23]

AIR (1962) SC 36, the honourable Supreme Court held that under Article 16(4) of the constitution, it was permissible to make reservation not only at the initial stage, but also of the posts filled in by promotion. Therefore, the Ministry of Home Affairs vide O.M.No.1/10/61, Est (o) dated 8th November 1963 fixed quota of Promotion by Selection, or on the basis of seniority-cum-fitness, at 12 1/2 per cent for Scheduled Castes and 5 per cent for the Scheduled Tribes only in class III and IV posts.[24]

However, on the request of the SC/ST Employees Welfare Association, the Govt. revised its policy in matter of promotion in 1968. Some State Govts. also followed the Central Government.

However in Indra Sawhney V. Union of India (Mandal Case)[25] the Hon'ble Supreme Court took up suo moto the issue of reservation of SC/ST in promotion and declared it unconstitutional. Eventually, the parliament through 77th Constitution Amendment Act, 1995 added a new clause 4A to Article 16 of the Constitution which enabled the state to provide for reservation for SC/ST in promotions. However, 16(4A) is confined to SCs and STs alone.

(7) Reservation till 01-07-1997 was computed on the basis of number of vacancies to be filled. However, the Supreme Court in the case of R.K. Sabarwal V. State of Punjab held that the reservation should be determined on the basis of number of posts in the Cadre and not on the basis of vacancies. Accordingly post based reservation was introduced w.e.f. 2-7-1997." The basic principle of post based reservation is that the number of posts filled by any category in a Cadre should be equal to the quota prescribed for that category."

(8) So far as the matter of reservation in promotion is concerned Clause 4-A of Article 16 as amended by 85th Amendment Act, 2001 has finally laid down the constitutional mandate in clear terms. Accordingly, there would be reservation, "in matters of promotion, with consequential seniority, to any class or classes of

posts in the services under the state for the Scheduled Castes and the Scheduled Tribes."

In pursuance of the above stated constitutional mandate, Government of India, DOPI issued Office Memorandum, NO.20011/1/2001/Estt, dated 21st January, 2002 to all the Ministries and Departments.

(9) So far as the upper limit is concerned, the Supreme Court pronounced in Devadasan V. Union of India, that "each year of recruitment will have to be considered by itself and the reservation for the backward communities should not be so excessive as to create a monopoly or to disturb unduly with the legitimate claims of other communities." Accordingly, the court held that the reservation of vacancies in excess of 50 percent, would according to the decision in Balaji's Case (AiR 1963 SC 649 not be constitutional."[26]

(10) It should be borne in mind that the Department of Personnel and Training, Government of India, issued O.M. No. 36012/31/90-Estt (SCT) dated 13th August 1990 and 25th Sept.1991 regarding reservation for Socially and Educationally Backward Classes in Civil Posts. Thus, the other Backward Classes were brought under the category of beneficiaries under Article 16(4) in the year 1991, as a sequel to The Mandal Commission Report. The said O.M. was challenged in the Supreme Court; but the Supreme Court upheld the said O.M. in 1992 (AIR 1992 SCC 217). However, after settlement of creamy layer issue a new O.M. dated : 08-09-1993 was issued.

(11) The rules and regulations framed by the Union Government in respect of reservations for SC/ST/OBC in Public employment are applied in the Public Offices or Offices and Institutions under the jurisdiction of the Union Government. The State /U.T. Governments also have framed their own rules and regulations in this respect on the same lines as of Union Government. Some of the State Governments have passed laws to deal with the matter of reservations.[27]

2.3 Certain Relevant Issues

In the light of this discussion, it is appropriate to address the following questions:-

(1) What is a fundamental right and how does it differ from ordinary right?

(2) Is reservation - in education and employment a fundamental right on the part of the backward classes ?

(3) Is it obligatory or discretionary on the part of the state to implement it ?

(4) Whether reservation policy goes against the principle of equality ?
(5) How far the SEBS or OBC Category is treated on par with the SC/ST Category?
(6) Is caste a valid criteron of classification ?
(7) Is meritorious backward class candidate entitled to be included in the general merit list ?
(8) Whether reservation policy is obligatory on unaided educational institutions ?
(9) Whether minority educational institutions are expected to implement reservation policy?
(10) How long the safeguards would continue ?

(1) What is Fundamental Right and how does it differ from ordinary right?

Before discussing whether reservation is a fundamental right or not, it is necessary to know as to what is fundamental right. According to Prof. Laski, rights are "those conditions of Social Life without which no man can seek, in general, to be himself at his best."[28] In the view of Dr. Babasaheb Ambedkar, "Fundamental Rights are the gift of the Law"[29] and they are "inalienable" and enforceable by the state.[30] Thus, fundamental rights are very essential for the development of human beings and no one can take away or abridge them without due process of law.

The Constitution of India has provided certain fundamental rights in its part III, from Article 12 to 35, they are : (1) Right to equality, (2) Right to freedom, (3) Right against exploitation, (4) Right to freedom of religion (5) Cultural and educational rights, and (6) Right to constitutional remedies.

The Constitution states in unequivocal terms under its Article 13(1) that, "All Laws in force in the Territory of India immediately before the commencement of this Constitution in so far as they are inconsistant with the provisions of this part, shall, to the extent of such inconsistency, be void. Moreover, (2) "The state shall not make any law which takes away or abridges the rights conferred by this part and any law made in contravention of this clause shall to the extent of the contravention, be void." This indicates that no law would be inconsistent with or abridging the content of the fundamental rights.

Further, the Constitution provides remedies for enforcement of rights conferred by Part III. Article 32(1) states that, "The right to move the Supreme Court by appropriate proceedings for the enforcement of the rights conferred by this part is guaranteed."

This amply proves that the makers of the Constitution gave utmost importance to the fundamental rights. They have not only made provision of remedies or empowered the Supreme Court to issue appropriate writs or orders for the enforcement of those rights, but they have made "Right to Constitutional Remedies" one of the fundamental rights itself. According to Dr. Babasaheb Ambedkar "Rights are real only if they are accompanied by remedies."[31] He rightly calls that provision under Article 32 as "Soul of the Constitution."[32]

The makers of the Constitution were quite aware of the fact that mere provision of fundamental rights would not be sufficient. In an economy based on private enterprise, the rich and powerful would misutilize their fundamental rights to exploit the poor and unemployed persons. Therefore, the Constitution provides under its Directive Principles of State Policy for "a social order in which justice social, economic and political, shall inform all the institutions of the national life."

Though the fundamental rights are not absolute and unlimited, they are, ordinarily beyond the reach of the legislature. It may, under its constituent power, amend any part of the Constitution, subject to the policy of "Basic Structure" and it may make any law under its legislative power, it can not deviate from the policy of directive principles of the state in governance of the country.

There are several kinds of rights, like legal and moral rights, political rights and civil rights, contract based and relation based rights. Ordinary rights are those which are not included in fundamental rights. Ordinary rights may be legal or statutory, but they have not been recoganized as fundamental. Presently right to property is ordinary, legal and constitutional, but it is not a fundamental right. The status makes the difference. Fundamental rights are essential, inalienable and inviolable. They form the part of basic structure of the Constitution. For the violation of fundaments right there is remedy under Article 32, which empowers the Supreme Court to protect them. There is remedy under Article 226 of the constitution to move to the High Court for protection of both the fundamenal right and oridinary rights. "The real distinction between the two," as observed by Dr. Babasaheb Ambedkar is, "that non-fundamental rights are created by agreement between parties while fundamental rights are the gift of the law."[33] Thus the difference between the two could be stated in terms of their source, status, estimation and remedy.

Thus, the fundamental rights are very essential, constitutional and inviolable. Therefore, they are mandatory on the part of the state, institutions and individuals, as such every body has to obey, protect and implement them in letter and spirit.

(2) Is reservation in education and employment a fundamental right on the part of the Backward Classes ?

The Policy of reservation in favour of the back-ward classes has been embodied in the Constitution, Article 15(4) and Article 16(4) under the Fundamental Rights Chapter. Hence, it is natural and consequent to believe that the Policy of reservation contemplated under the said articles is a fundamental right of the backward classes. It is fundamental, in the sense, it is inviolable, irrevocable and obligatory.

The fundamental rights guaranteed under Part III of the Constitution are guarantee against the action of the state. "The state" as used in part III of the Constitution includes the Union Government, State Governments and all local and other authorities within the Territory of India. It is however not certain whether the judiciary comes under "other authorities" of "the state". It is generally said that "the expression state as defined in Article 12 of the Constitution includes judiciary also".[34] Thus all the authorities within the Territory of India and under the control of the Government of India are called "The state". Thus the meaning of "the state" under the Constitution is some what different, from the theoritical meaning of the "state."

According to Article 13 of the Constitution "Laws in force" before the commencement of this Constitution and the Laws made by the state subsequently are expected to be consistent with the provisions of the fundamental rights otherwise they would be void to the extent of such inconsistency. According to Article 32, the righs guaranteed in the Constitution are justiciable, as such appropriate remedy can be sought in case of their violation.

Notwithstanding the strong and sound position of provisions of reservation, the honourable courts and the legal luminaries are of the opinion that the provisions of reservation are not mandatory. Some of the important decisions are as under :

(a) "Article 15(4) like Article 16(4) is an enabling provision, it does not impose an obligation, but merely leaves it to the discretion of the appropriate Government to take suitable action, if necessary." (Balaji Vs. State of Mysore)[35]

(b) "It must be remembered that Article 15(4) and Article 16(4) are not mandatory, but are merely enabling provisions. The State Government therefore may or may not make any rule or issue any executive direction for the purpose of reserving some posts for or extending other concessions to backward classes. It is also not in dispute that when the State Government can in its discretion make such rule or issue administrative instructions, it can also cancel or modify it."

(Dasu Rayudu Vs. Andhra Pradesh Public Service Commission.[36])

(c) "........ that Article 16 (4) does not confer any right on the Petitioner and there is no constitutional duty imposed on the Government to make a reservation for Scheduled Castes and Scheduled Tribes, either at the initial stage of recruitment or at the stage of promotion. In otherwords, Article 16(4) is an enabling provision and confers a discretionary power on the state to make a reservation of appoinments in favour of Backward Classes of citizens which in its opinion is not adequately represented in the service of the state." (C.A. Rajendran Vs.Union of India).[37]

(d) ".......... no writ can be issued ordinarily compelling the government to make reservations under Article 16(4) which is only an enabling clause." (P and T Scheduled Castes / Tribes Employees Welfare Association V. Unio of India).[38]

(e) "The Constitution, no doubt, has laid a special responsibility on the Government to protect the claims of SC/ST in the matter of Public appointment under various constitutional provisions of which we shall presently refer to a few."

Article 16(4) as manifested from the various decisions of this court referred to hereinbefore, is an enabling provision conferring a discretionary power on the state for making any provision or reservation of appointments or posts in favour of any backward class of citizens, which in the opinion of the state, is not adequately represented in the service under the state "Clause 4 of Article 16 has to be interpreted in the background of Article 335"... Reservation is not a constitutional compulsion but it is discretionary one."

(Mohan Kumar Singhania V. Union of India).[39]

(f) "We next come to the question whether Article 16(4) and Article 15(4A) guaranteed any fundamental right to reservation. It should be noted that both these Articles open with a non-obstante clause - "Nothing in this Article shall prevent the state from making any provision for reservation....". There is a marked difference in the Article 16(1) on the one hand and Article 16(4) and Article 16(4A). There is no directive or command in Article 16(4) or Article 16 (4A) as in Article 16(1). On the face of it the above language in each of Articles 16(4) and 16(4A), is in the nature of an enabling provision and it has been so held in judgements rendered by Constitution Benches and in other cases right from 1963."

(Ajit Singh V. The State of Punjab)[40]

(g) It was observed in M. Nagraj V. Union of India (2006) that "Articles 16(4A) and 16(4B) flow from Article 16(4) and if Article 16(4) is an enabling provision then Articles 16(4A), 16(4B) are also enabling provisions."[40(a)]

The judicial pronouncements in the above said cases are really surprising. They are more or less unanimous in saying that the constitutional provisions are merely "enabling" the state to provide for reservation for the backward classes in the educational institutions and in the employment. Even it has been categorically said that those provisions are mere "discretionary" as such the state may in its discretion make such rule or issue administrative instructions, it may also cancel or modify. Thus what is deliberately given by the Constitution has been made discretionary by the Judiciary.

(h) It is submitted that, the claim on reservation is not merely a declaratory right, it is a legal, constitutional and fundamental right. It is not merely a "directive" given to the state to provide for reservation. Had it been so, it would have been included in the chapter on Directive Principles of state policy. Although Article 46 has been included in the Directive Principles, Article 15(4) and 16(4) are provided in the fundamental rights. This amply indicates that the Constitution had deliberately included the said articles in the chapter on Fundamental Rights so as to give them mandatory position. It is included in the fundamental rights, as such it is a fundamental right. It is but a self-evident fact, which needs no other proof to prove it. The honourable Supreme Court pronounced in very explicit terms that, "..... even if a right is not specifically named (in Article 19(1), it may still be a fundamental right covered by some clause of that Article if it is an integral part of a named fundamental right or partakes of the same basic nature and character as that fundamental right."

(Maneka Gandhi V. Union of India).[41]

(i) According to Article 13 of the Constitution "Laws in force" before the commencement of this Constitution and the laws amde by the state subsequently are expected to be consistent with the provisions of the fundamental rights otherwise they would be void to the extent of such inconsistency. Hence no state can make any law antithetical to the fundamental right.

According to Article 32, the rights guaranteed in the Constitution are justiciable, as such appropriate remedy could be sought in case of their violation. What is said under Article 32(1) is this : "the right to move the Supreme Court by appropriate proceedings for the enforcement of the rights conferred by this part is guaranteed. Thus, Article 15(4) and 16(4) come under "the rights conferred by this part" and hence they are justiciable.

(3) Is Reservation Obligatory or Discretionary ?

Providing reservations under Article 15(4) and under Article 16(4) is constitutional, fundamental and justiciable. Undoubtedly those provisions "enable" the state to make any special provision or take affirmative action for the development of the "Social and Educationally Backward Classes" including the Scheduled Castes and the Scheduled Tribes. The provision signifies the 'will' and 'directive' of the Constitution to the state to take affirmative action. It does not mean that it is 'discretionary' on the part of the state.

In the words of Subba Rao J. "The expresson 'nothing in this article' is a legislative device to express its intention in a most emphatic way that the power conferred thereunder is not limited in any way by the main provision but falls outside it."[42] It has not really carved out an exception, but has preserved a power untrammelled by the other Provisions of the Article."

Even if it is assumed that the right to reservation is not a fundamental right, but it is merely a constitutional or statutory right; how could it be said that the constitutional or statutory provision is merely a "discretionary" provision ? Is it merely ornamental and not obligatory ? what is the substantial difference between a fundamental right and a constitutional or statutory right ? It is a matter of "status" and not of "fact". Fundamental rights are justiciable under Article 32 of the Constitution and we can directly invoke the jurisdiction of the Supreme Court in case of breach or transgression of such rights; whereas in other cases we have to approach to the High Courts under Article 226 for redress. There are certain constitutional rights, for example rights to citizenship (Article (5), right ot vote (Article 325, 326) right to property (Article 300A), Political rights and safeguards etc. etc. These provisions have given certain rights to the citizens and assign corresponding duties on the state. How could a legal right or duty be a matter of "discretion"?

Even the fundamental rights are not absolute. They are also subject to some reasonable restrictions. They may be of negative or positive nature. For example. Article 14 prevents the state from denying equal protection of the laws; whereas Article 19 confers the freedom of speech and expression. Judiciary is the guardian of the fundamental as well as constitutional rights of the individuals against the violation thereof by individuals or the state.

(4) Whether the Policy of Reservations goes against the Principle of Equality ?

The principle of equality is "the corner stone of our constitutional arch," as such it has been enumerated in the Preamble of the Constitution and it has been given the first and foremost place in the scheme of fundamental rights in our Constitution, under its Articles 14, 15, 16, 17 and 18. Article 14 declares that, "The state shall not deny to any person equality before the law or equal protection of the laws within the Territory of India."

According to M.V. Pylee, "Equality before the law is an expression of English Common Law while "equal protection of Laws" owes its orgin to the American constitution. Both the phrases aim to establish what is called the "equality of status and of opportunity," as embodied in the Preamble of the Constitution. While equality before the law is a somewhat negative concept implying the absence of any special privilage in favour of any individual and the qual subjection of all classes to the oridinary law, equal protection of laws is more positive concept implying equality of treatment under equal circumstances."[43]

However, the honourable Supreme Court has observed in Chiranjit Lal V. Union of India, that, "The principle does not take away from the state the power of classifying persons for legitimate purposes."

While reasonable classification is permissible, such classification must be based upon some real and substantial distinction bearing a reasonable and just relation to the object sought to be attained, and the classification can not be made arbitrarily and without any substantial basis.[44]

The Honourable Supreme Court in E.P. Royappa V. State of Tamil Nadu[45] pronounced the new concept of equality. Accordingly "Equality is a dynamic concept with many aspects and dimensions and it can not be 'cribbed, cabined and confined' within Traditional doctrinaire limits. From a positive point of view, equality is anti-thetic to arbitrariness. In fact equality and arbitariness are sworn enemies; onc bolongs to the rule of law in a republic while the other, to the whim and caprice of an absolute monarch. Where an act is arbitrary, it is implicite in it that it is unequal both according to political logic and constitutional law and is therefore violative of Article 14" and if it affects any matter relating to public employment, it is also violative of Article 16.

Thus, the classification must be based on -

(i) An intelligible differentia, which distinguishes persons or things that are grouped together from others left out of the group;

(ii) The differentia must have a rational relation to the object sought to be achieved by the Act.

(iii) The classification may be made on different basis, like geographical area, occupations etc.

(iv) The classification should not be arbitrary.

In the absence of equality, liberty and fraternity would be myths. According to Dr. Babasaheb Ambedkar, "Fratermity and Liberty are really derivative notions. the basic and fundamental conceptions are equality and respect for human personality. Fraternity and liberty take their roots in these two fundamental conceptions. Digging further down it may be said that equality is the original notion and respect for human personality is a reflexion of it. So that where equality is denied, everything else may be taken to be denied."[46]

The Constitution under its Article 14, 15(1), 15(4), 16(1), 16(4), 46, 330, 332, 335, 243 and others provide for promoting equality. Article 15(4) is not a "separate" part, it is a part of 15(1) and emanates from Article 14. Article 16(4) is a part of 16(1) and originates in Article 14. The provision of reservation contemplates to give equal opportunity to the equal and eligible persons. In the absence of Article 15(4) and 16(4) there would be inequality.

Some of the landmark decisions highlighting and upholding the principle of equality are given hereunder :

(a) "......there can be neither stability nor real progress if predominant sections of an awakened nation live in primitive conditions, confined to unremunerative occupations and having no share in the good things of life, while power and wealth are confined in the hands of only a few and the same is used for the benefit of the sections of the community to which they belong....., who today have a monopoly of education and consequently have predominant representation in the Government Services as well as in other important walks of life. It is cynical to suggest that the interest of the nation is best served if the barber's son continues to be a barber and a shepherd's son continues to be a shepherd.

.....We have pledged ourselves to establish a welfare state. Social Justice is an important ingredient of that concept. That goal cannot be reached if we overemphasize the "merit theory."

Advantages secured due to historical reasons can not be considered as fundamental rights guaranteed by the Constitution. The nation's interest will be best served taking a long-range view if the backward classes are helped to march forward and take their places in a line with the advanced sections of the people."

(Viswanath V. Government of Mysore).[47]

(b) "So in order to give a real opportunity to them (the backward classes) to compete with the better placed people CLS (3) and (4) are introduced in the article. CL (4) enables the state to make a provision for reservation of appointments or posts in favour of any backward classes of citizens. The predominent concept underlying the provision is equality of opportunity in the matter of employment, and without detriment to the said concept, the state is enabled to make reservations in favour of backward classes to give a practical content to the concept of equality."

The Constitution seeks to secure justice, social, economic and political to all citizens and provide equality of status and of opportunity to them all... (Trilokinath V. State of J. & K.)[48]

(c) "It has however been realized that in a country like India where large sections of the people are backward socially, economically, educationally and politically these declaration and guarantees will be meaningless unless provision is also made for the uplift of such backward classes who are in no position whatever to compete with the more advanced classes. Thus to give meaning and content to the equality guaranteed by Articles 14, 15, 16 and 29, provision has been made in Articles 15(4) and 16(4) enabling preferential treatment in favour of the "Weaker Sections."

(Hariharan Pillai Vs. State of Kerala)[49]

(d) "Article 15(4) will have to be given effect to in order to assist the weaker sections of the citizens, as the state has been charged with such a duty. No boubt, we are aware that any provision made under this clause must be within the well defined limits and should not be on the basis of caste alone. But it should not also be missed that a caste is also a class of citizens and that a caste as such may be socially and educationally backward. If after collecting the necessary data, it is found that the caste as a whole is socially and educationally backward, in our opinion, the reservation made of such persons will have to be upheld not withstanding the fact that a few individuals in that group may be both socially and educationally above the general average." (The State of Andhra Pradesh V. Balaram).[50]

(e) This sub-article (Art.16(4), "serves not as an exception but as an emphatic statement, one mode of reconciliating the claims of backward people and the opportunity for free competition that the forward sections are ordinarily entitled to." "The genius of Articles 14 to 16 consists not in literal equality but in progressive elimination of pronounced inquality. Indeed to treat sharply dissimilar persons equally is subtle injustice. Equal opportunity is a hope, not a menace." (State of Kerala Vs. N.M.Thomas).[51]

(f) "Ours is a country of great economic, social and cultural diversity. Often we take great pride in the country's cultural diversity. While cultural diversity adds to the Splendour of India, the others add to our sorrow and shame. The social and economic disparities are indeed despairingly vast. The Scheduled Castes, the Scheduled Tribes and the other socially and educationally backward classes, all of whom have been compendiously described as "The Weaker Sections of the Society," have long journeys to make society. They need aid : they need facility; they need launching. They need propulsion. Their needs are their demands. The demands are matters of right and not of Philanthropy. They ask for parity, and not charity. The days of Dronacharya and Ekalavya are over. They claim their constitutional right to equality of status and of opportunity and economic and social justice. Several bridges have to be erected, so that they may cross the Rubicon. Professional educaton and employment under the state are thought to be two such bridges. Hence the special provision for advancement and for reservation under Articles 15(4) and 16(4) of the Constitution."

(K.C.Vasanth Kumar Vs. State of Karnataka)[52]

(g) It is now well settled by decisions of this court that the reservation in favour of backward classes of citizens, including the members of the Scheduled Castes and the Scheduled Tribes, as contemplated by Article 16(4) can be made not merely in respect of initial recruitment but also in respect of posts to which promotions are to be made. (Comptroller and Auditor General of India Vs. K.S. Jagannathan)[53]

(h) "We too believe that Article 16(1) does permit reasonable classification for ensuring attainment of the equality of opportunity assured by it. For assuring equality of opportunity, it may well be necessary in certain situation to treat unequally situated persons unequally. Not doing so would perpetuate and accentuate inequality. Article 16(4) is an instance of such classification, put in to place the matter beyond controversy. The "backward class of citizens" are classified as a separate category deserving a special treatment in the nature of reservation of appointment/posts in the services of the state. Accordingly, we hold that clause [4] of Article 16 is not exception to clause (1) of Article 16. It is an instance of classification implicite in and permitted by clause (1) : (Indra Sawney V. Union of India)[54]

(i) "It is settled law that it should be read consistently with Article 46 of the Constitution to take special care of the educational and economic interests of the Scheduled Castes and the STs and to protect them from injustice and all forms of exploitations.

Appointment to an office or post under the state is one of the policies of the state to accord economic justice as part of social justice for integration of Scheduled Castes and Scheduled Tribes in the social mainstream, dignity of person and equality of status. It would be an opportunity to improve excellence, a fundamental duty. In the light of Article 16(4A) introduced by the Constitution (77th Amendment Act, 1995 the claims of the SC and the ST for promotion shall be taken into consideration in making appointment or giving promotion. It is constitutional duty coupled with power of the authorities implementing the rules of recruitment including promotion."

"Every Public Servant is a Trustee of the society and in all facets of Public administration, every public servant has to exhibit honesty, integrity, sincerity and faithfulness in implementation of the political, social, economic and constitutional policies to integrate the nation, to achieve excellence and efficiency in the Public administration. A Public Servant entrusted with duty and power to implement constitutional policy under Article 16(4), 16(4A), 15(4), 335 and all interrelated directive principles should exhibit transparency in implementation and of accountable for due effectuation of constitutional goals. Maintenance of the roster and strict adherence to it in accordance with the broucher issued by the Government of India in that behalf to implement.

The rule of reservation in promotion is the charge and trust put on Public Servants. The Constitution has trusted the Public Servant as honest administrator to effectuate Public Policy and Constitutional goals.

Omission thereof amounted to violation of constitutional duty and avoidance of implementation of the rule of reservation and the roster provided by the government." (Superintending Engineer Public Health V. Kuldeep Singh).[55]

(j) "In order to protect and promote the less forunate or unfortunate people who have been suffering from social handicap, educational backwardness besides other disadvantages, certain provisions are made in the Constitution with a view to see that they also have the opportunity to be on par with others in the society. Certain privileges and benefits are conferred on such people belonging to Scheduled Tribes by way of reservations in admission to educational institutions (professional colleges) and in appointments in services of state, the object behind these provisions is noble and laudable besides being vital in bringing a meaningful social change." (State of Maharashtra Vs. Milind and Others)[56]

(k) The Hon'ble Shri Balkrishna, C.J. has very rightly observed in Ashok Kumar Thakur Vs. Union of India.

That, .. "Reservation is one of the many tools that are used to preserve and promote the essence of equality, so that disadvantaged groups can be brought to the forefront of civil life. It is the duty of the state to promote positive measures to remove barriers of inequality and enable diverse communities to enjoy the freedoms and share the benefits guaranteed by the Constitution."[57]

(5) How far the SEBC Category is Treated on Par with the SC/ST Category?

It is a fact that the policy of reservation is not equally applicable to the SC/STs and SEBCs. For the purposes of constitutional safeguards under Article 15(4), 16(4) and 330, 332, 243D and 243T of the Constitution, the SC/STs are treated as one category and for the purpose of 15(4) and 16(4) only the SEBC or OBCs are treated as another category.

(a) **Definition :** According to Article 366(24) of the Constitution, "Scheduled Castes" means such castes, races or tribes as are deemed under article 341 to be Scheduled Castes for the purposes of this Constitution."

According to Article 366(25) of the Constitution, "Scheduled Tribes" means such Tribes or Tribal Communities or parts of or groups within such Tribes or Tribal Communities as are deemed under article 342 to be Scheduled Tribes for the purposes of this Constitution."

No such definition of S.E.B.C. or O.B.C. is given in the Constitution.

(b) **Criteria :** An inquiry into the history of the list of Scheduled Castes specified and enclosed as the Ninth Scheduled to the Government of India Act, 1935, reveals that the basis of enlisting certain castes as Scheduled Caste was "Untouchability". The present list of Scheduled Castes is but a modified version of the list prepared in 1935. In the opinion of Shri V.I. Muniswamy Pillai, a member of the Constituent Assembly, it was "untouchability", which brought out the special name of Scheduled Castes.[58] In the opinion of first commissioner for SC/ST, the Hutton's 1931 census criteria on the basis of which the list of Scheduled Castes was prepared in 1950 "appears to hold good for purposes of specifying the Scheduled Castes."[59] According to Prof. Marc Galanter, "the Scheduled Castes have been chosen primarily by the criterion of low social and ritual standing."[60]

The main criterion of Tribal Status, according to Dr.Babasaheb Ambedkar is their, "primitive uncivilized state."[61] According to Prof. Marc Galanter, the tribals are distinguished by their, "Tribal Characteristics" and by their spatial and cultural isolation from the bulk of the population.[62]

So far as "socially and educationally backward classes" are concerned, the criteria on which they are based is implied in the very nomenclature itself. It has been reportedly laid down by the Allahabad High Court that, social backwardness and educational backwardness are the two main creteria on which their category is based.[63] The Mandal Commission Report applied four social criteria, three educational criteria and four economic criteria for the purpose of identifying backwardness. The commission, in general found that if the progress of the caste supposed to be low is 25% less than the average progress of the people in that state, that caste fulfilled the criteria of backwardness.

(c) Constitutional Status

The President of India under Article 341 of the Constitution may specify certain castes, sub-castes or races or tribes as Scheduled Castes by public notification. The parliament may by law include in or exclude from the list any caste, sub-caste etc. The Constitution Order (S.C.) came into implementation in 1950.

In the same way the President under Article 342 of the Constitution may specify certain tribes or Tribal Communities as Scheduled Tribes by Public Notification. The parliament may by law include in or exclude from the list any Tribe. The S.T. Order came into operation in 1950.

Due to provision of political reservation for the Scheduled Castes ad aboriginal Tribes in the Act of 1935, it because imperative to make out the statewise list of the Scheduled Castes and the aboriginal Tribes (named later as the Scheduled Tribes) in the year 1936. However the matter of making the list of other Backward Classes came to light only after the commencement of the Constitution of India.

However, the list of other Backward Classes prepared in 1944 for the purpose of post-matric Scholarship Scheme and the list of other Backwards Classes prepared by the Commissioner for Scheduled Castes and Scheduled Tribes were brought into operations. Thus, the tribes who were left out for one reason or other from the list of Scheduled Tribes issued by the President have been included in the list of "Other Backward Classes" for the specific purpose by the Commissioner for SCs and STs. It was as under :-

Bihar	:	Bhogtas and Bhumij (except some parts of thestate)
Madhya Pradesh	:	Sub-Tribes of Gond Pandos.
Madras	:	Adiyans, Kadars, Kurichens, Paliyans Pulayans, Sugali, Yerukula, Yenadi.
Hyderabad	:	Erukula, Lambada, Yenadi.
Madhya Bharat	:	Rajasthan Bhilals, Bhilals-Minas, Dhamara Bhils, Bhilals, Bhils, Girasias Serias.
Saurashtra	:	Charans; Padhars, Rabaris, Sidhis.[64]

Subsequently, the President of India, under Article 340 of the Constitution appointed the first Backward Classes Commission on 29th Jan.1953 to investigate the social and educational criteria for other Backward Classes. The Commission submitted its report accordingly on 30th March 1955. The commission came to the conclusion that there were 2399 backward castes and they need special measures for the amelioration of their backwardness. The commission was headed by Kakasaheb Kalekar. There was, of course no unanimity in its decisions. Even its Chairman also differed in his opinion and conveyed so to the President after the submission of the authentic report. Consequently the said report was not even put before the Parliament for discussion on it. The main ground of difference was regarding the criteria on which backward classes were to be classified so. The main contention was whether caste should be a criterion of backwardness or not. The Union Government however could not come to any conclusion. Ultimately the Home Minister conveyed on 14th August 1961 to the individual state government to decide the criteria of backwardness in respect of their own state and prepare their own backward classes list accordingly.

Pursuant to the decision of the Union Government, various State Governments made certain efforts in that direction. See Table 2.3.

Besides, the other ten states including Harayana, Himachal Pradesh, Assam, Pondichery, Rajasthan, Orissa, Meghalaya and Delhi also adopted certain measures for the welfare of the backward classes.

(d) In view of failure of the first Backward Classes Commission in 1955, lack of uniformity in the State Governments on the issue of criteria of backwardness and measures to be adopted

TABLE 2.3

The Following Table Shows the efforts made by the State Governments During 1960 to 1980

Sr. No.	*State*	*State Action*	*Status*
1.	Andhra Pradesh	(1) 1964 List of 112 Castes	Invalidated by The Supreme Court in Sagar V.A.P. (AIR 1968 SC 1379)
		(2) 1968-1970, Andhra Pradesh Backward Classes Commission Chairman – Manohar Prasad Report, 1970.	Accepted with modification by the Govt. and upheld by the Supreme Court in State of A.P. Vs. P.V. Balaram (AIR 1972 SC 1375)
		(3) 1977 : A Committee of Vidhan Sabha. Chairman : Agisan Virappa Report, 1977	Accepted
2.	Bihar	(1) 1951 : List of 109 Castes	Invalidated by the Court in Nand Kishore Sharma V. State of Bihar (AIR 1965, Patrna, 372)
		(2) 1971-1976 : Backward Classes Commission. Chairman : Mungerilal Report, 1976 List of 128 Castes	Accepted by the Govt. but opposition from both High Castes and OBCs
3.	Gujarat	1972-1976 : Socially and Educationally Backward Classes Commission. Chairman : A.R. Bakshi List of 82 Castes Report, 1976.	Accepted by State Govt.

(Table Contd.)

(Contd. Table 2.3)

Sr. No.	State	State Action	Status
4.	Jammu and Kashmir	(1) 1967-68 : Commission. Chairman : Justice Gajendra Gadakar	Suggested for further inquiry.
		(2) 1969 : J &K Backward Classes Commission Chairman : J.N. Wajir Report, 1969.	Accepted by the State but invalidated by the Supreme Court in Janaki Prasad Vs. State of J&K (AIR 1973 SC 930)
		(3) 1976-1977 : Backward Classes Commission. Chairman : Dr. A.S. Anand	Accepted by the State Govt.
5.	Karnataka	(1) 1959 : Regionwise list with 164 Castes	Accepted, but invalidated by Mysore High Court in Ramkrishna Singh V. State of Mysore (AIR 1960 Mysore, 338)
		(2) 1960-1961 : Backward Classes Commission Chairman : Dr. R. Nagan Gowda Report, 1961. List of 214 Castes Under Art. 15(4) List of 185 Castes Under Art. 16(4)	Accepted by State Govt. but invalidated by the Supreme Court in Balaji Vs. State of Mysore. (AIR 1963 SC 649)
		(3) 1972-1975 : Karnataka Backward Classes Commission Chairman : L.G. Havanur Report, 1975	Accepted.

(Table Contd.)

(Contd. Table 2.3)

Sr. No.	State	State Action	Status
6.	Kerala	(1) 1961-1963 : Backward Classes Commission. Chairman : B.K. Shivanathan Report, 1963.	Accepted but invalidated by the High Court of Kerala in Jacob Mathew Vs. State of Kerala (AIR 1964 Ker.39)
		(2) 1964-1965 : Kerala Commisison for Reservation. Chairman : G. Kumar Pillai List of 91 Castes. Report, 1965.	Accepted with Modifications, but invalidated by The High Court of Kerala in Laila Chacko Vs. State (AIR 1967 Ker. 124)
		(3) 1967-1970 : Kerala Backward Classes Reservation Commission. Chairman : N.P. Damodaran Report, 1970.	Accepted
7.	Maharashtra	1961-1964 : Maharashtra Committee on Reservation for Backward Classes in Service. Chairman : B.D. Deshmukh Report, 1964	Accepted by the State Govt.
8.	Punjab	(1) 1951 : List of 14 Castes.	
		(2) 1965-1966 : Backward Classes Commission. Chairman : Vrishbhan	Accepted with certain modifications.
		(3) Report of the Vidhan Sabha Samiti. Report, 1976.	Not accepted by the Government.
9.	Uttar Pradesh	1975-1977 : Backward Classes Commission. Chairman : Chedilal Sathi Report, 1977.	Accepted with modification but invalidated by the Allahabad High Court in Chhotelal Vs. U.P. (AIR 1979 Allahabad, 135)
10.	Tamil Nadu	1969 – 1970 : T.N. Backward Classes Commission. Chairman : A.N. Sathanathan Report : 1971.	Accepted by the State Government.

Source : BCC 1980 Chapter II.

for their development, growing intervention and interpretations of certain facts by the Judiciary, growing laxity on the part of the government officials in implementing welfare measures and the mounting pressure of the backward classes for their development, the President of India had appointed the Backward Classes Commission, under Article 340(1) of the Constitution of India, under the Chairmanship of B.P. Mandal alongwith other five members on 21st March, 1979. After a detailed study, indepth survey, extensive tours and visits, direct interviews and collecting evidences, census reports and judicial decisions and collecting all relevant information, the Commission could finalize the basis or the criteria of backwardness, the statewise list of backward classes and the measures to be adopted for the development of the backward classes. The Commission had evolved four social criteria, three educational criteria and four economic criteria. They were as under :

(A) Social Criteria

(1) Castes / Classes considered as socially backward by others;

(2) Castes / Classes which mainly depend on manual labour for their livelihood;

(3) Castes/Classes where at least 25 per cent females and 10 per cent males above the state average got married at an age below 17 years in rural areas and atleast 10 per cent females and 5 per cent males do so in urban areas;

(4) Castes / Classes where participation of females in work is at least 25 per cent above the state average.

(B) Educational Criteria

(5) Castes / Classes where the number of children in the age group of 5-15 years who never attended school is at least 25 per cent above the state average;

(6) Castes / Classes where the rate of student drop-out in the age-group of 5-15 years is at least 25 per cent above the state average;

(7) Castes / Classes amongst whom the proportion of matriculation is at least 25 per cent below the state average;

(C) Economic Criteria

(8) Castes / Classes where the average value of family assets is atleast 25 per cent below the state average;

(9) Castes/Classes where the number of families living in the Kuccha houses is at least 25 per cent above the state average;

(10) Castes/Classes where the source of drinking water is beyond half a kilometre for more than 50 per cent of their households;

(11) Castes/Classes where the number of hoseholds having taken consumption loans is atleast 25 per cent above the state average.

While evaluating the above indicators, the commission had given different weightage to each of them. For social indicators or criteria they gave 3 points, for educatinal indicators they gave 2 points and for economic criteria they gave 1 point.

Moreover, the commission identified and listed non-Hindu backward classes, christians, sikhs and Buddhists on the basis of their observations.

The commission made the sample survey of one percent or so villages in 405 districts out of 407 Districts and collected the necessary data with the help of experts. Accordingly the commission observed that there were 52 per cent other backward classes in the total population.

(e) New Criterion of Creamy Layer

Further, the Expert Committee constituted for specifying the criteria for identification of socially advanced persons among the socially and educationally backward classes enumerted criterion of "creamy layer" in its report dated 10th March 1993, and stated that such creamy layer persons ought to be excluded from the beneficiary group under the said Article of the Constituion. Accordingly, the sons and daughters of those who are holding the

(i) Constitutional Posts like President and Vice-President of India, Judges of the Supreme Court and the High Courts, Chairman and members of the UPSC and State Public Service Commissions, Election Commissioner etc.

(ii) Sons and daughters of those who are holding group A / class I post of the All-India Central and state services, or Class-II post in the central and state services and persons serving in public sector undertakings;

(iii) Sons and daughters of those who are holding high rank in the armed forces,

(iv) Sons and daughters of those who are in lucrative profession, trade or industry;

(v) Sons and daughters of those who are holding landed property and getting irrigation facility,

(vi) Sons and daughters of those persons who earn the income of Rs. 4-5 lakh (from October 2008) per annum. Thus the creamy layer class is not entitled to reservation in employment.

However, the commission recommended 27 per cent reservation in employment and 27 per cent in educational institutions, in addition to certain other facilities for the backward classes at India Level. There were approximately 3744 socially and educationally backward castes in India. The commission submitted its report to the President of India on 12th December 1980.

Eventually, it came into implementation on 7th August 1990, during the Prime Ministership of Shri V.P. Singh.

Thus, there are three categories. "First, there are those castes designated as Scheduled Castes (SC) on the basis of "untouchability." Second, there are the Scheduled Tribes (ST), who are distinguished by their Tribal Culture and physical isolation and many of whom are residents of specially protected Scheduled Areas. Third, there are the "Backward Classes" (or, as they are sometimes called, "Other Backward Classes") a heterogeneous category, varying greatly from state to state, composed for the most part of castes (and some non-Hindu Communities) low in the traditional social hierarchy, but not as low as the SC. Also included among the other backward classes (OBC) are a few tribal and nomadic groups, as well as converts to non-Hindu religions from the SC; and in some areas the Denotified Tribes."[65]

In this respect, the Supreme Court has categorically said in Chuttar Singh V. State of Rajasthan (1977) that "Though OBCs are socially and educationally not forward, they do not suffer the same social handicaps inflicted upon Scheduled Castes and Scheduled Tribes.... The object of reservation for the Scheduled Castes and Scheduled Tribes is to bring them into the mainstream of national life, while the objective in respect of the Backward Classes is to remove their social and educational handicaps."[66]

Thus, SC, ST Category and SEBC Category are constitutionally on different footing; in the sense the reservation is available to the SC, ST in appointment or posts at the initial appointment as well as at the promotional stage; they are not subjected to 'creamy layer' policy and they are entitled to political reservations. On the contrary the SEBCs are entitled to reservation at the initial appointment stage but not at promotional stage. They are invariably subjected to 'creamy layer' policy. They are not constitutionally entitled to political reservation at the State and national legislature. So far as reservation in educational institution is concerned, all the three categories are entitled to the more or less equal benefit.

It seems that the Constitution contemplates some difference between "socially and educationally backward classes" under Article 15(4) and "Backward Classes" under Article 16(4). The Hon'ble Supreme Court held in Balaji case (1963) that, the 'backward classes of citizens' in Article 16(4) is the same as the "socially and educationally backward classes" mentioned in 15(4). However, in Indra Sawhney (1992), The Supreme Court held that "the backward classes of citizens" contemplated in Article 16(4) are not the same as 'socially and educationally backward classes' referred to in Article 15(4) the Term "Backward Classes of Citizens" in Article 16(4) is wider. It refers to the Scheduled Castes, Scheduled Tribes, other backward classes and the socially and educationally backward classes.

(f) According to section 2(g) of the Central Educational Institutions (Reservation in Admission) Act, 2006 (5 of 2007) "other backward classes" means the class or classes or citizens who are socially and educationally backward, and are so determined by the Central Government." Thus "Other Backward Classes" under Article 16(4) are equal to "socially and educationally backward classes, under Article 15(4) of the Constitution.

It is submitted that if the Other Backward Classes are entitled to socio-economic benefit under the Constitution, there is no harm in extending political benefits also as some of the State Governments have already started giving such benefits to them at the local level.

(6) Is Caste a valid criterion of Classification ?

We have accepted the principle of equality, but it does not mean equality amongst the unequals. Equality means equality amongst the equals. Indian Society, especially the Hindu Society is based on graded inequality. In the words of Dr. Babasaheb Ambedkar, "the Indian Society was formed with an ascending scale of reverance and a descending scale of contempt."[67] Every caste is characterized by its different occupation, low or high status, endogamy and observance of religious and traditional rituals. In order to bring equality in such a society, it is necessary to uplift the so called lower castes to the level of the castes enjoying higher position in all respects. Therefore our Constituent Assembly had resorted to the doctrine of classification of certain caste groups or social groups into "the socially and educationally backward classes, the scheduled castes and the scheduled tribes, for the purpose of the Constitution and provided them with certain special safeguars."

What could be the principle on which such a classification is based. In Chriranjit Lal V. Union of India (1950)[68] SCR 869, the Honourable Supreme Court held that the classification to be reasonable must be based on an intelligible differentia; and it should bear a reasonable and just relation to the object sought to be achieved.

In a caste society the intelligible differentia has always been caste. It was the caste which was the primary measure of man's status, intellectual ability, and occupation. However, with the remarkable change in our objective as specified in our Constitution, we have again to resort to caste as a criterion of classification and constitutional safeguards infavour of beneficiary groups.

However, it was decided by the Supreme Court in Chitralekha V. State of Mysore that, "the authority concerned may take caste into consideration in ascertaining the backwardness of a group of persons; but, if it does not, its order will not be bad on that account, if it can ascertain the backwardness of a group of persons on the basis of other relevant criteria."

"The important factor to be noticed in Article 15(4) is that it does not speak of castes, but only speak of classes. If the makers of the Constitution intended to take castes also as units of social and educational backwardness, they would have said so as they have said in the case of the Scheduled castes as the Scheduled Tribes. Though it may be suggested that the wider expression 'classes' is used in Clause (4) of Article 15 as there are communities without castes, if the intention was to equate classes with castes, nothing prevented the makers of the Constitution to use the expression "Backward Classes or Castes."[68(a)]

However, the Constitution under Article 15(1) has provided that, "The state shall not discriminate against any citizen on grounds only of religion race, caste, sex, place of birth or any of them." Article 16(2) also States more or less the same provision. The question is whether in a given situation the prohibited criteria of caste could be applied in finding out the real beneficiaries and provide them with the special safeguards.

The words 'only' used in the said Article itself indicates that caste can be one of the grounds, alongwith other grounds, for discrimination. Article 15(4) allows discrimination in favour of any socially and educationally backward classes, or for SC and STs for their advancement or development. The discrimination in their favour and not against them is termed as protective discrimination or affirmative action under Article 15(4) and 16(4).

The Champakam Dorairajan case the communal G.O. based on caste and religion was struck down as it was adjudged as violative of equality provision. In Balaji (1963) it was held that caste can not be the sole or dominant test. In P. Rajendran (1968) it was held that, "a caste is also a class of citizens and if the caste as a whole is socially and educationally backward reservation can be made in favour of such caste." In Indra Sawhney (1992), it was held that "occupation, caste nexus is true even today... It does not matter if he has earned money. He may not follow that particular occupation. Still, the label remains. His identity is not changed for the purpose of marriage, death, and all other social functions, it is this social class, the caste that is relevant." It was held in Ashok Kumar Thakur case (2008) that, "The list of socially and educationally backward classes of citizens are being prepared not solely on the basis of the caste and if caste and other considerations are taken into account for determining backwardness, it cannot be said that it would be violation of Article 15(1) of the constitution."[69]

According to E.D. Devadasan, "caste in its original sense can be confined to Hindus by religion," but that cannot be so in the case of Scheduled Castes. "The very term, "schedule" indicates as artificial creation and not the division according to religion".[70] The court observed that, "The Government was not concerned with what was the real caste, but only what shall be deemed to be scheduled castes in law." According to Prof. Parmananada Singh caste "under Article 341 need not be viewed in relation to Hinduism. It ought to be construed as a "secular" and "social group."[71] If the caste is deemed to be a social group and if it is found to be socially and educationally backward, there is no difficulty in treating that caste as a socially and educationally backward class.

In K.S. Jayasree Vs. State of Kerala, it was observed by the Supreme Court that, "In ascertaining social backwardness of a class of citizens it may not be irrelevant to consider the caste of the group of citizens, caste cannot, however, be made the sole or dominant test. Social backwardness in the ultimate analysis the result of poverty to a large extent. Social backwardness which results from poverty is likely to be aggravated by considerations of their caste. This shows the relevance of both caste and poverty in determining the backwardness of citizens. Poverty itself is not the determining factor of social backwardness. Poverty is relevant in the context of social backwardness. The commission found that the lower income group constitutes socially and educationally backward classes. The basis of reservation is not income but social and educational backwardness determined on the basis of relevant criteria. If any classification of backward classes of citizens is based solely on the caste of the citizens it will perpetuate the vice of caste system. Again, if the classification is solely on poverty it will not be logical."[72]

When we refer to "socially and educationally backward classes of citizens," the scheduled castes," and "the scheduled tribes", under Article 15(4) and 16(4) and other relevant articles of the Constitution, we refer to those specific classes of the society who had been traditionally subjected to invidious discrimination on the ground of their low caste status and untouchability imposed by the so called high caste people. It is that Traditional Stigma which still works badly. Some change is noticed in the outward social structure, but not in the basic ideology. Consequently, old prejudices against those backward classes are still alive and more virulent.

This situation has necessitated the state to intervenue by making relevant laws and arranging for law implementing machinery. The Constitution has played a magic in the life of the so called untouchables, tribals and backwards in introducing positive change. In consonance with its philosophy, the Constitution provides under its Article 17 for abolition of untouchability and declares its practice as an offence punishable by law. Thus, the parliament empowered under Article 17 of the Constitution had passed "the protection of Civil-Rights Act, 1955, to deal with the cases of untouchability. However, the offences under the said Act were continually increasing. Moreover, some other inhuman crimes were being committed against the SC and the STs by the Caste Hindus and the unsocial elements in the society. Such crimes are called atrocities, which include loot, arson, rape, boycott, murder crimes having demoralising and terrorising effects, abuse and insults and booking false cases aginast the SC/STs. Such crime are dealt with under the Scheduled Castes Scheduled Tribes (Prevention of Atrocities) Act, 1989."

The Devadasi system was made punishable offence under section 372 of the Indian Penal Code 1861. However, the Parliament empowered under Article 23 of the Constitution, passed the Immoral Traffic (Prevention) Act, 1956 to deal with the cases of prostitution in the name of religion.

In pursuance of demands made by some State Govts, the Parliament has enacted "The employment of manual scavengers and construction of dry latterines (Prohibition) Act, 1993; which came into implementation w.e.f. 26th January 1997.

In order to deal with juvenile delinquency, the Parliament has passed juvenile justice (care and protection of children) Act, 2000.

TABLE 2.4
Comparative Incidence of Crime Against Scheduled Castes

Sr. No.	*Crime-Head*	*Years*					*Variation in 2006 over 2005*
		2002	*2003*	*2004*	*2005*	*2006*	
1.	Murder	739	581	654	669	673	0.6
2.	Rape	1331	1089	1157	1172	1217	3.8
3.	Kidnapping and Abduction	319	232	253	258	280	8.5
4.	Dacoity	29	24	26	26	30	15.4
5.	Robbery	105	70	72	80	90	12.5
6.	Arson	322	204	211	210	226	7.6
7.	Hurt	4491	3969	3824	3847	3760	-2.3
8.	Protection of Civil Rights Act	1018	634	364	291	405	39.2
9.	SC/ST (Prev. of Atrocities) Act	10770	8048	8891	8497	9581	1.0
10.	Others	14383	11401	11435	11077	11808	6.6
	Total :	**33507**	**26252**	**26887**	**26127**	**27070**	**3.6**

NCR Bureau (i) : p.110 (2006).

TABLE 2.5

Comparative Incidence of Crime Against Scheduled Tribes

Sr. No.	*Crime-Head*	*Years*					*Variation in 2006 over 2005*
		2002	*2003*	*2004*	*2005*	*2006*	
1.	Murder	189	189	156	164	195	18.9
2.	Rape	597	597	566	640	699	9.2
3.	Kidnapping & Abduction	69	69	79	72	88	22.2
4.	Dacoity	37	37	40	27	12	-55.6
5.	Robbery	62	62	50	49	29	-40.8
6.	Arson	58	58	33	38	46	21.1
7.	Hurt	788	788	767	767	838	9.3
8.	PCR Act	47	47	11	162	49	-69.8
9.	SC/ST (Prev. of Atrocities) Act	1800	1800	115	1283	1232	-4.0
10.	Others	3127	3127	2658	2511	2603	3.7
	Total :	**6774**	**5889**	**5889**	**5713**	**5791**	1.4

TABLE 2.6

Disposal of Cases by Police For Crimes Committed Against Scheduled Castes During 2006

S. No.	Crime Head	Total No. of Cases for Investigation including Pending Cases from Previous Year	Cases withdrawn by Govt.	Investigation Ref. Used	No. of Cases in which Investigation: Charge Found False / Mistake of Fact or Law etc.	Final Report True Submitted	Charge Sheets submitted	Total (6+7+8)	No. of Cases Pending Investigation at the end of the year
1	2	3	4	5	6	7	8	9	10
1.	Murder (Sec. 302, 303 IPC)	810	0	0	46	29	581	656	154
2.	Rape (Sec. 376 IPC)	1453	0	1	117	40	1021	1178	274
3.	Kidnapping & Abduction (Sec. 363-369, 371-373 IPC)	338	0	1	44	36	201	281	56
4.	Dacoity (Sec. 395-398 IPC)	39	0	0	2	1	22	25	14

(Table Contd.)

(Contd. Table 2.6)

S.No.	Crime Head	Total No. of Cases for Investigation including Pending Cases from Previous Year	Cases withdrawn by Govt.	Investigation in Ref. Used	No. of Cases in which Investigation				No. of Cases Pending Investigation at the end of the year
					Charge Found False / Mistake of Fact or Law etc.	Final Report True Submitted	Charge Sheets submitted	Total (6+7+8)	
5.	Robbery (392-394, 397-398 IPC)	118	0	1	11	10	47	68	49
6.	Arson (Sec. 435, 438 IPC)	303	0	0	51	32	145	228	75
7.	Hurt (Sec. 323-333, 335-338 IPC)	4720	0	2	577	290	2849	3716	1002
8.	PCR Act 1955 for SCs	517	0	3	55	17	320	392	122
9.	SC/ST Prev. of Atrocities Act, 1989 for SCs	12781	5	11	1812	627	5968	8407	4358
10.	Other Crime	14129	0	13	2949	759	8132	11840	2276
11.	**Total :**	**35208**	**5**	**32**	**5664**	**1841**	**19286**	**26791**	**8380**

NCRB (ii) p. 427 (2006).

TABLE 2.7
Disposal of Cases by Police For Crimes Committed Against Scheduled Tribes During 2006

S. No.	*Crime Head*	*Total No. of Cases for Investigation including Pending Cases from Previous Year*	*Cases withdrawn by Govt.*	*Investigation Ref. Used*	*No. of Cases in Which Investigation*				*No. of Cases Pending Investigation at the end of the year*
					Charge Found False / Mistake of Fact or Law etc.	*Final Report True Submitted*	*Charge Sheets submitted*	*Total (6+7+8)*	
1	2	3	4	5	6	7	8	9	10
1.	Murder (Sec. 302, 303 IPC)	269	0	1	15	22	155	192	76
2.	Rape (Sec. 3716 IPC)	832	0	1	46	14	591	651	180
3.	Kidnapping and Abduction (Sec. 363-369, 371-373 IPC)	111	0	0	4	11	52	67	44
4.	Dacoity (Sec. 395-398 IPC)	16	0	0	0	3	2	5	11

(Table Contd.)

(Contd. Table 2.7)

S.No.	Crime Head	Total No.of Cases for Investig-ation including Pending Cases from Previous Year	Cases withdrawn by Govt.	Investiga tion Ref. Used	No. of Cases in Which Investigation				No. of Cases Pending Investigation at the end of the year
					Charge Found False / Mistake of Fact or Law etc.	Final Report True Submitted	Charge Sheets submitted	Total (6+7+8)	
5.	Robbery (392-394, 397-398 IPC)	40	0	0	0	9	13	22	18
6.	Arson (Sec.435, 438 IPC)	58	0	0	7	3	32	42	16
7.	Hurt (Sec.323-333, 335-338 IPC)	981	0	0	140	39	646	825	156
8.	PCR Act 1955 for SCs	207	0	2	147	0	26	173	32
9.	SC/ST Prev. of Atrocities Act, 1989 for SCs	1763	0	3	257	32	858	1147	613
10.	Other Crime	3067	0	24	641	48	1821	2510	533
11.	**Total :**	**7344**	**0**	**31**	**1257**	**181**	**4196**	**5634**	**1679**

NCR Bureau(ii) p. 437 (2006).

TABLE 2.8

Cases Registered by Police and Their Disposal Under the Scheduled Castes and The Scheduled Tribes (Prevention of Atrocities Act, 1989 During the year 2008) Scheduled Castes

S.No.	State/UT	No. of Cases Registered during 2008	No. of Cases with Police during 2008 including B.F.	No. of Cases Closed by Police After Investigation	No. of Cases Charge Sheeted in Courts	No. of Cases Pending with Police at the end of 2008
1.	Andhra Pradesh	3875	5046	1725	1697	1624
2.	Assam	104	262	59	37	166
3.	Bihar	3617	6438	742	1937	3759
4.	Chandigarh	2	4	0	2	2
5.	Chhatisgarh	600	710	32	590	88
6.	D&N Haveli	1	1	0	1	0
7.	Delhi	34	85	5	19	61
8.	Goa	4	7	3	3	1
9.	Gujarat	1228	1317	64	1116	137
10.	Haryana	339	384	68	277	39
11.	Himachal Pradesh	68	86	33	31	22
12.	Jharkhand	598	915	140	272	503

(Table Contd.)

(Contd. Table 2.8)

S.No.	State / UT	No. of Cases Registered during 2008	No. of Cases with Police during 2008 including B.F.	No. of Cases Closed by Police After Investigation	No. of Cases Charge Sheeted in Courts	No. of Cases Pending with Police at the end of 2008
13.	Karnataka	2343	2711	517	1788	406
14.	Kerala	519	722	219	275	228
15.	Madhya Pradesh	2965	3256	99	3003	154
16.	Maharashtra	1172	1546	128	1019	399
17.	Orissa	1836	2845	241	1367	1237
18.	Puducherry	2	2	0	0	2
19.	Punjab	101	241	83	86	72
20.	Rajasthan	4302	4568	2319	1952	297
21.	Sikkim	17	19	1	12	6
22.	Tamil Nadu	1615	2072	585	962	525
23.	Tripura	4	4	0	3	1
24.	Uttar Pradesh	7960	8588	1939	5941	708
25.	Uttarkhand	42	53	11	35	7
26.	West Bengal	19	34	4	8	22
	Total :	**33367**	**41916**	**9017**	**22433**	**10466**

(*Source* : National Crime Record Bureau, Ministry of Home Affairs).

Note :

(1) No case was registered under the Act in the States / UTs of Arunachal Pradesh, Manipur, Meghalaya, Mizoram, Nagaland, A&N Islands, Daman & Due and Lakshwdeep.

(2) The PoA Act does not extend to the State of Jammu & Kashmir.

TABLE 2.9

Cases Registered by Police and Their Disposal Under the Scheduled Castes and The Scheduled Tribes (Prevention of Atrocities Act, 1989 During the year 2008)

Scheduled Tribes

S.No.	*State / UT*	*No. of Cases Registered during 2008*	*No. of Cases with Police during 2008 including B.F.*	*No. of Cases Closed by Police After Investigation*	*No. of Cases Charge Sheeted in Courts*	*No. of Cases Pending with Police at the end of 2008*
1.	Andhra Pradesh	745	1007	267	408	332
2.	Andaman & Nicobar Islands	3	5	0	2	3
3.	Arunachal Pradesh	63	64	8	50	6
4.	Assam	130	224	31	35	158
5.	Bihar	99	235	29	53	153
6.	Chhattisgarh	614	703	37	587	79
7.	D&N Haveli	10	12	2	7	3
8.	Daman & Diu	0	2	0	0	2
9.	Goa	1	1	0	0	1
10.	Gujarat	222	237	7	215	15
11.	Himachal Pradesh	0	1	0	1	0
12.	Jharkhand	231	458	49	159	250

(Table Contd.)

(Contd. Table 2.9)

S.No.	*State / UT*	*No. of Cases Registered during 2008*	*No. of Cases with Police during 2008 including B.F.*	*No. of Cases Closed by Police After Investigation*	*No. of Cases Charge Sheeted in Courts*	*No. of Cases Pending with Police at the end of 2008*
13.	Karnataka	400	444	85	246	113
14.	Kerala	106	159	29	72	58
15.	Madhya Pradesh	1071	1177	24	1106	47
16.	Maharashtra	268	362	23	230	109
17.	Manipur	1	30	1	0	29
18.	Meghalaya	0	1	0	0	1
19.	Orissa	508	829	56	422	351
20.	Rajasthan	1038	1143	563	462	118
21.	Sikkim	12	16	1	6	9
22.	Tamil Nadu	14	20	4	14	2
23.	Tripura	14	15	0	10	5
24.	Uttar Pradesh	9	9	2	7	0
25.	West Bengal	17	32	1	10	21
	Total :	**5576**	**7186**	**1219**	**4102**	**1865**

(*Source* : National Crime Record Bureau, Ministry of Home Affairs).

Note :

(1) No case was registered under the Act in the States / UTs of Haryana, Mizoram, Nagaland, Punjab, Uttarakhand, Chandigarh, Delhi, Lakshawdeep and Puducherry.

(2) The PoA Act does not extend to the State of Jammu & Kashmir.

TABLE 2.10

Cases with Courts under The Scheduled Castes and The Scheduled Tribes (Prevention of Atrocities Act, 1989 During the year 2008)

Scheduled Castes

S.No.	State / UT	No. of Cases in Courts including B.F. in 2008	Cases Compounded or withdrawn	No. of Cases in which trials completed		No. of Cases Pending with Courts at the end of 2008
				Convicted	Acquitted or Discharged	
1.	Andhra Pradesh	5806	70	192	1323	4221
2.	Assam	162	0	7	19	136
3.	Bihar	8012	49	229	1015	6719
4.	Chhatisgarh	1620	46	122	235	1217
5.	Goa	4	0	0	0	4
6.	Gujarat	8311	9	38	986	7278
7.	Haryana	794	0	16	135	643
8.	Himachal Pradesh	225	7	3	47	168
9.	Jharkhand	852	34	30	158	630
10.	Karnataka	6877	20	47	1617	5193
11.	Kerala	1178	4	9	199	966
12.	Madhya Pradesh	14792	367	1665	2836	9924
13.	Maharashtra	5824	8	59	622	5135

(Table Contd.)

(Contd. Table 2.10)

S.No.	State / UT	No. of Cases in Courts including B.F. in 2008	Cases Compounded or withdrawn	No. of Cases in which trials completed		No. of Cases Pending with Courts at the end of 2008
				Convicted	Acquitted or Discharged	
14.	Orissa	6243	9	89	691	5454
15.	Punjab	318	0	9	47	262
16.	Rajasthan	10042	140	711	835	8356
17.	Sikkim	26	0	12	3	11
18.	Tamil Nadu	3286	14	126	641	2505
19.	Tripura	14	0	0	6	8
20.	Uttar Pradesh	30112	42	3283	2704	24083
21.	Uttarakhand	300	0	37	44	219
22.	West Bengal	26	0	1	4	21
23.	Chandigarh	4	0	0	0	4
24.	D & N Haveli	5	0	0	1	4
25.	Daman & Diu	1	0	0	1	0
26.	Delhi	57	0	3	2	52
27.	Puducherry	7	1	0	2	4
	Total :	**1104898**	**820**	**6688**	**14173**	**83217**

(*Source* : National Crime Record Bureau, Ministry of Home Affairs).

Note :

(1) No case was registered under the Act in the States of Arunachal Pradesh, Manipur, Meghalaya, Mizoram, Nagaland, A&N Islands and Lakshadweep.

(2) The PoA Act does not extend to the State of Jammu & Kashmir.

TABLE 2.11

Cases with Courts under The Scheduled Castes and The Scheduled Tribes (Prevention of Atrocities Act, 1989 During the year 2008)

Scheduled Tribes

S.No.	State /UT	No. of Cases in Courts including B.F. in 2008	Cases Compounded or withdrawn	N.o. of Cases in which trials completed		No. of Cases Pending with Courts at the end of 2008
				Convicted	Acquitted or Discharged	
1.	Andhra Pradesh	1313	14	40	352	907
2.	Arunachal Pradesh	216	0	0	0	216
3.	Assam	151	0	4	16	131
4.	Bihar	174	4	2	12	156
5.	Chhattisgarh	2050	62	159	335	1494
6.	Goa	1	0	0	1	0
7.	Gujarat	1827	6	8	253	1560
8.	Himachal Pradesh	10	0	1	2	7
9.	Jharkhand	646	37	16	80	513
10.	Karnataka	806	3	5	136	662
11.	Kerala	254	1	4	37	212
12.	Madhya Pradesh	4962	143	504	753	3562

(Table Contd.)

(Contd. Table 2.11)

S.No.	State/UT	No. of Cases in Courts including B.F. in 2008	Cases Compounded or withdrawn	N.o. of Cases in which trials completed		No. of Cases Pending with Courts at the end of 2008
				Convicted	Acquitted or Discharged	
13.	Maharashtra	2050	1	26	199	1824
14.	Meghalaya	1	0	0	0	1
15.	Orissa	2450	0	37	199	2214
16.	Rajasthan	2239	19	192	252	1776
17.	Sikkim	14	0	5	3	6
18.	Tamil Nadu	64	0	0	8	56
19.	Tripura	29	0	3	13	13
20.	Uttar Pradesh	103	0	9	5	89
21.	Uttarakhand	14	0	3	0	11
22.	West Bengal	28	0	0	2	26
23.	A&N Islands	23	0	0	0	23
24.	D & N Haveli	21	0	0	4	17
25.	Daman & Diu	2	0	0	0	2
26.	Lakshadweep	1	0	0	0	1
	Total :	**19449**	**290**	**1018**	**2662**	**15479**

(*Source* : National Crime Record Bureau, Ministry of Home Affairs).

Note : (1) No case was registered under the Act in the States / UTs of Haryana, Meghalaya, Mizoram, Nagaland, Punjab, Chandigarh, Delhi and Puduchery.

(2) The PoA Act does not extend to the State of Jammu & Kashmir.

If the objects and provisions of the enormous body of legislation and the spiralling incidents of offences under those Acts are taken into account, the present social status of the SC/ST would be better known. It needs no other evidence to corroborate the fact of social backwardness. See Table 2:4, 2:5, 2.6, 2:7, 2:8, 2:9, 2:10 and 2:11.

Apart from all the measures taken by the state for the improvement of educational level of the Scheduled Castes, Scheduled Tribes and the other Backward Clases, there could not be significant improvement in the situation.

Under Article 21-A, it is a mandatory obligation on the state to provide free and compulsory education to all children between six to fourteen years. Other countries spend 6 per cent to 8 per cent of Gross Domestic Product on education. However we spend just 4 per cent of GDP.

While laying down the principle of determining educational backwardness, the honourable judges of the Supreme Court in OBC Reservation Case (2008) pronounced that "matriculation examination can no longer be considered to be an appropriate bench mark. It has to be at the most graduation."[73]

TABLE 2.12

Following Table Shows the Percentage of Graduates and above (Year 2004-2005)

S.No.	*Social Group*	*General Education Urban Male*	*Gen. Education Urban Female*
1.	Scheduled Caste	6.6	3.9
2.	Scheduled Tribes	10.8	7.4
3.	Other Backward Classes	10.6	6.0
4.	Socially Advanced	23.8	18.2
5.	All Social Groups Combined	16.2	11.5

Source : The Supreme Court on OBC Reservation by Malik and Malik, 2008, p. 323.

The above figures explicitly indicate that the Backward Classes are educationally backward as compared to the socially advanced classes even in general education.

Thus, the caste factor is very much active and effective. Lower the caste, more would be the disadvantages. In order to neutralize the adverse effects of lower caste status, it is imperative to classify the society on the basis of low status of the caste along with other factors like educational and economic status and it is necessary to undertake reformative measures.

(7) Is meritorious backward class candidate entitled to be included in the general merit list ?

The main purpose of providing reservation under Article 15(4) and under Article 16(4) of the Constitution is to facilitate "the advancement" of any Socially and educationally backward classes of citizens or the Scheduled Castes and the Scheduled Tribes. Under Article 46 of the Constitution, "the state shall promote with special care the educational and economic interests of the weaker sections of the people, and, in particular, of the Scheduled Castes and the Scheduled Tribes." Reservation is, of course not meant for restricting their advancement. Therefore, the candidate of merit of general standard ought to be included in the general merit list for the purpose of educational admission or for public employment.

Under Article 29(2) of the Constitution, every qualified candidate is equally entitled to get admission into "any educational institution maintained by the State or receiving aid out of State funds," and it will not be denied to such person on grounds only of religion, race, caste, language or any of them." The right protected under this Article is a fundamental right available to any person having requisite qualification and compentitive merit.

The question of admission on merit was raised in some cases.[74] In P. Sudarshan Vs. State of Andhra Pradesh, it was held that, "the selection cannot be made in separate compartments in such a way as to allow Backward Class candidates to compete for both general and reserved seats to the detriments of others. Reservations are to operate as a guaranteed minimum. Backward Class candidates, it was held, may obtain additional seats by merit but can not require that reservations operate as a guarantee of seats over and above those acquired by merit."[75]

Later on, the situation changed after 1970. The 'over and above' arrangement in admission came into operation in states like Andhra Pradesh, Punjab, Tamil Nadu and U.P. So also 'over and above' reservations in employment are found in Andhra Pradesh, Kerala, Punjab, Tamil Nadu and in Maharashtra.[76] Thus, there seems to be consensus on treating meritorious candidates in general merit list, without interference with the reserved quota. However, this arrangement seems to be not popular and not in practice uniformally.

So far as elections to the Lok Sabha or State Assemblies are concerned, any member of the reserved category may contest for the reserved seat or general seat. If he gets elected to the general seat, his election would be over and above the seats reserved for that particular community.

During the Constituent Assembly Debates, Dr. Babasaheb Ambedkar explained that "It is accepted that the Scheduled Castes and the Scheduled Tribes shall be entitled to contest seats which are not reserved seats; which are unreserved seats. That is contained in the report of the Advisory Committee which has already been accepted by the House. The reason why that particular provision has not been introduced in article 292 is because it is not germane at this place. The proposition will find its place in the law relating to election with which this Assembly or the Assembly in its legislative capacity will have to deal with."[77]

Accordingly the Representation of Peoples Act, 1951 provided under its section 55, that, "For avoidance of doubt it is hereby declared that a member of the Scheduled Castes or of the Scheduled Tribes shall not be disqualified to hold a seat not reserved for members of those castes or tribes, if he is otherwise qualified to hold such seats under the Constitution and this Act."

It is true that several candidates belonging to reserved category contest election for general seat for the Union or State Legislatures; but a very few of them get elected. However, they are not counted against the reserved quota for that community.

On the ground of analogy, it could be said that the backward candidates securing higher rank or merit in the qualifying or competitive examination ought to be included in general category, for the purpose of admission in the educational institutions and in the recruitment to any service. If irrespective of their higher merit, they are included in the reserved quota, it would be injustice on their part and denial of constitutional right to them.

(8) Whether Reservation Policy is obligatory on unaided educational institutions :

The Constitution under its Article 15(4) has provided that, "Nothing in this article or in Clause (2) of Article 29 shall prevent the state from making any special provision for the advancement of any socially and educationally backward classes of citizens or for the Scheduled Castes and the Scheduled Tribes."

Thus, the provision under the Article is very wide. There is nothing to restrict or abridge its application only to aided or unaided educational institutions. It provides for social and educational advancement of the weaker sections of the society. Reservation is, inter alia, a tool, a device to undertake and fulfil the purpose of the Article. Hence it is accepted and applied in respect of aided as well as unaided educational institutions.

However, it was held by the hon'ble Supreme Court in T.M.A. Pai Foundation Vs. State of Karnataka,[78] that, "The establishment and running of an educational institution where a large number of persons are employed as teachers or administrative staff, and an activity is carried on that results in the imparting of knowledge to the students, must necessarily be regarded as an occupation," within the meaning of Article 19(1)(g). The right to establish and administer broadly comprises of the following rights.

(a) to admit students.
(b) to setup a reasonable fee structure.
(c) to constitute a governing body.
(d) to appoint staff (Teaching and non-teaching); and
(e) to take action if there is dereliction of duty on the part of any employee.

The similar ruling was given in P.A. Inamdar Vs. State of Maharashtra[79] and specifically held that state regulation of admission in such institutions would not be regarded reasonable restriction on the fundamental right of occupation under Article 19(6).

According to Article 19(1)g, "All citizens shall have the right to practise any profession or to carry on any occupation, trade or business." It is surprising to know that education is an "occupation". With due respect to the hon'ble Supreme Court it can be said that it is inconceivable.

The second reasoning with reference to 19(6) is also equally inconceivable. This interpretation given by the apex court would have adverse effect on the social and educational advancement of the weaker sections of the society. Consequently, the parliament has introduced Article 15(5) in the Constitution by the Constitution 93rd Amendment Act, 2005. The said Article runs as under :

"Nothing in this article or in sub-clause (g) of clause(1) of article 19 shall prevent the state from making any special provision by law for the advancement of any socially and educationally backward classes of citizens or for the Scheduled Casts or the Scheduled Tribes in so far as such special provisions relate to their admission to educational institutions including private educational institutions, whether aided or unaided by the state other than the minority educational institution referred to in Clause (1) Article 30."

Thus, all the public as well as private educational institutions irrespective of the fact that they receive State aid or not, are brought under one category so far as regulation of admissions as per reservation policy is concerned. There is no distinction between the educational institutions on the ground of aided and unaided category. The state is empowered to regulate by law the admissions based on the policy of reservation.

The object of Article 15(5) is, obviously to "neutralize" the adverse effect of the ruling of the Supreme Court in T.M.A. Pai Foundation case and P.A. Inamdar case on reservation policy; and "ensure" that nothing in Article 19(1)g shall prevent the state from making any provision in respect of reservation in admission.

Any educational institution whether it is "aided or unaided" cannot be a criterion on the basis of which there could be distinction for the purpose of reservation policy. Whether such educational institution is a recognized institution by the competent authority is the reasonable criterion. Its existence is taken into account only on the basis of its recognition. Thus, once the institution is duly recognized, it gets its corporal status. It becomes a corporated person or a legal person. Whether such institution gets grants-in-aid or not is immaterial.

The 93rd amendment is an Act of the Parliament. The Parliament may in exercise of its constituent power amend any provision of the constitution in accordance with Article 368 of the Constitution; and its validity, cannot be challenged on the ground that it violates a fundamental right. The purpose of the said amendment is to achieve the constitutional objective of securing justice to the underprivileged people. Moreover, the very language of the amendment is very much clear, unambiguous and explicit. In view of this where is the scope for its interpretation ? It is, obviously the duty of all the people to honour the provisions of the Constitution and implement it expeditiously.

(9) Whether minority educational institutions are expected to implement reservation Policy?

In our country there are certain communities known as minorities on account of their less numerical strength in the total population, mostly Hindus with reference to the concerned state. The Constitution of India under its Articles 29 and 30 deals with cultural and educational rights of the minorities.

The question what is a 'minority' was raised in the Kerala Education Bill case in 1958.[80] The Supreme Court held that a 'minority' means a community which is numerically less than 50 percent of the population of that state. The Supreme Court observed that as ".. the Bill extends to whole state of Kerala, consequently the minority must be determined by reference to the entire population of that state." According to Justice Nasirullah Beg, "so far as religious minorities are concerned, the main religious minorities are Muslims, Christians, Sikhs, Buddhists, Jains and a microscopic minority of Parsis."[81] According to D.D. Basu, "it should refer to any community which is numerically less than 50 per cent of the population of the state concerned."[82]

In order to instill trust and confidence in such minorities and associate them with the national stream, some special rights are given to them by our Constitution. Among others Article 30(1) of the Constitution provides that, "All minorities whether based on religion or language, shall have the right to establish and administer educational institutions of their choice."

It is, of course a fundamental right of the minorities based on language or religion. Like all fundamental rights, this right is also subject to certain limitations. The right to 'establish' and 'administer' any educational institution under Article 30(1) is subject to Article 29(2), which states that, "No citizen shall be denied admission into any educational institution maintained by the state or receiving aid out of state funds on grounds only of religion, race, caste, language or any of them."

In St. Stephen's College V. University of Delhi (1992)[83] it was held by the Supreme Court that, the right to select students for admission was a part of administration, as such it was an important facet of its fundamental right. However, the Supreme Court observed that, "The state may regulate the intake in this category with due regard to the need of the community in the area which the institution is intended to serve. But in no case such intake shall exceed fifty percent, of the annual admission. The minority institutions shall make available at least fifty per cent of the annual admission to members of communities other than the minority community. The admission of other community candidates shall be done purely on the basis of merit."

However, in T.M.A. Foundation V. State of Karnataka (2003) the Supreme Court pronounced that, it would be open, to the state authorities to insist on allocating a certain percentage of seats to those belonging to weaker sections of society; from amongst the non-minority seats." In P.A. Inamdar V. State of Maharashtra (2005)[84] the Supreme Court held that, '..... neither the policy of reservation can be enforced by the state nor any quota or percentage of admissions can be carved out to be appropriated by the state in a minority or non-minority unaided educational institution." So far as NRIs concerned, the hon'ble court stated that, "A limited reservation of such seats, not exceeding 15% in our opinion may be made available to NRIS depending on discretion of the management subject to two conditions, first, such seats should be utilized bonafide by the NRI only and for their children or wards. Secondly within this quota, the merit should not be given a complete go-by."[85]

In this background the Parliament has introduced Article 15(5) by the Constitution 93rd Amendment Act, 2005 to enable the state to make special provision for the advancement of the weaker sections of the society regarding admission to educational institutions including private educational institutions, whether aided or unaided "Other than the minority educational institutions referred to in Clause (1) of Article 30."

Later, the Supreme Court pronounced in M.S. Catholic Vs. T. Jose (2007) as under :

"The right conferred on minorities under Article 30 is only to ensure equality with the majority and not intended to place the minorities in a more advantageous position vis-a-vis the majority. There is no reverse discrimination in favour of minorities. The general laws of the land relating to national interest, national security, social welfare, public order, morality, health, sanitation, taxation etc. applicable to all, will equally apply to minority institutions also."

"But if any such regulation interfere with the overall administrative control by the management over the staff, or abridges / dilutes, in any other manner, the right to establish and administer educational institutions such regulations, to that extent, will be inapplicable to minority institutions."[86]

Under Article 15(4), the "special provision" is wide one, as it is prima facie applicable to all the institutions including the minority institutions. However, Article 15(5) applies to the institutions, "other than the minority educational institutions, referred to in Clause (1) of Article 30". Is there any contradiction between the said two provisions ? If yes, as to why the Parliament allowed such situation to exist at all ? If there is no contradiction or we have to give harmonious construction to the constitutional provisions, then what could be the actual position at present.

Till now, the minority institutions had the right of admitting the students belonging to the minority group to the extent of 50 per cent of its strength. They were, of course required to admit the non-minority students on the remaining seats. Now the question is, has the 93rd Amendment done any thing new ?

This particular point was discussed in detail in Ashok Kumar Thakur Vs. Union of India.[87] The Hon'ble Chief Justice K.G. Balkrishnan pronounced that, "no educational institution or any aggrieved party has come before us challenging the constitutional amendment on these grounds. The challenge is made by the petitioners objecting to the reservations made under Act 5 of 2007. Therefore, the Plea that Article 15(4) and 15(5) are mutually contradictory and, therefore Article 15(5) is not constitutionally valid and cannot be accepted...... Article 15(5) is also to be taken as an enabling provision to carry out certain constitutional mandate and thus it is constitutionally valid and the contentions raised on these grounds are rejected."

It has been further observed that, "The exemption of minority educational institutions has been allowed to conform Article 15(5) with the mandate of Article 30 of the Constitution. Moreover, both Articles 15(4) and 15(5) are operative and the plea of non-severity is not applicable."

Moreover, it was obsered that "if at all there is any violation of Article 14 or any other equality Principle, the affected educational institution should have approached this Court to indicate their rights. No such petition has been filed before this court. Therefore, we hold that the exclusion of minority educational institutions from Article 15(5) is not violation of Article 14 of the Constitution as the minority educational institutions, by themselves, are a separate class and their rights are protected by other constitutional provisions."

It is submitted that this problem could be solved properly by resorting to the decision given by the Supreme Court in St. Stephen's College Case (1992) (Supra). So far as fifty percent quota in admission is concerned the Minority institutions would have absolute freedom to select their own eligible students and in respect of other seats they would follow the rules laid down by the concerned State Government.

It may not be out of order to state that there are certain underprivileged groups in both, majority and minority communities. There are more than fifty Muslim castes and some SC/ST/OBC Christian Castes in the OBC list of the concerned state. If the minorities including Muslims, Christians, Jains and others, with the concurrence of the National Commission for Minorities and other agencies generously accept to give a due share in admission in their rich and standard educational institutions, the backward classes of their respective religion would be greatly benefitted alongwith other backward classes. They may, by this way, graciously serve the interests of their own community as well as the national interest.

It is the duty of all the right thinking people and institutions to implement certain welfare measures, like reservation in educational institutions, public offices and providing other amenities to the weaker sections of the society in the interest of social justice. After all the problem of weaker sections of the society is the problem of the nation as a whole and it ought to be solved in its right earnest.

(10) How long the safeguards would continue ?

It is, however a fact that there is nothing to indicate in Article 15(4), Article 16(4), Article 46 and Article 335 as to how long the special safeguards would be in continuation.

However, Article 15(4) of the Constitution refers to the advancement of socially and educationally backward classes not adequately represented in the services under the state. Article 46 states that, "the state shall promote with special case the weaker sections of the people, and shall protect them from social injustice and all forms of exploitation." These provisions, of course contain the constitutional verdict on the problem as to how long the safeguards ought to be in continuation.

It has been very categorically stated that the backward classes ought to attain "advancement" in educational and other fields. It could be logically and reasonably inferred that educational facilities would continue under Article 15(4) of the Constituion. The underlying content of Article 16(4) is they should be "adequately represented in the services." It could be inferred that till that stage is achieved the reservation in services of the state would continue. Article 46 refers to promotion of educational and economic interests and freedom from exploitation. Thus, the constitution is more objective oriented rather than limitation of time. These provisions really reflected the prudence and wisdom of the founding fathers of the Constitution of India.

While laying down the guide lines in this respect, the hon'ble Supreme Court stated in K.C.Vasantkumar V. State of Karnataka (1985)[88] that, "thousands of years of discrimination and exploitation cannot be wiped out in one generation. But even here economic criterion is worth applying by refusing preferred treatmet to those amongst them who have already benefitted by it and improved their position. And finally reservation must have a time span otherwise concessions tend to become vested interests."

However, the hon'ble Supreme Court observed in Ashok Kumar Thakur V. Union of India (2008)[89] that, "This compensatory state action can be continued only for a period till that inequality is wiped off..... But at the outset, it may not be possible to fix a time-limit or a period of time." However "the matter could be examined by parliament at a future time."

The reservationists plead their case on the ground of caste and inequality and the past sufferings in the caste society. However, the anti-reservationists argue that caste is the creation of past generation, as such, how could present generation be held responsible for the past. It is, however a fact that, the present generation is the successor of the past. They enjoy ancestral legacy of high caste status, large property and Luxurious living standard and enjoy power and prestige in the society. Is it not the gift of the old generation. If the ancestors could not repay and repent for their acquisitive and exploitative nature, it is the successors who must fulfil, at least partially, that obligation.

It is argued that, the present unemployment among the Caste Hindus is due to the policy of reservation. Hence, hereafter the constitutional safeguards be invariably discontinued. There is no substance in this argument. Very few of Dalits, Tribes and backwards could avail of the benefits of constitutional safeguards; that too very late. They could not fulfil their own quota. Private sector is still far from them. For the problem of increasing unemployment the blame may be given to the national planning, economic policy, growth of population and certain other factors and not to reservation policy.

So long the caste system is in vogue, the sense of superiority and inferiority would be prevailing. All the backward classes suffer, more or less exclusion, deprivation and oppression. The instances of untouchability, atrocities, honour killing and Brahmanic and feudal domination are increasing. Thus, the social backwardness of the so called low caste is still in vogue. So far as educational backwardness is concerned, the SC, ST, OBCs are comparately more backward than the so called high castes. Due to poverty and pressing conditions the backward classes neither avail of quality education nor higher education. In the opinion of the honourable Supreme Court (Ashok Kumar, 2008)[90] the elementary education or secondary education cannot be the criterion of forwardness. The criterion of forwardness is minimum graduation or professional qualification. If this yardstick is applied, the SC, ST and OBCs are educationally backward as compared to others. Therefore, so long the Backward classes remain socially and educationally backward, their claim for special safeguards would be in vogue.

2.4 Who is Responsible : Union or State ?

Who is responsible for implementation of various constitutional provisions, statutory provisions, policies and programmes and developmental schemes with special reference to the Scheduled Castes, Scheduled Tribes and other Backward Classes is a pertinent question. Whether it is the responsibility of the Union or State or of both.

The Constitution under its Article 1 states very categorically that, "India, that is Bharat shall be a Union of States." It is the responsibility of India, that is Bharat to run the administration, defend the state, protect the individual rights and see the welfare of all the people, especially the weaker sections of the society. According to Article 53(1) of the Constitution, "The executive power of the union shall be vested in the President and shall be exercised by him either directly or through officers subordinate to him in accordance with this constitution." Ours being a parliamentary Government, the Prime-Minister and his council of ministers execute the Policy on behalf of the President. At the state level, according to Article 154 of the constitution, "The executive power of the state shall be vested in the Governor and shall be exercised by him either directly or through officers subordinate to him in accordance of this Constitution. Thus, the Chief-Minister and his council of Ministers execute the Policy on behalf of the Governor appointed by the President of India.

Thus, the President of India is the head of the state and responsible for the administration of the country. However, for the sake of administrative convenience, the subjects are divided into (1) Union list consisting of 97 subjects, (2) State list consisting of 66 subjects and (3) Concurrent list consisting of 47 subjects. There is only one reference relating to "nomadic and migratory Tribes" in union list. There is no reference relating to advancement of the weaker sections of the society in the seventh schedule. Ultimately we have to resort to entry No. 97 of the union list, which states, "Any other matter not enumerated in list II or list III" form part of Union List, and take out the inference that the subject of SC/ST/OBC belongs to Union list.

Under Article 17 (abolition of untouchability) and under Article 23(1) (prohibition of Traffic in human beings) and by virtue of Article

35(i)(ii), "The Parliament shall have and the state legislature of a state shall not have power to make laws." Thus, these two subjects are by specific provision are part of union list. But the co.operation of the state in implementation of some provisions of those Acts is very much required. It could be said that the right to education, employment and temple entry were denied on account of untouchability. With the abolition of untouchability all other civil-rights are accrued to the so called (ex) untouchables.

According to Article 46 of the Constitution (Directive principles of state policy), "the state shall promote with special care the educational and economic interests of the weaker sections of the people, and in particular of the Scheduled Castes and the Scheduled Tribes, and shall protect them from social injustice and all forms of exploitation."

For the purpose of Part III and Part IV unless the context otherwise requires, "The State" includes the Government and Parliament of India and the Government and Legislature of each of the states and all local or other authorities within the Territory of India or under the control of the Government of India." This is a very comprehensive definition of "the state," as such the duties and responsibilities under Part III and Part IV bestowed upon all the authorities under the control of the Government of India.

Presently, the Ministry of Social Justice and empowerment is the Nodal Ministry, looking after the welfare of the SC and OBCs and the Ministry of Tribal Welfare is looking after the Tribal Welfare. In the states also there are separate ministries responsible for the welfare of the SC/ST/OBCs within their respective jurisdiction. So far as the state of Jharkhand, Madhya Pradesh and Orissa are concerned, there is specific mention that there shall be a minister in charge of Tribal Welfare who may in addition be in charge of the welfare of the Scheduled Castes and backward classes.

At the bottom level we have adopted the Panchayat System and Municipalities. The Parliament by virtue of Article 40 of the Constitution, has passed the 73rd and 74th Constitution Amendment Acts in 1992 and introduced Part IX and Part IXA which respectively relate to Panchayats and Municipalities. Both the subjects are in the state list, as such they are empowered to define the details regarding powers and functions of those institutions. The Panchayats and Municipalities are also bound to discharge their duties and responsibilities laid down under the Constitution as well as their respective state laws.

India, that is Bharat is a Union of States. We have adopted a quasi-federal government. In the words of Dr. Babasaheb Ambedkar, the Chairman of the Drafting Committee of the Constitution, "Though the country and the people may be divided into different states for convenience of administration the country is one integral whole, its people a single people living under a single imperium derived from a single source."[91] He explained that, "the Draft Constitution has sought to forge means and methods whereby India will have federation and at the same time will have uniformity in all the basic matters which are essential to maintain the unity of the country. The means adopted by the Draft Constitution are three (1) a single judiciary, (2) uniformity in fundamental laws, civil and criminal, and (3) a common all India civil service to man important posts."[92]

The Constitution of India, under its Article 256, imposes an obligation on the states to ensure compliance with the laws made by Parliament and any existing laws, and it empowers the union to give such directions to the states as may appear to the Government of India to be necessary for that purpose. The directions may relate inter alia to execution of schemes for the welfare of Scheduled Tribes (Article 339). There is a specific responsibility of the state under various provisions of the Constitution to see the welfare of the weaker sections of the society including Scheduled Castes and Scheduled Tribes.

The non-compliance of the directions in general by the states would meet dire consequences including dismissal of government under Article 356. The increasing dependence of the State Governments on central financial assistance including grant-in-aids and overdrafts etc. may be used to influence the states and get compliance of the directions given by the union. Thus there are so many instruments or devices with the Union Government to ensure the compliance of its directions from the State Governments.

Thus, it is the Union Government which is ultimately responsible and accountable to take all the necessary steps to secure justice, social, economic and political to all the people, with special reference to the historically disadvantaged people.

Conclusion

It is a universally known fact that the Scheduled Castes, Scheduled Tribes and other Backward Classes had suffered a lot in the Indian Social System. In order to bring about a positive change in their life and develop them socially, educationally and economically the founding fathers of our Constitution provided some special safeguards in the Constitution. The provisions under Article 15(4) and Article 16(4) and other relevant provisions form part of

Fundamental Rights under the constitution of India. Therefore, it is mandatory on the part of the state to implement them in letter and spirit.

The special safeguards, including reservations in educational institutions and reservations in employment under the state are not fully based on caste, but on victim's social and educational backwardness. Caste is but a criterion to measure social backwards and social status. The special safeguards are expected till the backward classes achieve advancement and equal status in the society. It is obviously the responsibility of the state to secure justice to the backward classes.

It all depends on the interpretation of the relevant constitutional provisions, the relevant statutory provisions, rules and regulations in the real perspective and the implementation of those provisions in the real sense. It is but imperative to see that the reservation would certainly bring silent but perfect revolution in the society.

References

1. Added by the 1st Constitution Amendment Act, 1950. AA Added by the 1st Constitution Amendment Act, 1950.
2. Added by the 93rd Constitution Amendment Act, 2005. Added by the 93rd Constitution Amendment Act, 2005.
3. Galanter Marc : Competing Equalities : p. 373. Oxford University Press, Delhi, 1984.
4. AIR 1951, SC 226.
5. Constitutent Assembly Debates : Vol.VII, pp. 655, 661.
6. Galanter Marc : Competing Equalities, p. 368.
7. RCSC ST : 1955: p. 121.
8. Report of the Committee on Untouchability, Economic and Educational Development of the Scheduled Castes 1969, Government of India. pp. 206, 207.
9. AIR 1964 SC 1823, 1833.
10. See letter by R.K. Kshirsagar in response to an Article Written by K.S. Ramakrishnan, Published in the Indian Express (Bombay) on 20th May, 1985.
11. Galanter Marc : Competing Equalities : p. 173.
12. AIR 1963 SC 649, 663.
13. AIR 2003 SC Para. pp. 65-68, pp. 390-400.
14. Ashok Kumar Thakur V. Union of India. (2008) 6 SCC p. 450.

14a. Indian Express, Mumbai, dated 13-04-2012.

14b. Indian Express, Mumbai, dated 02-04-2012 Article by Yamini Lohia, "The higher education myth."

15. Added by the 77th Constitution Amendment Act, 1995, and 8th Constitution Amendment Act, 2001.
16. Added by the 81st Constitution Amendment Act, 2000.
17. Proviso added by the 82nd Amentment Act, 2000.
18. Brochure 1982. p. 7. Department of Personnel and Training, Govt. of India.
19. *Ibid.*, p. 8.
20. *Ibid.*, pp. 290-91.
21. *Ibid.*, pp. 291-92.
22. *Ibid.*, p. 197.
23. AIR 1962 SC 36.
24. Brochure 1982, p. 197.
25. AIR 1993 SC 493, 631.
25a. Brochure 2011. p. 5.
26. AIR 1964. SC 179, 187, 188.
27. Those State Governments are :-
    (1) Government of Orissa (38/1975)
    (2) Government of West Bengal (1976)
    (3) Government of Assam (12/1979)
    (4) Government of Tripura (5/1991)
    (5) Government of Bihar (1991)
    (6) Government of Karnataka (7/1991 and 1994)
    (7) Government of Madhya Pradesh (21/1974 and 1995)
    (8) Government of Uttar Pradesh (4/1994)
    (9) Government of Tamil Nadu (45/1994)
    (10) Government of Kerala (16/1995)
    (11) Government of Maharashtra (8/2004)
    (12) Government of Punjab (2006).
28. Laski H.A. Grammer of Politics. p. 91. George Allen and Unwin Pvt. Ltd. London, 1950.
29. DBAWS Vol. 13, p. 63.
30. *Ibid.,* Vol. 1 : p. 409.
31. *Ibid.,* Vol. 1 : p. 406.
32. CAD. Vol. VII : p. 953.
33. DBAWS Vol.13 : p. 63.
34. Pande J.N.Constitutional Law of India. p. 60. Central Law Agency, Motilal Nehru Rtd. Allahabad (2000).
35. AIR 1963 SC 649, 664.
36. AIR 1967 AP 353 (363).
37. AIR 1968 SC 507 (513).
38. AIR 1989 SC 139 (142).
39. AIR 1992 SC 1;3, 25; 26.
40. Civil Appeal No.3792-3794/1989(1996) 2 SCC 775.

40a. M.Nagaraj & Others V. Union of India. AIR 2007 SC 71.
41. AIR 1978 SC 597, (640).
42. T.Devadasan V. Union of India. AIR 1964 SC 179, 190.
43. Pylee M.V. India's Constitution. p. 84. Asia Publishing House, Bombay (1962).
44. Chiranjit Lal V. Union of India. (1950) SCR 869.
45. AIR 1974 SC 555, 583.
46. DBAWS.Vol. 3, p. 66.
47. AIR 1964 Mysore 132 to 136.
48. AIR 1967 SC 1273 (1285).
49. AIR 1968 Ker 42 (47-48).
50. AIR 1972 SC 1375 (1395).
51. AIR 1976 SC 535, 537.
52. AIR 1985 SC 1495 (1507-1508).
53. AIR 1987 SC 537, 547.
54. AIR 1993 SC 477, 539.
55. AIR 2001 SC 393. AIR 1997 SC 2133.
56. State of Maharashtra Vs. Milind and Others.
57. (2008) 6 SCC Part 2, p. 446.
58. CAD Vol. IX, p. 1640.
59. RCSCST 1952 p. 11.
60. Galanter Marc : Competing Equalities. p. 135.
61. DBAWS.Vol. I. p. 52.
62. Galanter Marc : Competing Equalities p. 147.
63. Chotelal V.U.P. AIR 1979 ALL 135.
64. RCS CST, 1953, p. 191, 196, Govt. of India.
65. Galanter Marc : Competing Equalities : pp. 42, 43.
66. AIR 1997 SC 303.
67. DBAWS Vol.1, p. 51.
68. (1950) SCR 869. 68(a) AiR 1964 SC 1823, 1833.
69. (2008) 6 SCC p. 499.
70. Devadasan E.D. Christian Law in India. pp. 351-52. DSI Publications : S.R. Chetty Street, Madras. (1974).
71. Singh Paramanand: Reservation and Discrimination in India. p. 122. Deep & Deep Publications, New Delhi.
72. AIR 1976 SC 2381.
73. (2008) 6 SCC 1 p. 46.
74. Raghuramula V. Andhra Pradesh. AIR 1958 A.P. 129. p. Sudarshan V. State of A.P. AIR 1958 AP 59. Chamraja V. State of Mysore, AIR 1967 Mys. 21.
75. Galanter Marc : Competing Equalities. pp. 455, 56.
76. *Ibid.*, p. 459.
77. DBAWS. 13 : 849.
78. AIR 2003 SC 355. pp. 380, 387.
79. AIR 2005 SC 3226.

80. AIR 1958 1958 SC 956.
81. Beg Nasirullah J. Rights of Minorities under the Indian Constitution. p. 4. Buddha Vihar, Lucknow (1976).
82. Basu D.D. Constituional Law of India. p. 93.
83. AIR 1992 SC 1630 (1663).
84. AIR 2003 SC 355, 417.
85 AIR 2005 SC 3226 (3264).
86. AIR 2007 SC 570 (577, 578).
87. (2008) 6 SCC p. 486, 487.
88. AIR 1985 SC 1495 (1507).
89. (2008) 6 SCC p. 522.
90. *Ibid,* p. 45, 608, 626.
91. DBAWS Vol. 13, p. 68.
92. *Ibid*, p. 58.

3

Reservation, Merit and Efficiency

It is a fact that the anti-reservationists argue their case, 'inter alia, on the ground of merit and efficiency. They obviously argue that due to the policy of reservation, the Scheduled Castes, Scheduled Tribes and the socially and educationally backward classes, though comparatively less meritorious and inefficient are admitted in the educational institutions and so also in the public services, as a result the meritorious candidates belonging to the higher classes suffer injustice and this causes loss to academic standard and administrative efficiency. How far, the plea of merit in respect of social justice is reasonable is a question. It is therefore proposed to inquire into this complicated matter which has conspicuously attracted the attention of the whole nation.

3.1 Reservations for Justice

It is the primordial need and a genuine demand of the human beings to secure justice, in the pursuit of which they had deliberately constituted the state. Therefore, the state is inherently under the obligation to distribute justice to the people, under it, so that they may live with peace, prosperity and pleasure.

What is justice is a prime question which has to be addressed.

(a) The word 'Justice' has been derived from the Greek word 'Dikaiosume', which signifies the wider meaning than the English Word 'Justice'. It is synonymous with morality.

(b) Plato the ancient Greek philosopher subscribes to the idea of justice as something moral, just virtuous or equitable. He states that justice is the "giving to everyman his due."[1] According to Plato the individual must be good, not only because of external restrains, but by his inner motives. According to him, 'virtue is knowledge'. Mere excellence or efficiency makes man a good craftsman, a good carpenter, but not necessarily a good and virtuous man. Platonic justice implies not of legal justice but moral and universal justice. It implies the functional specialization and non-interference in the activities others performing.

(c) J.S. Mill had given five attributes of justice. They are summarized as under -

- (i) It is unjust to deprive any one of his personal liberty, his property or any other thing which belongs to him by law.
- (ii) However, one could be deprived of his legal rights, if the law which confers on him those rights is a bad law.
- (iii) Each person should obtain that, whether good or evil, which he really deserves.
- (iv) It is unjust to break faith with any one or to violate an engagement.
- (v) It is inconsistent with justice to be partial, to show favour or preference to one person over another. In other words there should be equality of opportunity to all.[2]

(d) According to Dr. Babasaheb Ambedkar, "Justice is simply another name for liberty, equality and fraternity." According to him (1) liberty connotes civil and political liberty : civil liberty includes liberty of movement, liberty of thought, reading and writing, and liberty of action. Political liberty consists in right to share in the framing of laws and in the making and unmaking of governments. It is not mere non-intervention by the state in the private life of the individuals, but it is restructuring the whole of society in such a way which could be conducive for the welfare of the individuals. (2) Equality means, "moral equality." It is essentially an ethical value which recognizes equality of opportunity for each and every one. It is true that men are not equal in physical strength, talents, industry and in tests and attitudes. However, the principle of equality denies the undue right to the strong to exploit the weak. It envisages equal opportunities to all without making any unjust distinction between man and man, on the ground of caste, class, creed or sex. (3) Fraternity means, fellow feeling'. It is feeling of brotherhood with all human beings. It is "a sentiment which leads an individual to identify himself with the good of others."

However, he gives much importance to equality. He thought that, "fraternity and liberty are really derivative notions. The basic and fundamental conceptions are equality and respect for human personality. Fraternity and liberty take their roots in these two fundamental conceptions. Digging further down it may be said that equality is the original notion and respect for human personality is a reflexion of it, so that where equality is denied, everything else may be taken to be denied."[3]

(e) According to John Rawls Justice as fairness is inclusive of two Principles.
"First : each person is to have an equal right to the most extensive basic liberty compatible with a similar liberty for others.
Second : Social and economic inequalities are to be arranged so that they are both (a) reasonably expected to be to everyone's advantage, and (b) attached to positions and offices open to all."[4] Thus (1) The idea of fairness is central to justice. (2) The nature of objectivity must establish public framework based on reasons and evidence after discussion and due reflection. (3) People must have moral power and sense of justice. (4) Priority to liberty in the assessment of justice. (5) need of procedural fairness. (6) importance of equity in social arrangements so that attention is drawn particularly to the predicament of the worst off people. (7) Freedom of opportunity to do what they would like with their own lives."[4[a]]

(f) The Constitution of India, envisages inter alia under its preamble : "Justice : social, economic and political". However, it is not fully confined to social justice, economic justice and political justice. It goes beyond that, it further envisages, "Liberty of thought, expression, belief, faith and worshop; Equality of status and of opportuity". Fundamental rights and Directive Principles of state policy are the means to achieve the goal of justice, in its broad sense.

Thus, justice is a very comprehensive term; which cannot be defined in exact terms, but it can be perceived as something, 'due,' 'fairness' and reasonableness. It includes 'Distributive Justice' and corrective justice, legal justice and moral justice. It includes, social justice, economic justice and political justice.

In India, where the society is based on graded inquality, abject poverty and feudal principles, the concept of social justice assumes importance. According to V.R. Kshna Iyer, Social Justice is the balancing wheel between freedom, political and economic and indeed, makes for survival of democracy."[5]

In order to bring about a necessary social change and establish 'fraternity' in the society, the constitutional and legal instruments are required to bring into application through administrative machinery.

The inhuman practice of untouchability, which has ruined the very life of the so called untouchables has been abolished and its practice has not been only forbidden but made it an offence punishable by law under Article 17 of the Constitution. The protection of Civil Rights Act, 1955 and the prevention of (SC ST) Atrociies Act, 1989 are in operation. However, the Scheduled Castes, Scheduled Tribes and other backward classes being subjected to untouchability exclusion and exploitation respectively for quite a long period, are unable to secure justice at their own. The Constitution therefore provides certain safeguards or compensatory measures so that they may secure social, educational, economic and political justice.

The special safeguards, obviously include educational safeguards under Article 15(4) and 15(5) and service safeguards under Article 16(4), 16(4A), 16(4B), Article 320(3) and Article 335 of the Constitution. In addition to these social and economic safeguards, political safeguards or reservations are provided to the SCs and STs under Article 330 and 332 of the Constitution. More over SC/STs are eligible to avail of reservations in the Zilla Parishads and local Self-Governments in the States respectively under 243D and 243T of the Constitution. Even the Constitution has allowed reservation in the Zilla Parishads and local self-Governments in favour of the Backward Classes under the said articles.

3.2 Reservation in Educational Institutions

In order to spread education among the SC/ST/OBCs the constitution has made certain provisions under Article 15(4), 15(5) in particular and under Article 21(A), 29(2) and Article 45 and Article 46 in general.

Education which was in state list was brought under the concurrent list in 1976 by 42nd Constitution Amendment Act, 1976. Later, the Union Government has passed, "the Central Educational Institution (Reservation in Admission) Act, 2006 in respect of Central Government Institutions only. Further it has passed the right of children to free and compulsory Education Act, 2009 only for the students of 8th to 14th year."

The Union Government has instructed all the State Governments and Universities to reserve 15% seats for SC and 5% for STs. Later on, the OBCs also got 27% reservations in educational institutions. Some of the State Governments have passed the laws for providing reservations to the SC/STs in the professional institutions. Others have made the rules only.

(a) Compelling Situation

It is because of poverty and ignorance of the SC/ST/OBCs in particular, they remained educationally backward in comparative terms and in absolute terms. Generally at the school enrolment level they come in good number, but as they come to higher level, their strength is dwindled. Most of the students are dropped out of the school due to acute poverty, pressing conditions, and ignorance. They are, of course, far away from quality education due to their inability to pay higher tuition fees and other fees, they are not exposed to modern amenities, infrastructural facilities, expanding avenues and modern technological advancement. Therefore, the SC, ST, OBC students are woefully constrained to lose confidence and suffer from inferiority complex, as such they cannot exemplify their inner qualities and intelligence to a great extent.

On the other hand the general category students having capacity to pay capitation fees and the NRI students paying big donations are able to seek admission into quality education institutions and purchase merit by paying accumulated wealth of their parents. Still they inconceivably criticise on the students crossing hurdles race through out and seeking with great difficulty admission on merit-cum-reservation basis.

(b) Law on standard of eligibility : Article 15(4)

So far as standard of eligibility is concerned the Ministry of Education have issued circular No.33-3/62-u-v(1) dated 28th September 1962 to all State Governments / Union Territory Administrations and Universities requesting them to follow the rule of minimum essential qualification. It is "Where admissions are restricted to candidates having a minimum percentage of Marks, a reduction of 5% for Scheduled Castes / Scheduled Tribes may be allowed provided that the lower percentage prescribed does not fall below the minimum required to pass the qualifying examination." Thus, the SC/ST candidates might not be able to secure competitive marks or marks equal to general candidates, they had to fulfil the condition of minimum standard for getting admission. Once they are admitted to any particular course, they have to attend the classes and comply with the condition of minimum attendance in the class, they have to undergo the regular course, appear for home examinations, tests and tutorials like general students. When they appear for the annual examinations or examination at the end of the particular course, they have to qualify for the examination. For the purpose of passing the course, everyone has to secure certain prescribed percentage of marks in the final examination. There is no concession or relaxation of marks for passing the final year examination and getting degree or diploma whatever it may be. Thus, so far as passing the course is concerned, equal standard is maintained.

Even some of the students of reserved category have been competing the general candidates, achieving merit and distinction even after crossing several obstacles and barriers.

Moreover, according to Section 4 of the Central Educational Institutions (Reservation in Admission) Act, 2006, reservations provided under Section 3 of the said Act would not apply to -

(a) a Central Educational Institution established in the tribal areas referred to in the sixth schedule to the Constitution;

(b) the institution of excellence, research institutions, institutions of national and strategic importance specified in the schedule to this Act;

Provided that the Central Government may as and when considered necessary, by notification in the official Gazettee, amend the schedule;

(c) a Minority Educational Institution as defined in this Act;

(d) a course or programme at high levels of specialization, including at the post-doctoral level, within any branch or study or faculty, which the Central Government may, in consultation with the appropriate authority, specify.

It implies that the SC, ST and OBC students are not treated as eligible for getting admission to the higher course of study. Thus the doors of institutions of excellence, specialization and strategic courses are still not opened for the candidates of reserved categories on ill conceived presumption of lower standard of such candidates.

TABLE 3.1
Proportion of Literacy

Year	*SC*	*ST*	*General*
1961	10.27	8.54	24.00
1971	14.71	11.29	29.35
1981	21.38	16.35	41.30
1991	37.41	29.60	52.21
2001	54.69	46.10	65.38

TABLE 3.2

Number and Percentage Share of Graduates in various Disciplines in the Sample (NSSO 1999-2000)

Castes / Communities	*Agriculture*		*Engineering*		*Medicine*		*Other Subjects*		*Caste / Communities Share of Total Urban Population (Percent)*
1. Hindu ST	26	2.4	18	1.3	10	1.8	229	1.3	2.6
2. Hindu SC	41	3.8	30	2.2	10	1.8	629	3.6	12.9
3. All Muslims	101	9.4	68	5.0	54	10.0	1006	5.7	17.0
4. Hindu OBC	108	10.0	202	14.9	56	10.4	2402	13.7	24.2
5. Hindu U.C.	669	62.1	908	66.8	350	65.3	11529	65.9	36.9
6. All Christian	90	8.4	70	5.2	35	6.6	707	4.0	2.8
7. All Sikhs	18	1.7	30	2.2	11	2.1	419	2.4	1.6
8. All Others	25	2.4	33	2.4	10	1.9	581	3.3	2.0
9. Total :	1078	100	1359	100	535	100	17501	100	100

(*Source* : Satish Deshpande in his Article, "Exclusive Inequalities", Pub. in Economic and Political Weekly, June 17-23, 2006 Vol. XLI No. 24, p. 2439).

"In the total sample (about 1.51 Lakh persons in Urban India) there were 1,359 persons with engineering degrees, of which as many as 908 belonged to Hindu UC; the next highest figure is 202 for Hindu OBCs - less than one-fourth the former figure. Similarly, Hindu OBCs account for 56 doctors out of the sample total of 535, but the Hindu UCS have as many as 350 doctors, or more than six times the OBC figure. Among the non-technical graduates 11,529 out of 17,501 are Hindu UC, which is more than four and half times the figure for the OBCs at 2,402."

Thus the percentage of SC and STs is very meagre in the total urban population according to the said survey.

3.3 Reservaton in Public Services (16(4))

(a) From 1950 to 1970, the relevant rules and regulations in respect of reservations in services were made. However, during that period the SC and STs were neither educationally eligible nor they had the knowledge of reservation policy of the Government. Therefore educated / qualified candidates from the SC/STs were not available in sufficient number during those days. Later on the qualified candidates were available, but they were treated as 'not suitable' in most of the cases. Even though their representation was very meagre, the anti-reservationists raised huge cry, freak talks and lose allegations

TABLE 3.3
Reservation for Scheduled Castes and Scheduled Tribes in Services under the Central Government Important Dates

S. No.	*Item*	*Resolution*	*SC*	*ST*
1.	**Direct Recruitment**			
	(a) By open competition	42/21/49 NGS dtd. 13.09.1950	12 1/2%	5%
	(b) Otherwise than by Open Competition	--	16 2/3%	5%
	(a) By Open Competition	27/25/68 Est. dtd. 25.03.1970	15%	7 1/2%
	(b) Otherwise than by Open Competition		16 2/3%	7 1/2%
2.	**Posts filled by Promotion**			
	(a) Promotion by Departmental Exam	OM No.5/4/55 SCT dtd. 04.01.1957	12 1/2%	5%
		OM No.1/10/61 Estt. dtd. 08.11.1963		
		Class I-II	No Reservation	
		Class III-IV	12 1/2%	5%
		OM No.1/12/67 Estt. dtd. 11.07.1968	12 1/2% Class II	5%

(Table Contd.)

(Contd. Table 3.3)

S. No.	Item	Resolution	SC	ST
		Class III	12 1/2%	5%
		Class IV	12 1/2%	5%
	(b) Promotion by Selection	01.09.1969 Estt.		
		dtd. 26.03.1970		
		Class I	12 1/2%	5%
		Class II	12 1/2%	5%
		Class III	12 1/2%	5%
		Class IV	12 1/2%	5%
	(c) Promotion by Seniority Subject to fitness	27.02.1971 Estt. dtd.27.11.1972	15%	7 1/2%
	(d) Promotion to Selection Grade	08.11.1973 Estt. dtd.12.09.1974	15%	7 1/2%
3.	Reservation in Public Sector Undertakings	OM 05.01.1963 SCT dtd.04.03.1964	12 1/2%	5%

(Table Contd.)

(Contd. Table 3.3)

S. No.	*Item*	*Resolution*	*SC*	*ST*
4.	Reservation in Autonomous Bodies (Municipal Corporations, Co.op. Institutions, Universities, etc.)	OM No.39/40/74 SCT dtd.39.09.1974	15%	7 1/2%
5.	Reservation in Voluntary Agencies Receiving Grants-in-Aid	OM No.27/12/73 Estt. dtd.07/10/1974	15%	7 1/2%
6.	Reservation in Public Services to the SEBCs or OBCs	OM No.36012/31/90 Estt. (SCT) dtd.13.08.1990 & dtd.08.09.1993 to the Extent of 27% for OBCs	36012/2/93 Estt. (SCT)	

Source : Brochure on SC/ST in Services.
Ministry of Personnel, Public Grievances etc.
Dept. Personnel and Training, Govt. of India, New Delhi.

against reservations. Consequently anti-reservation agitations were erupted on large scale especially in Bihar, Gujarat, Maharashtra and other states. The Mandal Commission came into implementation actually in 1993. Subsequently, the new economic policy brought many limitations on reservation. Thus the policy of reservation is being implemented unduly slowly. Still there is no comprehensive law covering all the aspects of reservations at central level.

The following table shows how late the SC, ST and OBCs have started taking benefits of reservations. Further it shows as to how the State is not very serious about the implementation of the policy of reservation enshrined in the Constitution. See Table No. 3:3.

3.4 Law on Standard of Suitability (16(4))

So far as the standard of suitability is concerned the Ministry of Home Affairs Vide O.M. No. 8/10/66-Est(C) Dated 15th May 1967 stated as under :

(a) Direct Recruitment by Examination

If according to their normal positions in the examination candidates belonging to Scheduled Castes and Scheduled Tribes obtained less vacancies than the number reserved for them, the Union Public Service Commission or other recruiting authority will have full discretion in order to make up the deficiency to recommend Scheduled Caste and Scheduled Tribe candidates who may obtain a low place in the examination, except where such authority considers that the minimum standard necessary for the maintenance of efficiency of administration has not been reached.

(b) Direct Recruitment Otherwise than by Examination

"The appointing authorities will have discretion to select, for vacancies reserved for Scheduled Castes and Scheduled Tribes, candidates belonging to these communities who may be of a lower standard than candidates of other communities, so long as the Scheduled Caste and Scheduled Tribe candidates have the prescribed minimum educational, technical and other essential qualifications and the appointing authorities are satisfied that the lowering of standard will not unduly affect the maintenance of efficiency of administration.

Further, the Department of Personnel and Training, Govt. of India made the clarification in respect of educational standards of the SC/ST candidates for any post, vide 36011/8/84-Estt(SCT) dated 17th Oct., 1986 that "a minimum number of marks or a minimum grade is also prescribed as part of the educational qualification in the recruitment rules. In such cases, the minimum marks / grade so prescribed shall also uniformly apply to all candidates including SC and ST candidates."[6]

However, "the state may lower barriers to opportunity exclusively for backward classes," like concessions in examination fees, application fees, lower age etc. The state may, "to insure the inclusion of these groups, employ some lower standard of selection at the intake point."[7] It was held in Janaki Prasad case, that, "where appointments and promotions to responsible public offices are made, greater circumspection would be required in making reservations for the benefit of any Backward class because efficiency and public interest must always remain paramount. It is implicit in the idea of reservation that a less meritorious person is to be preferred to another who is more meritorious."[8]

In S.S. Sharma V. Union of India, The Supreme court had accepted, "that relaxed eligibility criteria would be justified in the case of candidates of backward classes."[9]

In P&T SC/ST Employee Welfare Association V. Union of India, it was held that,"the employees belonging to the SC and the STs may be promoted to the higher cadre on completion of a shorter period of service than what is prescribed for others. In this particular case it is open to the Government to direct that while all others would be entitled to be promoted to the higher cadre on completion of 16 years of service the members belonging to the Scheduled Castes and the Scheduled Tribes may be promoted to the higher cadre on completion of say 12 or 13 years of service."[10]

3.5 Carry forward and Dereservation

It should be noted that if the candidates belonging to SC and STs were not available or they were not found suitable for a particular post or service the posts so reserved for them were permitted to be dereserved till 1989. This became a way to avoid the entry of SC STs in the services on the ground of non-availability of candidates or suitable candidates. Therefore, the Department of Personnel and Training issued a memorandum banning on deservation in direct recruitment to vacancies under the Government, vide letter No.36012/6/88 Estt. SCT dated 25th April 1989. The vacancies which could not be filled up shall remain unfilled until the next recruitment year and such vacancies would be treated as 'backlog' vacancies to be carried forward, and if such vacancies remained unfulfilled for three successive years, then the seats earmarked for SC could be filled by ST candidate or Vice-Versa.[11]

So far as dereservation of vacancies falling in Promotion Quota is concerned, Department of Personnel and Training through its letter No. 390 11/7/90 Estt. Govt. of India, dated 8-2-1991 directed to all Ministries / Departments of Govt. of India that in view of non-availability of candidates for promotion in the zone of consideration, the post can be dereserved with the prior approval of the competent authority.[12]

3.6 Reservation in Promotions

So far as reservation in promotion is concerned, the SC/ST candidates who have not acquired the general qualifying standard to departmental examination, could also be considered for promotion provided they are not found unfit for such promotion, Vide O.M. No. 8/12/69 Estt/SCT/dated : 23rd December 1970.[13]

In State of Kerala V.N.M.Thomas, the question was whether the Kerala Government's recruitment/rule for promotion with relaxation of period in passing departmental examination was valid or not. The Supreme Court held that such relaxation was valid in respect of promotion.[14]

Later on, the hon'ble Supreme Court in Mandal Commission Case had declared that reservations under Article 16(4) can not be made in promotions.[15]

Further, relaxation of qualifying marks in any examination or lowering the standards of evaluation was held invalid in S.Vinodkumar V. Union of India.[16]

Eventually, the parliament has passed the 77th Constitution Amendment Act, 1995 and added clause 4A to Article 16 of the constitution. Further the suitable proviso was added to Article 335 by 82nd Constitution Amendment Act, 2000. In pursuance of the said proviso, the Govt. of India, DOPT issued O.M. No. 36012/23/96-ESTT dated 3rd October 2000 providing for relaxation in qualifying marks in any examination or lowering the standard of evaluation for reservation in promotion in favour of the Scheduled Castes and the Scheduled Tribes.[17] Thus, both the provisions under Article 16(4A) and the proviso to Article 335 are in favour of only SCs and STs.

(1) However, in SBI SC/ST Employees Welfare Association V. State Bank of India (1996) 4 SCC 119, it was decided by the Supreme Court that, the Policy of reservation in promotion was not violative of Article 16(4) and 16(4A) but the vacancies lapsed due to non-availability of SC/ST candidates could not be revived.[18]

(2) However, it was held in Union of India V. Virpal Singh Chauhan (1995) that, "While the rule of reservation shall be applied

and the roster followed in the matter of promotions to or within a particular service, class or category, the candidate promoted earlier by virtue of rule of reservation / roster shall not be entitled to seniority over his senior in the feeder category and that as and when a general candidate who was senior to him in the feeder category is promoted, such general candidate will regain his seniority over the reserved candidate notwithstanding that he is promoted subsequent to the reserved candidate. There is no unconstitutionality involved in this."[19]

It was reiterated in Ajit Singh Januja Vs. State of Punjab (1996) that "the rule of reservation gives accelerated promotion but it does not give the accelerated 'consequential seniority'. If a Scheduled Caste / Scheduled Tribe candidate is promoted earlier because of the rule of reservation/roster and his senior belonging to the general category is promoted later to that higher grade the General Category candidate shall regain his seniority over such earlier promoted Scheduled Caste / Tribe Candidate."[19(a)]

(3) In view of the above said decisions, the parliament, however passed the 85th Amendment Act, 2001 and introduced in Article 16 (4A) "in matters of promotion with consequential seniority," and settled the issue of 'consequential seniority' without any doubt or ambiguity.

(4) Again the question of constitutional validity of the Constitutional Amendments to Article 16(4) was raised in M.Nagaraj and others V. Union of India (2006)[20]. In this case the hon'ble Supreme Court made it clear that, "The impugned Constitutional amendments by which Articles 16(4A) and 16(4B) have been inserted flow from Article 16(4). They do not alter the structure of Article 16(4). They retain the controlling factors or the compelling reasons, namely, backwardness and inadequacy of representation which enables the states to provide for reservation keeping in mind the overall efficiency of the state administration under Article 335. These impugned amendments are confined only to SCs and STs."

"As stated above the impugned provision is an enabling provision. The state is not bound to make reservation for SC/ ST in matters of promotions. However if they wish to exercise their discretion and make such provision, the state has to collect quantifiable data showing backwardness of the class and inadequacy of representation of that class in public employment in addition to compliance of Article 335. It is made clear that even if the state has compelling reason as stated above, the state will have to see that its reservation provision does not lead to excessiveness so as to breach ceiling limit of 50% or obliterate the creamy layer or extend the reservations indefinitely."

"Subject to above, we uphold the Constitutional Validity of the Constitution (seventy seventh Amendment Act, 1995, The Constitution (Eighty First Amendment) Act, 2000, the Constitution (Eighty second Amendment) Act 2000, the Constitution (eighty Fifth Amendment) Act, 2001."

(5) Eventually, the hon'ble Supreme Court held in U.P. Power Corporation V. Rajesh Kumar (April 2012)[21] that "we are of the firm view that a fresh exercise in the light of the judgement of the Constitution Bench in M. Nagaraj is a categorical imperative. The stand that the Constitutional amendments have facilitated the reservation in promotion with consequential seniority and have given the stamp of approval to the Act and the Rules cannot withstand close scrutiny in as much as the Constitution Bench has clearly opined that Articles 16(4A) and 16 (4B) are enabling provisions and the state can make provisions for the same on certain basis or foundation. The conditions precedent have not been satisfied. No exercise has been undertaken. What has been argued with Vehemence is that it is not necessary as the concept of reservation in promotion was already in vogue. We are unable to accept the said admission, for when the provisions of the Constitution are treated valid with certain conditions or riders, it becomes incumbent on the part of the state to appreciate and apply the test so that its amendments can be tested and withstand the scrutiny on parameters laid down therein."

In the ultimate analysis, we conclude and hold that section 3(7) of the 1994 Act and Rule 8A of the 2007 Rules are ultra vires as they run counter to the dictum in M. Nagaraj."

(6) It became a matter of great concern to the members of both Houses of Parliament when the issue was raised by the BSP Leader Mayawati in Rajya Sabha and Congress M.P. P.L. Punia in Loksabha on 29th April 2012. However, the State Minister in Prime-Minister's Office V. Narayan Samy assured to take appropriate steps very soon in the interest of Social Justice.[22] Thus the issue of reservation in Promotion of SCs and STs in the Public Services stands unsettled even after making suitable Constitutional amendments.

(7) It is, however difficult to comprehend the principles laid down in the Nagaraj case (2006) and affirmed in UP Power Corporation Case (2012) by the hon'ble Supreme Court. It is but a fact that the Scheduled Castes and the Scheduled Tribes have been subjected to 'Untouchability' and 'Tribalism' respectively. In order to improve their socio-economic condition and bring them to the main stream, the Constitution has provided certain special safeguards to them. The President of India, empowered under Article 341(1) and Article 342(1) of the Constitution promulgated the SC and ST orders in 1950 after consultation with the concerned Governor which facilitate to identify those Castes and Tribes.

Now, in view of the above said Judgements is it again imperative to 'Identify' SC/STs and 'Test' their 'backwardness' by collecting quantifiable data for the purpose of special safeguards ?

The criterion of listing the SC/STs was their traditional low social status. Backwardness, social or economic cannot be relevant in respect of SC/STs. No doubt Untouchability and Tribalism are no more legally in existence, but they are in real existence. In a caste society social-status and not individual status is relevant. Almost all the members of the so called lower castes are subjected to more or less same deprivation and inhuman treatment irrespective of educational or economic status of its individual members.

Their present backwardness could be easily perceived in their slums and wretched localities. The prejudice and hatred against them could be easily preceived from increasing incidents of caste-violence and atrocities perpetrated on them; as reported periodically by the National Human Rights Commission. So far as their employment position is concerned the Brochure on Reservation brought out by the Department of Personnel and Training, Govt. of India gives certain information and statistics. It is good if the additional information in this respect is brought out by the state for the information and guidance of all the concerned authorities and general public. However, it need not be imperative. It is submitted that want of certain data regarding the present position of the disadvantaged groups ought not to be a stumbling block in the way of justice to them.

3.7 Quantum of Reservation

It is, however, necessary to know the quantum of reservations so as to know the probable effects of the SC/ST incumbents on the administrative efficiency.

(1) It should be noted that from 13-09-1950 to 25-03-1970 the quota of reserved posts for the Scheduled Castes was 12 1/2 percent in respect of recuitment by open competition in other cases it was 16 percent. The quota of reserved posts for the Scheduled Tribes was fixed at 5 percent for any type of recruitment.

However, from 25-03-1970, the quota of reserved posts for the Scheduled Castes was raised from 12 1/2 to 15 percent in case of recruitment by open competition and in other cases it was fixed at 16 2/3 percent, and for the Scheduled Tribes the quota of reserved posts was fixed at 7 1/2 percent. The same quantum of reservations is in existence since then.

(2) The Mandal Commission Report was accepted on 7th Aug.1990 by the Union Government (O.M. No. 360/2/31/90-ESTT(SCT) dated 13th Aug.1990 and 25th Sept.1991). Accordingly the quantum of reservation for the Backward Classes was fixed at 27%.

Presently, the quantum of reservation is as under -

Scheduled Castes	:	15% from 1970.
Scheduled Tribes	:	7 1/2% from 1970.
Other Backward Classes	:	27% from 1991.

(3) According to the 'carry forward' rule (vide O.M.No.2/11/1955 RPS dated 7th May 1955 if a sufficient number of suitable candidates belonging to SC/ST is not available from the respective classes in a particular year, such shortfall in the number of SC/ST is to be carried forward upto two subsequent recruitment years, before the reservation is finally treated as lapsed.[23]

The period of carry forward of reservations was further extended for three consecutive years vide O.M.No.27/25/68 Est(SCT) dated 25th March 1970.[24]

In Devasasan V. Union of India, the Supreme Court said that "each year of recruitment must be considered by itself and the reservation for the backward communities each year should not be excessive so as to creat a monopoly or to interfere unduly with the legitimate claims of other communities. Accordingly, the court held that the reservation ought to be less than 50 percent, but how much less than half would depend upon prevailing circumstances in each case."[25]

In Akhil Bharaliya Soshit Karmachari Sangh V. Union of India, the carry forward rule was upheld. It was held that the carry forward rule shall not result, in any given year, in the selection or appointments of SC and ST candidates considerably in access of

50%."[26] In Indra Sawhney V. Union of India the Supreme Court held that the reservation should not exceed 50 percent."[27]

The issue of "carry forward and quota" has been finally settled by the constituion (81st Amendment) Act, 2000. Accordingly, the vacancies remained unfilled would not be considered together with the vacancies of the year in which they are being filled up for determining the ceiling of 50% reservation on total number of vacancies of that year.

However, the Supreme Court reiterated in M.Nagaraj V. Union of India. (2006)[28] that the ceiling limit of 50% the concept of creamy layer and the compelling reasons, namely narrow backwardness, inadequacy of representation and over all administrative efficiency are all constitutional requirements without which the structure of equality of opportunity in Article 16 would collapse."

3.8 Scope of Reservations

Sor far as the applicability of reservation is concerned, there seem to be five categories of services :

(1) General Services.
(2) Temporary and Emergency Services.
(3) Scientific and Technical Services.
(4) Judicial Services, and
(5) Military Services.

(1) In respect of General Services including the services under the Public Sector Undertakings, there is no exemption or exclusion from the preferential discrimination or reservation. It would include the services under the Union Government and the State Governments/Union Territories Governments. Even the statutory bodies like University, Corporations and local self governments are also bound to apply the rules of reservations to the services under them.

(2) However, the following services are exempted from the reservations -

(a) (1) Vacancies filled by transfer or deputation.
   (2) Temporary appointments of less than 45 days duration.
   (3) Those work-charged posts which are required for emergencies like flood relief work, accident restoration and relief work etc.

(b) In case where only one vacancy occurs and it is reserved for SC/ or ST or OBC, it should be treated as unreserved and filled accordingly and the reservation should be carried forward to subsequent recruitment year. "In the subsequent recruitment year, even if there is only one vacancy, it should be treated as "reserved" against the carried forward reservation from the initial recruitment year, although it may happen to be the only vacancy in that recruitment year."[29]

(3) Scientific and Technical Posts Required for Research or Guiding Research

So far as 'Scientific and Technical' posts are concerned the reservation orders infavour of Scheduled Castes and Scheduled Tribes were not applicable in the case of appointments to posts for conducting research, or far organizing guiding and directing research vide O.M. No. 9/2/63 SCT(1), dated 2nd Nov.1963.[30]

It was clarified in 1964 that for being exempted from the reservation, a post must satisfy the following two conditions.

(1) It should be a post classified as 'Scientific or Technical' in terms of cabinet secretariat memorandum of 1961; and

(2) It must be a post for conducting research or for organizing, guiding and directing research.

However, it was decided in 1975 that the scheme of reservation would apply to Scientific and Technical Posts upto and including the lowest grade of clas 1 in the respective services, vide M.O. No. 9/2/73, Est.(SCT) dated 23-06-1975.[31]

Thus, according to the said order those Scientific and Technical Posts which satisfy the following conditions are to be exempted from the purview of reservation :-

(i) The posts should be in grades above the lowest grade in class 1 of the service concerned.

(ii) They should be classified as "Scientific or Technical" in Terms of Cabinet decision of 1961.

(iii) They should be posts for conducting research or for organizing, guiding and directing research.

In Indra Sawhney Vs. Union of India (1993) it was laid down that in certain services where on account of the nature of duties attached to them or the level (in the hierarchy) at which they are obtained, merit alone would count. Further the hon'ble Supreme Court observed in K. Duriasamy V. State of Tamil Nadu (AIR 2001 SC 718) that, "It is by now a proposition well settled, that the super speciality level in particular and even at the Post-Graduate level reservations of the kind known as 'protective discrimination' in favour of those considered to be backward should be avoided as being not permissible.[32]

(4) Judicial Services

Judiciary is one of the three branches of the Government. It is the prime organ of the body politic which interprets the law and distributes justice to the people. Justice is the foundation of the state, therefore, judiciary assumes a unique position in the state. The Judicial Power is an important Power as such it is respected by all the people.

At the Union Level there is a Supreme Court. Its Constitution, Powers and functions are provided under Part V : Chapter IV of the Constitution of India. At the State Level there are High Courts whose, constitution, powers and functions are provided under Part VI : Chapter V of the Constitution, and at the District and Taluka Level there are District Courts and Sub-ordinate Courts, whose constitution, powers and functions are provided under Part VI : Chapter VI of the Constitution.

Generally, persons of high qualification, merit and integrity and experience are appointed as judges subject to constitutional and statutory provisions at various level. Although there is a mandatory provision of reservation under Article 16(4), Article 46 and Article 335 of the Constituion no reservation is provided in Judicial Services of the Country; allegedly on ground of having no such provision in the Constitution so far as Judiciary is concerned. Apex Court of the Country itself holds the view that there is no place for reservation in the judicial appointments at any level.

However, it seems that the people who think that there ought to be equitable distribution of Political Power, economic power, administrative power and judicial power, they demand for reservations in educational institutions, and public services including judicial services among all the classes including the backward classes. Thus, because of persuasions and pressures from the socially conscious people in the society for reservations of vacancies for the Scheduled Castes and the Scheduled Tribes the men in power were convinced to concede the said demand.

It seems on the Report of the committee on untouchability etc. constituted under the Chairmanship of Shri L. Elayaperumal (1969) that, "the Home Ministry suggested to the Registrar of the Supreme Court the framing of suitable rules to provide reservation for SC and ST in the courts services. But nothing has been done so far in this regard."[33]

The Commissioner for the SC and STs states in his report for the year 1975-76 & 1976-77. Part (1) that, the High Power Committee Meeting was held under the Chairmanship of the Prime Minister, on 12th Nov.1976 to review the position regarding reservations for SC/ST in the services under the High Courts.

"The Committee was informed that -

(i) Provision for reservation in services under the High Courts existed in more than half the states and action was being initiated by some more states to provide reservation.

(ii) It had been clarified to the state Governments that in the matter of appointments to the sub-ordinate Judicial Service of the state, Article 234 can be invoked for making reservations for Scheduled Castes and STs and that in the case of Higher Judicial Service, Article 309 can be invoked.

(iii) The Minister for law and justice had earlier written to the Chief Ministers of all the states requesting them to ensure that the High Courts adopt the State Govts/Central Govt orders for providing reservation for SC and STs in the Ministerial Judicial and Higher Judicial Services under the High Courts both at the time of initial recruitment and in promotions; and

(iv) The Chief Justices of High Courts had also been requested to take necessary effective steps in this regard."

It seems on the said report that some of the State Governments have accepted the Policy of reservation in the State Judicial Services and in the ministerial posts at the initial appointments.

The hon'ble Commissioner for SC ST (1977) had recommended in his said Report that,"The High Courts which have not accepted the principle of reservation or have not so far started giving effect to the reservation orders both at the time of initial recruitment and promotion in the Ministerial, State Judicial and High Judicial Services, should do so without any further delay. In various categories of posts the backlog should be calculated and duly qualified, eligible Scheduled Caste and Scheduled Tribe candidates should be considered against reserved quota without sacrificing efficiency in Judiciary...... the Ministry of Law should take suitable steps in this regard and also explore the possibility of providing reservations in nomination from the Bar."[34]

Again, this matter reportedly came up for discussion in the High Power Committee Meeting held on 20th October 1978 under the Chairmanship of the Prime-Minister. The Minister of Law "pointed out that constitutionally, no reservation could be madein the matter of appointment of Judges to the High Courts or Supreme Court." Although some of the other Ministers agreed to have reservation in Judiciary, the Prime Minister said that, "one had to proceed with caution in the matter."[35]

The High Commissioner for SC ST Shri Shishir Kumar (1980) opined that, "It is rather unfortunate that the Ministry of Law have held the view that the High Court is considered as a "State", and, therefore, the appointment of Chief Justice and other Judges to the High court could not be considered as services under the "State" since the High Court itself is to be regarded as the "state". It is, high time that the issue be settled once for all, if necessary by making a Presidential reference to the Supreme Court to decide whether appointment of Judges to the High Courts and Supreme Court is outside the purview of the Provisions made in Articles 16(4) and 335 of the Constitution."[36]

It seems on the Report of the Commission for SC ST (Second Report) submitted by Bhola Paswan Shastri that, only Nine High Courts, Allahabad, Andhra Pradesh, Delhi, Gauhati, Kerala, Madras, Orissa Punjab and Rajasthan have provided reservation for SC/STs in the State Higher Judicial Services; and 14 High Courts - Allahabad, Andhra Pradesh, Delhi, Gauhati, Kerala, Madras, Orissa, Punjab, Rajasthan, Calcutta, Himachal Pradesh, Karnataka, Patna and Haryana have provided reservations for SC/STs in the State Judicial Services.[37]

The Commission for Scheduled Castes and Scheduled Tribes in its Third Report (1980-81) submitted by K. Rajamallu has strongly recommended to the Government of India that :-

"(i) suitable provisions should be made for appropriate reservation for Scheduled Castes and Scheduled Tribes among the Judges of High court and Supreme Court.

(ii) suitable provisions should be made for reservation for the Scheduled Castes and Scheduled Tribes in the Judicial Services of the State where it has not yet been provided. The percentage of reservation in these services should also be on the lines of percentage in other services of the state."[38]

According to the Broucher, published by the Lok Sabha Secretariat, New Delhi, 1986 "The Government, however, addressed the Chief Ministers of States and the Chief Justices of High Courts in August, 1980 saying, inter-alia, that it should be possible for them to locate persons from the Bar belonging to Scheduled Castes, Scheduled Tribes, minority communities, backward classes and other weaker sections who were suitable for appointment as High Court Judges. They were advised to keep this thing in view while making recommendations."[39] Further, it is learnt that, "The then Law and Justice Minister Dinesh Goswani has written to the State Governments and Chief Justices of High Courts to recommend suitable names of persons from among six categories who can be considered for appointment of Judges in the high court."[40]

In this respect, one Sunil Gupta raised two inconceivable arguments against reservation in Judiciary. He states that, "whether a meritorious person can be discarded and dropped from consideration in favour of some less fit, less meritorious person only for the reason that the former does not fall in one or the other of the six categories whereas the latter does." Here he prejudicially takes for granted that the reserved category candidates are less meritorious than others, which basic presumption itself is wrong. His other argument is the judge of the High Court may "strike down a law, may even a constitutional amendment, made by a whole parliament and all the State Assemblies put together in exercise of their sovereign legislative and constituent powers. The superiority of the judiciary is axiomatic."[41] Here he wants to maintain the 'monopoly' of exercising the constituent power by the non-reserved candidates which is against the principle of democrary.

This amply shows that the men in power are not determined to provide for reservations in the judiciary. Even the judiciary is unwilling to have reservations in Judiciary. All three branches of the Government, Executive, Legislative and Judiciary ought to implement mandate of the Constitution. There is reservation in administration, there is reservation in the legislature but not in judiciary. It is very much unreasonable and against the spirit of the constituion, implying in Article 16(4), 46 and 335.

The comprehensive definition of "the state" under Article 12 makes all the difference.[42] We have to define "the state" and "state" in their proper perspective; otherwise it would be very much problematic. It is a well known fact that "state" is constituted by four elements, population, territory, government and sovereignty. Its existence is recognized by the World States. Whereas by virtue of the definition of 'the State' under Article 12, "the Government and Parliament of India and the Government and the legislature of each of the States and all local or other authorities within the territory of India or under the control of the Government of India are 'the State'. This broad definition is meant only for the purpose of Part III (Fundamental Rights and Part IV Directive Principles of State Policy) of the Constitution in a limited "context". This definition connotes the correct meaning only if "unless the context otherwise requires" is taken into account. Thus the definition of "the State" is for a definite purpose, and it cannot be construed so in general.

Consequently, the judiciary is a part of the Government, which is one of the constitutent elements of State. So how the judiciary itself can be a State ? If it thinks so, in the light of Article 12, every "authority" or "Local Body" would be "the State". If the Supreme Court denies to implement the Policy of Reservation being "the State", then how the "other authorities" would agree to the same.

It is expedient to take into account that, "India, that is Bharat, is a sovereign, socialist, secular, Democratic, Republic", no autority is Supreme or Parallel, but every authority or entity is under the Sovereign State of India. Therefore, this anamoly has to be removed by proper construction of "the State" taking into account "unless the context otherwise requires."

It seems that the Govt. of Bihar had very strongly insisted on providing reservations in the Subordinate Judicial Services of the State. It provided under section (4) of the Bihar Reservation of vacancies in posts and services for SC and ST and OBCs Act 1991 for reservation in State Judicial Services. However, the Supreme Court by majority held that the said provision was unconstitutional being violation of Articles 223, 234 and 235 and 309 of the Constitution. (The State of Bihar V. Balmukund Sah, AIR 2000 SC 1296).[43] It was argued before the Supreme Court by the appellant state that the state legislature was competent to make enactment in connection with appointments to the Public Services under list II Entry 41of the seventh scheduled and "Judicial Service" is also a Public Service of the State." It was strongly argued that, "The reasoning of the High Court that the Act does not cover "Judicial Service" is patently erroneous and that this Act is not bound by any fetters of Articles 233 or 234 and is an exercise of paramount legislative power conferred on stae authorities under Article 309 first part read with Entry 41 list II Seventh Schedule of the Constitution." Notwithstanding these learned arguments, the hon'ble Supreme Court dismissed the state appeal made against the High Court Judgement given previously.

It was held by majority of the Judges of the hon'ble Supreme Court, that Article 309 of the Constitution which deals with the matter of 'Public Service' does not include 'Judicial Service'. "Article 309, which, on its express terms, is made subject to other provisions of the Constitution, does get circumscribed to the extent to which from its general field of operation is carved out a separate and exclusive field for operation by the relevant provisions of Articles dealing with sub.ordinate Judiciary as found in chapter VI of Part VI of the Constituion."

It was held by the majority Judges of the honourable Supreme Court in the said case that, "no recruitment to the post of a District Judge can be made by the Governor without recommendation from the High Court. Similarly appointments to subordinate Judiciary at grass-root level also cannot be made by the Governor save and except according to the rules framed by him in consultation with the High Court and the Public Service Commission."

"However, so far as the question of exercising that enabling Power under Article 16(4) for laying down an appropriate scheme of reservation goes, as seen earlier, we cannot be oblivious of the fact that the High Court, being The high constitutional functionary, would also be alive to its social obligations and the constitutional guidelines for having schemes of reservation to ameliorate the lot of deprived reserved categories like the SC, ST and other Backward Classes. But for that purpose, the Governor can in Consultation with the Court, make appropriate rules and provide for a scheme of reservation for appointments at grass-root level or even at the highest level of the District Judiciary but so long as this is not done, the state legislature cannot, by upsetting the entire apple-cart and totally by pasing the constitutional mandate of Articles 233 and 234 and without being required to consult the High Court, lay down a statutory scheme of reservation."

However, the minority judgement delivered by the honourable justice R.P.Sethi appended with the majority judgement given by the honourable justice S.B.Majumdar and others in the above referred case of course goes against the majority Judgement.

It is evident that the minority judgement is greatly relied on the decision given previously by the Supreme Court in B.S. Yadav Vs State of Haryana (AIR 1981 SC 561) which states that, "On a plain reading of Articles 235 and 309 of the Constitution, it is clear that the Power to frame rules regarding seniority of officers in the judicial service of the state is vested in the Governor and not in the High Court." (p. 576)

"Who has the power to pass such a law ? Obviously not the High Court because, there is no power in the High Court to pass a law in the exercise of power conferred upon it in that behalf may have the force of law. There is a distinction between the power to pass a law and the power to make rules which by law, have the force of law. Besides, "Law" which the second part of Article 235 speaks of, is law made by the legislature...."

"Article 235 does not confer upon the High Courts the Power to make rules relating to conditions of service of Judicial Officers attached to District Courts and the Courts Subordinate thereto."

"Who, then, possess that Power ? Article 309 furnishes the answer. It provides that Acts of the appropriate Legislature may regulate the recruitment and conditions of service of persons appointed posts in connection with the affairs of the Union or of any State. Article 246(3) read with Entry 41 in list II of the Seventh Schedule, confers upon the State legislatures the power to pass laws with respect to "State Public Services" which must include the Judicial Services of the State."

"The proviso to Article 309 provides, in so far as material, that until the State Legislature passes a law on the particular subject, it shall be competent to the Governor of the state to make rules regulating the recruitment and the conditions of service of the Judicial officers of the state."

Eventually referring to Section 4 of the impugned Bihar Act which has been declared ultravires of the Constitution, the minority Judgement pronounced that, "Interpretation of Section 4 as put in by the High Court if accepted, would not only frustrate the purpose and object of the Bihar Act No.3 of 1992 but also be contrary to the mandate of the Constitution as enshrined in its part III and further declared in part IV, Article 46 and Article 335 of the Constitution."

Thus, the majority Judgement in the present case has undoutedly invalidated the Bihar Reservation of vacancies in posts and services (for Scheduled Cstes, Scheduled Tribes and other Backward Classes) Act, 1991, but has not restricted the State Government to make necessary provision for reservation of vacancies which could be made only after following the procedure laid down by Article 233 and Article 234 of the Constitution or it could be made by bringing in necessary amendment in the relevant articles of the Constitution by Law. Reservation is, however a fundamental right of the disadvantaged sections of the society, as such it ought be respected and applied in all the three branches of the Government in the interest of Justice.

(5) Armed Forces : It is the policy of the Government, "to make recruitment to the Armed Forces as broad-based as possible and to provide equal opportunities to all citizens irrespective of caste, creed or domicile. Merit and physical standards are stated to be the only criteria for recruitment.[43(a)] Hence, there is no specific reservation in the armed forces.

However, the role played by the Mahar Regiment in armed operations in India and abroad are really noteworthy. Their bravery, valour and sacrifice for the nation won several gallantary awards worth their name. They have proved their bravery beyond doubt.[44]

In Indra Sawhney V. Union of India, the Supreme Court expressively stated that, "We are of the opinion that there are certain services and positions where either on account of the nature of duties attached to them or the level (in the hierarchy) at which they obtain, merit (as explained herein above), alone counts. In such situations it may not be advisable to provide for reservations.

Some of Them are

(1) Defence services including all Technical posts therein but excluding civil posts.

(2) All technical posts in establishment/engaged in Research and Development including those connnected with atomic energy and space and establishments engaged in production a defence equipment.

(3) Teaching posts of professors and above, if any.

(4) Posts in super-specialities in Medicine, engineering and other scientific and technical subjects.

(5) Posts of Pilots (and Co-Pilots) in Indian Airlines and Air India. The list given above is merely illustrative and not exhaustive."[45]

3.9 Merit and Efficiency

Merit includes physical and mental ability of a person. It is taken into account while making appointments and promotions in the services. The merit is, however, judged on the basis of written and oral test, performance test and physical test. The mental ability or intelligence is the major component of merit.

(1) It is very difficult to define it in exact terms. According to Kundu and Tutoo Intelligence and intellect are not one and the same thing. Intelligence is wider in meaning than intellect. Intellect means cognitive powers or activities like perceiving, observing, remembering, imagining, and thinking, but intelligence on the other hand means not only intellectual activities but also the capacity for solving practical problems of life as well.[46] According to Binet, as observed by Gardner Murphy, "at least three things would be involved in real intelligence;

(1) The ability to follow directions;

(2) The ability to make and maintain a given mental set, that is to keep going along the lines laid down earlier in prosecution of the task;.

(3) Auto-criticism or the capacity to see where one is making a mistake and to rectify it.[47]

The intelligence of a person could be measured in terms of I.Q. (Intelligence Qutient). The normal I.Q. (ranging from 90-109) higher, 110-119 high and 120-139 superior) is an indicator of higher intelligence.

The second major component of merit is the standard of values. A value means, "a conception or standard, cultural or merely personal by which things are compared and approved or disapproved, relative to one another, held to be relatively desirable or undersirable, more meritorious or less, more or less correct."[48] The sublime values including honesty, integrity and a sense of justice are very much required in administration.

(2) So far as administration is concerned merit includes administrative merit. Before and after recruitment to a particular post, the incumbent should have adequate knowledge of his work-subject and knowledge of the rules and regulations which he has to apply and the rules he is subjected to. He should administer the rules and regulations skillfully, intelligently and judiciously. He should try to fulfil the object of his service.

What is efficiency ? The dictionary meaning of efficiency is "an ability to accomplish a job with a minimum expenditure of time and effort." It is performing or functioning in the best possible and least wasteful manner, having and using requisite knowledge, skill and industry.

There is correlationship between merit and efficiency. Merit includes efficiency and efficiency depends on merit. Both are more or less inter related terms. However, merit is the quality of an individual whereas efficiency is the quality of a group. Efficiency does not merely include speedy disposal of work, but it includes a greater amount of expediency, propriety, a sense of jutice, devotion to work, sympathy for the poor and needy and a staunch national spirit. Merit enables personnel to achieve efficiency. Merit depends on several things including family background, education, culture and environment.

The efficiency of the administration could be properly safeguarded by prescribing a minimum standard of qualification and proper training or orientation of the employees at the one hand and at the other by proper supervision, coordination, motivation and guidance by the superior authority.

(3) Shri Giriswar Misra and Lal Bachan Tripathi (1980), who had studied 'psychological consequences of prolonged deprivation' on the scheduled and low castes in comparison to others, came to the conclusion that, "birth in a particular caste is not a decisive contributor towards cognitive growth. The more direct determinant of one's performance on a general mental ability test is his experimental richness which one accumulates from environment."[49]

According to R.R.P. Sinha, who had studied the 'Tribal and Non-Tribal Intelligence' (1980)" there exists no innate difference between the intelligence test scores of people belonging to two different racial groups, Tribals (Orans) and non-Tribals (Hindus and Muslims) and that whatever differences exist are due to difference in their environmental and cultural conditions.[50]

Thus, intelligence cannot be attributable to a particular caste or community. It is dependent on certain variables like family background, education, environment, cultural conditions etc. Merit is a relative factor. It cannot be expressed in absolute terms.

(4) Whether the theory of merit could be explained in terms of race ? Are the caste Hindus or Savarnas and the SC/STs or Avarnas are racially different ?

If it is believed that the Savarnas and Avarnas belong to two distinct races, one is superior and other is inferior, then is it virtually different from the racism of Nazis ? Is it not reminding the two nation theory of Jinnah and racist theory of the Whites ? Is it not reminding the Britisher's Theory that the Indians were not capable to rule over themselves ?

Even if it is assumed for the sake of argument, that there were initially two or more races in India, the question is, are they still pure without intermixture of blood. In the course of history, several people intruded India, such as Greek, Parthain, Shak, Kushan, Hun, Arab, Yavan, Turk, Mogal, Portugese, Dutch, French and British. Did they not intermix with the native people? In this respect Shri S.V. Ketkar has rightly stated that there is no Varna or caste which can claim purity of blood.[51]

From anthropological point of view, there is no exclusively distinct blood group of a particular caste. All the blood groups such as A, B, Rh etc. are found in all the castes, creeds and religious groups. The characteristics like skin colour, height, character, intelligent quotient, diseases etc. are generally due to heredity and environment. In this respect, John Buethner-Janusch has rightly stated that, "Most of the traits of character and personality that appear to differ among human populations are clearly culturally determined and formed.[52]

Several social scientists like Garth, Hirsch, Klinebarg, Lee and McGurk found that the different I.Q. could be attributed to the educational and environmental differences.

(5) In this respect it is very important to note the opinion of the renowned social scientists, who met in Paris in 1950, who issued a statement on race which in part, is as follows :

"Whatever classification the anthropologist makes of man, he never includes mental characteristics as part of those classifications. It is now generally recognized that intelligence tests do not in themselves enable us to differentiate safely between what is due to innate capacity and what is the result of environmental influences; training and education. Wherever it has been possible to make allowances for differences in environmental opportunities, the tests have shown essential similarity in mental characters among all human groups. In short, given similar degrees of cultural opportunity to reveal their potentialities, the average achievement of the members of each ethnic group is about the same.[53]

(6) Now, the question is as to who is to decide the merit of the SC/ST employees ? Are the same persons who have been trampling them since quite a long and who are acutely apathetic to the SC/STs eligible to judge their merit ? Had there been any fact finding committee appointed in this respect and had it inquired into this matter ? If not, how could the anti-reservationists oppose reservations on the ground of deficiency of merit on the part of the SC/ST employees. When the administrative efficiency is a collective responsibility, how it could be said that only a few SC/ST employees, that too at lower level affect the efficiency of the whole administration.

(7) It is allegedly said that due to SC/ST employees many accidents take place. It has been allegedly said the reserved category staff was mainly responsible for the railway accidents.[54] Accidents are but mischance which may occur by any person irrespective of his caste. Many a time, the other party is also equally or partially responsible for the accidents. Thus accidents may take place due to negligence of a person and contributory negligence of another person. Many a time the lower grade employees, who generally belong to SC/ST are required to carry out more hazardous work that too for maximum hours causing physical strain and mental stress which may lead to accidents. Probably due to strenuous nature of work, adverse work condition and lack of proper training, they could be involved in hazardous mishas. It is, however, difficult to establish caste accident relationship.

(8) Could any one claim in absolute terms that the employees of the general category are meritorious and efficient ? It is reliably learnt that there were 224.012 Lakhs of sick units till March 1998, in which 15,682 crores of bank credit (at the end of March 1998) was locked up.[55] The big industrial units are virtually manned by the high caste Hindus. If they claim to

be meritorious and efficient, how there could be such a large number of sick units in India. Are they not responsible for the inefficiency in those industrial units and improper use of huge public fund? It is said that some of the cooperative sugar factories and banks are not working properly. Are they managed by the SC/STs. Some of the medicines are reportedly of Sub-standard and harmful to the patients. Whether those pharmaceutical companies are managed by the so called low caste people ? These are all the results of human weaknesses which are, of course, not attributable to any caste.

(9) Those who are admitted on big donations to the professional colleges like Medical and Engineering belong to the high caste rich strata of the society. What worth they would contribute for the benefit of society when they would be recruited in the services of the State ?

The whole administration in our country is greatly infested with certain bad elements. The increasing incidents of red-tappism, corruption, sale of office, inefficiency, scams and scandals, increasing menace of black money are threatening to the very concept of socio-economic and administrative justice. Who are responsible for inefficient and corrupt administration in India ? Are not those who are charged with the duty of framing the policy and executing it responsible for the same ?

(10) In the educational field also the claim of merit by the so called high caste people is a myth. According to Jayati Ghosh, the entrance tests held at national level, test not intelligence or ability in the subject per se, but a certain aptitude for answering such tests. This is itself a skill that can be learnt, and there are now training institutes all over the county, especially in certain cities for this purpose. Such training in turn costs time and money, which effectively excludes most potential candidates.

So the flourishing "coaching" industry for these competitive exams amounts to another form of exclusion, or "reservation" for those who can afford to spend enough time and resources to ensure this prior coaching."

The said author further states that, reservation exists "for those who can come in through "NRI Quotas" which are now to be found in many institutions, or in institutions which require capitation fees or charge very large annual fees from students.[56] Thus the argument of merit is empty one.

The students of weaker sections have to cross several obstacles in their way, including poverty, sub-standard schools, especially the vernacular schools, unhealthy atmosphere, lack of books and means of transportation, prejudicial attitude of the village and school and their own inferiority complex. Still they come to a certain stage of competition. It is their merit.

It is generally argued that due to reservations persons of lower qualifications are selected. In view of Marc Galanter, "the translation of lower academic accomplishment into inefficiency in administration is difficult to trace. It is not clear how well academic performance co-relates with administrative talent."[57]

"Normally efficiency is, "in the words of K.R.Sunda, "evaluated 'on the job'. In the case of Scheduled Castes and Scheduled Tribes this draconian condition helps the selector quite often prejudiced to deny their claims on predetermined "born inefficient myth."[58] The SC/ST employees have to struggle for getting education and appointment. After the appointment he is looked down upon with bias and apathy by his superior and even by his inferior in the administrative hierarchy. He has to undergo a 'hurdles race', and prove his suitability.

Meritarians argue that it is because of the appointments of SC/STs on reservation basis, the administration has been losing efficiency. However, the following tables show that their reprsentation was below the quota fixed for them. How could a very tiny minority representation of SC/STs affect adversely on the whole administration. So far as higher positions are concerned there was either marginal represention or no representation. In such a situation how could they charge the SC/ST incumbents of low efficiency?

Following tables show the representation of SC/STs in : (1) Central Government Services and (2) Public Sector Banks.

TABLE 3.4
Representation of SCs/STs in Central Government Services

Group	*SCs*		*STs*	
	1.1.1965	*1.1.2008*	*1.1.1965*	*1.1.2008*
A	1.64	12.50	0.27	4.90
B	2.82	14.90	0.34	5.70
C	8.88	15.70	1.14	7.00
D	17.75	19.60	3.39	6.90

Source : Brochure on Reservation, Govt. of India, 2011, p. 7.

(i) All figures are in percent.

(ii) The reservation of OBCs has not been quantified.

TABLE 3.5

The Following Table shows the Percentage of SC/ST Population, Quota of Reservations and Posts filled in 1952, 1962, 1972, 1983, 1994 and 2004 Central Government

Class	1952 (1-12-1952)		1962 (1-1-1962)		1972 (1-1-72)	
	SC Population 15.05 Res. Quota 12.50 Posts filled	*ST* Population 06.31 Res. Quota 05.00 Posts filled	*SC* Population 14.64 Res. Quota 12.50 Posts filled	*ST* Population 06.80 Res. Quota 05.00 Posts filled	*SC* Population 14.60 Res. Quota 15.00 Posts filled	*ST* Population 06.94 Res. Quota 07 1/2 Posts filled
I	00.75	017	01.26	--	03.34	00.50
II	01.29	0.35	02.88	--	03.66	00.46
III	03.42	0.58	07.74	--	09.94	01.64
IV	19.59	0.94	17.35	--	21.78	03.85

(Table Contd.)

(Contd. Table 3.5)

Class	*1983 (1-1-83)*		*1994 (1-1-1994)*		*2004 (1-1-2004)*	
	SC Population 15.75 Res. Quota 15.00 Posts filled	*ST Population 07.76 Res. Quota 0.7 1/2 Posts filled*	*SC Population 16.50 Res. Quota 15.00 Posts filled*	*ST Population 08.10 Res. Quota 7 1/2 Posts filled*	*SC Population 16.20 Res. Quota 15.00 Posts filled*	*ST Population 08.20 Res. Quota 7 1/2 Posts filled*
I	06.71	01.41	10.25	02.92	12.20	04.10
II	10.16	01.46	12.06	02.81	14.50	04.60
III	14.61	04.14	15.73	05.38	16.90	06.70
IV	19.53	05.51	20.46	06.15	18.40	06.70

Source : Compiled.

It seems that the representation of SC/STs in Central Government Services is slowly improving. However, when the theory of merit and efficiency was invented and being argued very strongly, the representation of SC/STs was very poor and negligible.

TABLE 3. 6
Representation of SCs/STs in Central Government Services as on 3.5.2012

Group	*SCs*	*STs*
A	11.9%	4.4%
B	14.3%	5.4%
C	16.2%	7.3%
D	18.4%	6.5%

Source : Minister Narayan Swamy, Minister for Personnel Rajya Sabha Discussion on 3.5.2012 (Indian Express : 4th May 2012).

In the words of Dr.Babasaheb Ambedkar, it could be said that, "No body will have any quarrel with the abstract principle that nothing should be done whereby the best shall be superseded by one who is only better and better by one who is merely good and the good by one who is bad.

But the argument completely fails to carry coviction when in practice one finds that having regard to the historical circumstances of India everytime the 'best man' is chosen he turns out to be a man from the governing class. This may be alright from the point of view of the governing class. But can it be alright from the point of view of the servile class ?"[59]

There is a provision under Article 320 (4), that even without consulting Public Service Commission, the state may take necessary steps to make appointment under Article 16(4) and Article 335 of the Constitution. However, it is difficult to know whether this provision has been ever implemented. See Table No. 3:7.

3.10 Judicial Verdict on Merit and Efficiency

(1) In T.Devadasan V. Union of India (AIR 1964 SC 179) the Hon'ble Justice Subbarao observed on the validity of relaxation of any rule in favour of the SC/ST candidates, that, "The expression 'nothing in this article' inCl.(4) in Article 16 is a legislative device to express its intention in a most emphatic way that the power conferred thereunder is not limited in any way by the main provision but falls outside it. It has not really carved out an exception, but has preserved a power untrammelled by the other provisions of the Article."[60]

TABLE 3.7
Statement Showing the Representation of SCs/STs in the Service of Public Sector Banks

Year	Total Strength	Officer SC	%	ST	%
1969	24546	33	0.13	--	--
1975	65100	553	0.84	87	0.13
1980	132964	4047	3.04	864	0.64
1981	147778	5661	3.85	1303	0.88
1982	161631	7463	4.62	1741	1.08
1983	172844	8752	5.06	2309	1.33
1984	190753	10867	5.70	2799	1.46
1985	109081	14008	7.03	3542	1.78
1986	206660	15089	7.30	3810	1.84
1987	211353	16523	7.81	4148	1.96
1988	215959	18037	8.35	4748	2.19
As on 1.1.90	232852	20537	8.81	5759	2.47
As on 1.1.91	237057	21756	9.17	6432	2.17
As on 1.1.92	231490	22232	9.60	7004	3.03
As on 1.1.93	233880	23224	9.93	7357	3.45
As on 1.1.94	249016	25515	10.24	8333	3.34
As on 1.1.95	250806	26861	10.71	8818	3.52
As on 1.1.96	252898	28102	11.11	9235	3.65

(Table Contd.)

(Contd. Table 3.7)

Year	Total Strength	Clerks			
		SC	%	ST	%
1969	90789	412	0.45	--	--
1975	90789	9815	5.30	1271	0.68
1980	184862	35493	11.95	5258	1.77
1981	296963	41042	12.60	7172	2.20
1982	325476	45516	12.99	9137	2.60
1983	350307	50696	13.48	11080	2.95
1984	376097	55634	13.92	13244	3.31
1985	399411	59152	14.13	15407	3.65
1986	418365	39641	13.63	15924	3.70
1987	434057	63088	14.53	16041	3.69
1988	435740	60716	13.93	16733	3.85
As on 1.1.90	463492	65017	14.02	19793	4.27
As on 1.1.91	468321	66584	14.20	20886	4.45
As on 1.1.92	447238	63570	14.21	19763	4.42
As on 1.1.93	449468	64750	14.41	20036	4.46
As on 1.1.94	470873	66051	14.45	21500	4.56
As on 1.1.95	473429	66787	14.53	21990	4364
As on 1.1.96	473133	69493	14.69	22269	4.71

(Table Contd.)

(Contd. Table 3.7)

Year	*Total Strength*	*Sub-Staff (Including / Sweep)*			
		SC	*%*	*ST*	*%*
1969	42809	2632	6.15	--	--
1975	90760	14835	16.34	1534	1.69
1980	121808	24556	20.15	2545	2.08
1981	117034	20395	17.43	4019	3.43
1982	141036	31619	22.42	6038	4.28
1983	153280	35154	22.93	6068	3.96
1984	158465	37834	23.87	6722	4.24
1985	168386	42068	24.98	7312	4.34
1986	175541	43781	24.94	7715	4.39
1987	183900	46752	25.42	8032	4.36
1988	188290	48100	25.55	8400	0.46
As on 1.1.90	205635	54146	26.33	11039	5.36
As on 1.1.91	210229	35902	26.59	11579	5.00
As on 1.1.92	201197	53850	26.76	10950	5.44
As on 1.1.93	204858	55820	27.25	11464	5.60
As on 1.1.94	215819	60098	27.85	12419	5.75
As on 1.1.95	217509	61012	28.05	12430	5.72
As on 1.1.96	218980	62400	28.49	12794	5.54

(14 Nationalized Banks, SBI and its Associate Banks) NC SC ST Fourth Report, p. 198.

In Chandra Sekhara V. State of Mysore, AIR 1963 Mys.292 the Hon'ble Justice Somnath Iyer observed that, fixing a lower minimum level of marks in a competitive examination in favour of SC/ST candidates is outside the power of the State, since it is not a 'reservation in any sense of the term under Article 16(4)."[61]

However, it has been rightly observed by the Hon'ble Supreme Court in N.M. Thomas Vs. State of Kerala, that "the temporary relaxation of test qualification made in favour of SC and ST is warranted by their inadequate representation in the services and their overall backwardness." Rule 13-AA (relaxation of period) does not impair the test of efficiency in administration in as much as members of Scheduled Castes and Tribes who are promoted have to acquire the qualification of passing the test. The only relaxation which is done in their case is that they are granted two years more time than others to acquire the qualification. From the point of view of time a differential treatment is given to members of Scheduled Castes and Tribes for the purpose of giving them equality consistent with efficiency. Rule 13-AA and the two orders are therefore valid."[62]

(2) The decisive guidelines given by the Supreme Court in K.C.Vasant Kumar V. State of Karnataka[63] are of great significance in the matter of reservations. So far the plea of merit and efficiency is concerned the Hon'ble Justice Chinnappa Reddy has very rightly observed, which could be epitomized as under -

(a) The demand of reservation is a matter of right and not of philanthrophy. "They ask for parity, and not charity."

(b) "The disastrous consequences of the so called meritarian principle to the vast majority of the under-nourished, poverty-stricken, barely literate and vulnerable people of our country are too obvious to be stated." "There is no merit in a system which brings about such consequences."

(c) A child of the Scheduled Caste or Tribe who has been brought up in an adverse situation securing 40 to 50 percent of the marks is meritorious than a child of the higher caste who has been brought up in a favourable situation securing even 70 to 90 percent of the marks in a competitive examination; as a child of SC or ST has "to jump so many hurdles."

(d) "The requirements of efficiency may always be safeguarded by the prescription of minimum standards."

(e) "The truth is that the civil service is no paradise and the upper echelons belonging to the chosen classes are not necessarily models of efficiency."

(f) To think that the high caste people are meritorious is "a vicious assumption, typical of the superior approach of the elitist classes."

(g) "There is neither statistical basis nor expert evidence to support those assumption that efficiency will necessarily be impaired if reservation exceeds 50% if reservation is carried forward or if reservation is extended to promotional posts."

(h) "The mere securing of high marks at an examination may not necessarily mark out a good administrator. An efficient administrator, one takes it, must be one who possesses among other qualities the capacity to understand with sympathy and, therefore, to tackle bravely the problems of a large segment of population consisting the weaker sections of the people."

(i) "Different minimum standards and different modes of selection may be prescribed for different posts and for admission to different courses of study having regard to the requirements of the posts and the courses of study."

(j) "We do not, therefore, mean to say that efficiency is to be altogether discounted. All that we mean to say is that it cannot be permitted to be used as a camouflage to let the upper classes take advantage of the backward classes in its name and to monopolise the services, particularly the higher posts and the professional institutions."

(3) The Honourable Supreme Court has pronounced in Indra Swhney V. Union of India (Decision on Mandal Commission) that, "it is wrong to treat merit as synonymous with efficiency in administration and that merit is but a component of the efficiency of an administrator. Even so, the relevance and significance of merit and at the stage of initial recruitment can not be ingnored. It cannot also be ignored that the very idea of reservation implies selection of a less meritorious person. At the same time, we recognise that this much cost has to be paid, if the constitutional promise of social justice is to be redeemed. We also firmly believe that given an opportunity, members of these classes are bound to overcome their initial disadvantages and would compete with and may, in some cases, excel-members of open competitor candidates. It is undeniable that nature has endowed merit upon members

of backward classes as much as it has endowed upon members of other classes and that what is required is an opportunity to prove it. It may not, therefore, be said that reservation are anti-meritarian. Merit there is even among the reserved candidates and the small difference, that may be allowed at the stage of initial recruitment is bound to disappear in course of time. These members too will compete with and improve their efficiency alongwith others."[64]

3.11 Onus of Proof

The main allegation of the anti-reservationists on the basis of which they oppose the policy of reservations is that the SC/ST employees generally lack merit and efficiency. However, they do not care to prove their allegation. The onus of proof lies on the part of the person who makes any statement or allegation against any other person.

The allegations made recklessly without proof are irresponsible statements; which a sensible person cannot dare to utter. It is because of such irresponsible statements based on prejudice, the violent agitations take place, causing irreparable damage not only to the private and public property but to the unity and harmony in the society.

Conclusion

(i) The policy of reservation came into implementation in direct recruitment in 1950, but in promotion in 1963 and in Public Sector undertakings in 1969.

(ii) There was no relaxation in standard of qualification in direct recruitment. In promotional matter the time limit in passing the departmental examination was somewhat relaxed, but there was no exemption at all.

(iii) From 1950 to 1970 the percentage of reservation for SC and ST was only 12 1/2 and 5 percent respectively. After 1970 it was increased for SC to 15 percent and for ST to 7 1/2 percent. The SEBC came into beneficiary category in 1991 and the quota was 27 percent. In no point of time the reservation quota was fully filled up.

(iv) The scientific and technical services, judicial services and defence services are purposely kept out of the reservation policy. Even if there is any recruitment of SC/ST in those services, it is only on the basis of general standard and merit.

(v) So far as merit and efficiency is concerned the SC/ST and OBC are not lagging behind the candidates of general category.

The weaker sections are quite competent to prove their merit and efficiency provided they get opportunities on par with others. Merit and efficiency should include national character, commitment to the constitutional philosophy and compassion to the needy brethren. It is because of merit they cross several barriers in their way and come up to the general standard.

(vi) The anti-reservationists make allegations against the backward class employees, but they have not proved so. Their allegations are not based on facts, but on age-old caste prejudice. It should be borne in mind that administrative merit and efficiency consists of several things including educational qualification, technical knowledge, proper training and orientation, a good system of communication, natural and social circumstances, objective supervision and above all the integrity of men in power.

Merit and efficiency cannot be a monopoly of any caste. The SC/ST/OBC employees also possess requisite qualification for their respective jobs. They should not be prejudicially under- estimated. They should be given opportunities for full exposure of their merit and efficiency. Any baseless allegation against them must be treated as an unsocial act. The SC/ST/OBC people want their just and equal share in the power. It is their legitimate claim and in no condition they would waive it.

While taking into account the criteria of merit and efficiency of the administrators, the level of their compassion towards the poor masses and love for the nation ought to be considered. The level of I.Q. or merit is not taken into account in a caste ridden society. Henceforth in addition to I.Q. (Intelligent quotient) C.Q. (Compassion quotient) ought to be considered in counting merit of the people. Our objective, our commitment is to secure justice : social, economic and political. Hence, any thing or principle ought to be viewed within that parameter.

References

1. Sabine G.H. A History of Political Theory. p. 55. Oxford and IBH Pub. Company Calcutta (Third, 1961).
2. Warnock Mary (Ed) Utilitarianism by John Stuart Mill. pp. 296-301. Collins and Sons, London (1962).
3. Dr. Babasaheb Ambedkar : writings and speeches Vol. III : pp. 25, 38, 98, 25, 97, 44. Government of Maharashtra.
4. Rawls John : A Theory of Justice. p. 60. Universal Law Pub. Company, Karnal Rtd., Delhi. (2000, 2005)

4a. for details see the Idea of Justice by Amartya Sen PP.62-64. Pengnin Books. (2010).
5. Iyer, V.R. Krishna (J) : Some Half-Hidden Aspects of Indian Social Justice. P.36. Eastern Book Company, Lucknow (1979).
6. Brochure (1993) P.107. DOPT, Government of India, 1993.
7. Galanter Marc : Competing Equalities. P.421. Oxford University Press, Anasari Rtd, Darya Ganj, New Delhi (1984)
8. AIR 1973 SC 930, 939.
9. AIR 1981 SC 588, 594.
10. AIR 1989 SC 138, 142.
11. Brochure (1993) p. 227.
12. *Ibid*. p. 229.
13. Brochure (1982) p. 110.
14. AIR 1976 SC 490.
15. AIR 1993 SC 477, 493.
16. (1995) 6 SCC 684 (1996) 6 SCC 580.
17. Brochure (2011-Part 1) p. 26.
18. (1996) 4 SCC 119.
19. AIR 1996 SC 448, 455.
19a. AIR 1996 SC 1189, 1201.
20. AIR 2007 SC 71, 106.
21. AIR 2012 SC 2753.
22. Lokmat (Aurangabad) dated 1-5-2012.
23. Brochure (1982) p. 176.
24. *Ibid*. p. 178.
25. AIR 1964 SC 179.
26. AIR 1981 SC 298, 327.
27. AIR 1993 SC 477, 566.
28. AIR 2007 SC 71, 106.
29. Brochure (2011 Part 1) p. 13. DOPI Govt. of India 2011.
30. Brochure. (1982) p. 16.
31. *Ibid*. p. 20.
32. AIR 2001 SC 718, 721.
33. Report of the Committee on Untouchability etc.1969. p. 273
34. RCSC ST; 1975-76 & 1976-77 (Part 1) p. 41, 42.
35. RCSC ST; 1978-79 (Part-1) p. 77.
36. RCSC ST; 1978-79 (Part-1) p. 77.
37. RC SC ST; (Second Report of the Commission) 1979-80. p. 240.
38. RC SC ST; (1980-81). p. 110.
39. Welfare of SC & STs. 1986. p.18. Lok Sabha Secretariat, New Delhi.
40. Indian Express dated 22-03-1990.
41. Indian Express. dated 27-03-1990.
42. RC SC ST (26th Report) Part I, p. 77 (1980)

43. AIR 2000 SC 1296, 1311, 1320, 1321, 1374.
43a. Report of the Committee on untouchability, Economic and Educational Development of the S.C., p. 274. (Govt. of India) 1969.
44. For detailed information see "forefront for Ever", The History of the Mahar Regiment" by V. Longer (1981) The Saugar Regimental Centre, Saugar (M.P.)
45. AIR 1993 SC 576.
46. Kundu C.L. and Tutoo D.N. : Educational Psychology. p. 294. Sterling Publishers Pvt. Ltd. Green Part Extension, New Delhi. (1988)
47. Murphy Gardner : An Introduction to Psychology p. 336. Oxford and IBM Pub. Calcutta (1968)
48. Johnson Harry M. Sociology : A Systematic Introduction.p. 49 Allied Publishers, New Delhi. (1970)
49. Misra Giriswar and Tripathi L.B. Psychological Consequences of Prolonged Deprivation p. 176.
National Psychological Corporation, Kacheri Ghat, Agra (1980).
50. Sinha R.R.P. : Tribal and Non-Tribal Intelligence p. 81. Classical Publications, New Delhi. (1980)
51. Ketkar S.V. : Maharashtrian Dnyan Kosh Part 23, p.192-93.
52. Buettner-Januseh : Origins of Man. P.622. Wiley Eastern Pvt. Ltd. New Delhi. (1969)
53. As quoted by R.R.P. Sinha in Tribals and non-Tribals intelligence (1980) p. 18-19.
54. For details see an article "Job Reservations in Railway and Accidents" in Indian Express, 19-9-1990.
55. Statistical Outline of India (1999-2000).
Tata Services Ltd., Bombay House, Mumbai (1999).
56. EPW : June 17-23, 2006 p. 2430.
57. Galanter Marc : Competing Equalities : p. 113. Oxford University Press, Delhi : 1984.
58. Paper presented by K.R. Sunda at the UGC Sponsered Seminar on constitutional safeguards and Social Justice, held at Dr. Babasaheb Ambedkar College of Arts and Commerce, Nagasenvana, Aurangabad on 29-31 March 1997 (Unpublished).
59. DBAWS : Vol.9, p. 229.
60. AIR 1964 SC 179, Para 23.
61. AIR 1963 Mys.292.
62. AIR 1976 SC 490. (491)
63. AIR 1985 SC 1495.
64. AIR 1993 SC 576.

4

Constitution : The Value-Based Supreme Law

It is is woefully observed that the very foundation of our polity is being challenged today by the arch enemies of constitutionalism. For some time they challenged to the constitutional provisions aimed at bringing about socio-economic equality such as provisions for reservations to the Scheduled Castes and Scheduled Tribes, the Governments decisions taking over private property for public benefit, provisions regarding the minorities and many other provisions. Now they are up with arms against the whole edifice of constitutional validity. They are openly arguing for changing the Constitution and framing a new Constitution.

4.1 Foundation of the Polity

The Constitution is not only the fundamental document of Supreme legal importance, but it is the very foundation of our polity, that "we the people of India" have accepted for us and for the posterity. It envisages to form a new social order based on justice, liberty, equality and frternity. In the words of Justice Krishna Iyer, "ours is a very progressive Constitution. Its basic values are so great, so sublime that we should be proud to say that we have such a Constitution."[1]

(1) It has been rightly said by Robert Dahl that, "One cannot decide whether one is better than another without invoking standards of value."[2] It is, of course true in respect of both the individuals and the nation.

What does mean by value is a pertinent question. A value is, in the words of Harry M. Johson, "a conception of standard, cultural or merely personal by which things are compared and approved or disapproved relative to one another, held to be relatively desirable or undersirable, more meritorious or less, more or less correct."[3] Thus values are ideals or objectives which are generally accepted and observed in high esteem by the people in a given society.

(2) Obviously, every social order is based on the existing law including the constitutional law and customs, as well as on certain prevailing morals, ideals and values. The values accepted by the people would prevail irrespective of legal sanction, which they get it subsequently. "Every legal disposition," according to Thomas Cowan, "is a value judgement. Every statute envisages two types of relevant human behaviour, the good and the bad. It enjoins the good and proscribes the bad."[4] The Constitution being the supreme law of the land may accord legal sanction to the prevailing values by embodying them in itself and it may, in the pursuit of happiness and welfare of the people, generate new values.

(3) The Constitution of India is the deliberate creation of the collective wisdom of the Constituent Assembly headed by Dr.Rajendra Prasad, which fistly met on December 9, 1946 and put the seal of finality on the Draft Constitution drafted and submitted by the Chairman of the Drafting Committee, Dr.Babasaheb Ambedkar, on November 26, 1949. However, it came into implementation on January 26, 1950. During the period of struggle for freedom or even before that certain values were deliberately evolved by the social reformers and political leaders in our country. Even it could be said that their freedom struggle was for certain values. The framers of the Constitution have incorporated all those values which were evolved during the period of struggle for national independence and the values they felt necessary for constituting a strong and welfare state. It should be borne in mind that while "generating the values" it has discarded certain traditional values based on theology to the extent they contradict modern values.

4.2 Important Values

The values envisaged by the Indian Constitution can be categorised as social, political, economic, religious and cultural values. They are as under

(a) (1) Among the social values mention must be made of "Social Justice" "Equality," Abolition of untouchability and gender equality. The Constitution in its preamble inter alia, pledges to secure "social justice" to all its citizens. The principle of "Social Justice" enunciated in the preamble of the Constitution has its roots in the Objectives Resolution moved by Pandit Nehru in the Constituent Assembly.[5] There was of course, a persistent demand for social justice from the social reformers since a very long. Therefore the Constituent Assembly has incorporated it in the Constitution.

According to justice P.B.Gajendragadkar, "Social Justice" implies, "removing all inequalities and affording equal opportunities to all citizens in social affairs as well as economic activities."[6] Justice V.R. Krishna Iyer observed that, "social Justice is the balancing wheel between freedom, political and economic and indeed, makes for the survival of democracy."[7]

It could be inferred from the provisions of the Constitution that it includes "equality before law (Art.14), Prohibition of discrimination on grounds only of religion, race, caste, sex, place of birth or any of them (Art.15(1). Special treatment for socially and educationally backward classes (Art.15(4); equality of opportunity (Art.16(1), providing reservations in services for the backward classes (Art.16(4); abolition of untouchability (Art.17), renouncing practices derogatory to women (Art.15A(e), etc.

(2) The Constitution gives great importance to the principle of equality. "Equality" means equality of status and of opportunity. It is true that men are not equal in physical strength, talent, industry and in Tests and attitudes. However, the principle of equality denies the undue right to the strong to exploit the weak. In the society where the principle of equality is recognized, every body is equal in status, irrespective of his or her caste, creed, religion, sex or place of birth. There will be perfect rule of law. Everyone is equal before the law or there will be common law for all without any discrimination.

Equality recognizes no caste discrimination; graded inequality and untouchability. Every body has equal opportunity to seek education to get employment and to participate in the administration of the country. He has equal 'dignity' as a human being. We have accepted the principle of common citizenship and adult suffrage. Therefore, every one has one vote and it has one value; irrespective of one's post, property or power.

Although the Constitution has not specifically and outrightly abolished the caste system, it has removed its very vigour and its discriminatory basic characteristics. It has provided fundamental rights to the people without any discrimination and provided equal opportunity of development including the right to protective discrimination or special safeguards.

(3) "Untouchability" is a stigma attached to a section of the society, which has dehumanised it. According to Dr.Babasaheb Ambedker it was born some time about 400 A.D.[8] He said that, "untouchability" is the notion of defilement, pollution, contamination and the ways and means of getting rid of that defilement. It is a case of permanent, hereditary stain which nothing can cleanse."[9]

In order to get rid of it, Dr.Babasaheb Ambedkar and other social reformers launched the anti-untouchability movement through out India in the pre-independence period and they became successful in their venture. Ultimately, the Constitution of India, under its Article 17 abolished the inhuman practice of untouchability. The said Article states that, "Untouchability" is abolished and its practice in any form is forbidden. The enforcement of any disability arising out of 'untouchability' shall be an offence punishable in accordance of law." In pursuance of this provision, the Parliament has passed the protection of Civil Rights Act, 1955, and it is in implementation. Later on the Parliament has passed the SC, ST prevention of Atrocities Act, 1989 to deal with the cases of atrocities on the Scheduled Castes and Scheduled Tribes.

Thus, the Constitution of India has incorporated a sublime human value in it and maintained equality and human dignity in the society. It has given human identity and all the resultant rights to the so called untouchables facilitating them to regain their very persona.

(4) The Constitution maintains gender equality. In the pre-independence era, the women were treated as inferior and lower than the males. They had no civil rights.[10] However, the Constitution of India brought them upto the level of the males and gave them equal civil and political rights. They have got full opportunity to develop their personality The state is empowered to make "any special provision for women and children." (15(3)), the state would see that, "men and women equally have the right to an adequate means of livelihood " (39(a)), and 'equal pay for equal work for both men and women' (39(d)) and "That the health and strength of workers, men and women, and the tender age of children are not abused."(39(a)).

(b)(1) Among the political values that the Indian Constitution enshrines in it, mention must be made of "Democracy," National integration," "Decentralization," "Neutrality" and "Constitution-alism." The Constitution declares India as a "Democratic Republic." The term "Democracy" is derived from the Greek words "Demos" and "Kratos". The former meaning the people and latter rule. Thus Democracy means the rule of people. According to Abraham Lincoln Democracy is "A Government of the people, by the people, and for the people."[11]

In democracy the Sovereign Power vests with the people in general. Therefore as J.S. Mill States that, "There is no difficulty in showing that the ideally best form of government is that in which the sovereignty, or supreme controlling power in the last resort, is vested in the entire aggregate of the community, every citizen not only having a voice in the exercise of that ultimate sovereignty, but being, at least occasionally, called on to take an actual part in the government by the personal discharge of some public function, local or general."[12]

According to Dr.Babasaheb Ambedkar, Democracy is "a form and a method of government whereby revolutionary changes in the economic and social life of the people are brought about without blood shed."[13] Thus democracy is a form of Government based on public opinion and meant for public good. Ours is a democratic Republic as the head of the state is elected one. Our democracy is known as Parliamentary democracy because the Parliament consisting of elected representatives of the people elect the head of the executive, called Prime-Minister, and it enjoys Supreme Power. Our Democratic Republic provides fundamental rights to the people, which are inviolable (Art.13) by the state. Indian democracy is, of course, based on "equality" (Preamble and Art.14), "Liberty" (Preamble and Art.19) and "Fraternity" (Preamble and Art. 51 A(e)). The principles of "one man one vote" and "one man one value" form the basis of "Democratic Republic."

(2) "National Integration" is an important political value of associated life. "National integration" could be defined in the words of G.S. Ghurye as "a pscychological and educational process...... involving the development of a feeling of unity, solidarity and cohesion in the hearts of people, a sense of common citizenship and a feeling of loyality to the nation.[14] It is a self-evident fact that there are several inherent dangerous forces in our society, such as casteism, communalism, plurality of language, regionalism, economic inequality and many others which threaten national integration. In order to find out the ways and means of making "the people of India", "we, the people of India" or "the nation" an agency called "National Integration Council" has been constituted in the year 1961. However, the Constitution, in furtherence of national unity and integrity provides that India is "a union of states" (Art.1); its citizens will abide by "the Constitution," respect "the National Flag" and

"the National Anthem" (Art 51 A(a); and uphold and protect "the sovereignty, unity and integrity of India" (Art. 51 A(c). Further it states that the people will have "to defend the country" (51 A(e). However, national integration will be possible if the people faithfully develop "the scientific temper", Humanism " and "the spirit of inquiry" and reform" (Art. 51 A(h).

(3) "Decentralization" of power is thought as a necessary element to promote the spirit of democracy throughout the country. According to the Encyclopedia of social sciences, "the process of decentralization denotes the transference of authority, legislative, judicial or administrative from a higher level of government to a lower."

The Constitution provides for division of power between the union and states, according to which the Centre-State relations are governed. It provides for the organization of "village Panchayats" (Art.40); as such we have accepted the Panchayat Raj System and local self governments to work at the grassroot level within the limited jurisdiction of (delegated) powers stipulated under 11th Schedule (Art. 242G) and 12th Schedule (Art. 242W).

(4) "Neutrality" is a principle applied in the formation of foreign policy of our country. Neutrality, "implies the impartiality of one state toward two or more belligerent states.[15] The Constitution gave the Directive under Article 51 to (a) "Promote international peace and security, (b) foster respect for honourable relations between nations, (c) foster respect for international law and treaty obligations in the dealings of organized people with one other; and (d) encourage settlement of international disputes by arbitration." Accordingly, our country has adopted the policy of neutrality or non-alignment in its international affairs.

(5) "Constitutionalism" has been defined under the Encyclopedia of social sciences as "the name given to the trust which men repose in the power of words engrossed on Parchment to keep a government in order."

It precisely denotes a rule against absolutism. "Constitutionalism", as Friedrich states, "has been traced in relation to liberalism, to rationalism, to individualism. Each one of these general philosophies has indeed contributed its fair share to the making of Constitutionalism."[16]

According to Barnes, Carter and Skidmore, "Some constitutions include guarantees of rights and freedom, as either negative restrictions on government or positive commands to it. Where there are present, and there is some way to enforce them, then we can speak of a constitutional government, or constitutionalism."[17]

Our Constitution is a written document and we must have indomitable faith in it. It is a "way to enforce" the guarantees of rights and freedom as included in the Constitution. It could be preserved by resorting to an appropriate writ for the judicial pronouncement as to invalidity of any law or rule conflicting with the fundamental rights of the people. It is but resorting to Constitutional means for the protection of the rights; and abandoning Satyagraha, disobedience etc. which have been rightly called by Dr.Babasaheb Ambedkar as "grammar of anarchy."[18]

(c)(1) Among the economic values "Socialism" which has been deliberately inserted in the Preamble of the Constitution by the Constitution 42nd Amendment Act, 1976, forms an important place. There already existed certain Directives to the state which indicated "a socialist bias"[19], for example Article 38 directs the State to promote "a social order" in which justice, social, economic and political shall inform all the institutions of the national life. Further, Article 39 provides extensively for adequate means of livelihood, distribution of the ownership and control of the material resources so as to serve the common good; adoption of such an economic system which does not allow concentration of wealth and means of production, equal pay for equal work for both men and women and protection of children and youths from exploitation. Besides, Article 39(A) guarantees legal aid to the poor, Article 41 Guarantees right to work, Article 42 guarantees just and human conditions of work, Article 43 guarantees living wages and Article 43A guarantees participation of workers in the management of industries. It directs the state to promote with special care the educational and economic interests of the weaker sections, in particular of the Scheduled Castes and the Scheduled Tribes (Article 46). In the opinion of Dr. Babasaheb Ambedkar all these directives were "socialistic" in nature and content, and if they were not so, he said that, "I fail to understand what more socialism can be."[20]

However, at the initiative of Pandit Nehru the All India Congress in its Avadi Session held in January 1955 passed an important resolution to lead India towards "Socialistic pattern of Society"[21] in which certain big industries would be controlled by the state; and equal distribution of national wealth would take place; and progress would be made by adopting planning. Nevertheless, in order to stress the importance of socialism, a final recognition has been given under the 42nd Amendment Act passed in 1976.

The Constitution has accepted the value of socialism in recognition to the principle : "Political democracy cannot last unless there lies at the base of it social democracy."[22] However, the model of socialism stated in the Constitution is unique one. It does not resemble with that of western model. In order to secure the socialistic social order our country adopted the system of 'mixed economy' and 'planning' for the purpose of economic development and land reforms Acts, abolition of privy purses etc. for the purpose of arresting the growth of feudalism and capitalism.

(2) Economic Justice cannot be separated from social and political justice. The makers of the Constitution found that there was utmost need of economic justice to the Indian people. The princes were to take away a significant portion of amount from the Consolidated fund of India. The land-lords were to usurp the landed income at the cost of poor farmers and landless agricultural labourers. Priestly class and village heads were to exploit the people. The moneylenders were to grab the agricultural produce. This was sheer negation of economic justice.

Therefore the Constitution directed under Article 38 that, "The state shall strive to promote the welfare of the people by securing and protecting as effectively as it may a social order in which justice, social, economic and political, shall inform all the institutions of the national life." Thus the new social order, in place of old decadent unsocial order, was proposed to take place. This was a revolutionary proposal that found prime palce in the Constitution.

Undoubtedly, the new social order has not come into reality till now. However, efforts are being made towards that directions irrespective of certain odds and counter revolutionary moves of the reactionary forces which are operating under different banners and different garbs. Now, it is imperative on the part of the progressive forces to unite their might to bring into reality the constitutional ideal.

(d) (1) In the sphere of religion the principle of "secularism" has been accepted by the Indian Constitution. The term "secularism" has been included in the Preamble by the 42nd Amendment Act, in 1976 in formal recognition to that effect. According to Encyclopedia of Religion and Ethics, "secularism is wholly unconcerned with that (unknown) world and its interpretation. It deals with the known world; interpreted by experience, and neither offers nor forbids any opinion regarding another life."

Dr. Babasaheb Ambedkar has connotatively stated that a secular "state shall guarantee to every Indian citizen liberty of conscience and the free practice of his religion, No person shall be compelled to become a member of any religious association. The state shall not recognize any religion as state religion. Every religious association shall be free to regulate and administer its affairs, within the limits of the laws applicable to all."[23] According to

Lakshmi Kant Maitra, a member of the Constituent Assembly, "By secular state, as I understand it, is meant that the state is not going to make any discrimination whatsoever on the ground of religion or community against any person professing any particular form of religious faith. This means in essence that no particular religion in the state will receive any state patronage whatsoever. The state is not going to establish, patronise or endow any particular religion to t he exclusion of or in preference to others and that no citizen in the state will have any preferential treatment or will be discriminated against simply on the ground that he professed a particular form of religion. In other words, in the affairs of the state, the professing of any particular religion will not be taken into consideration at all. This I consider is the essence of a secular state."[24] According to M.P. Sharma, "The secular state implies a state which is neutral in maters of religion and faith. Religious neutrality of the state, however, does not prevent it from regulating any economic political or other secular activity associated with religious practice, or from providing for social welfare and reform."[25] In the words of Dr.V.P. Luthera, "a secular state is one which is separated from, unconnected with and not devoted to religion."[26]

(2) The Constitution secures to all the citizens the right to freedom of religion and conscience, subject to public order, morality and health (Art. 25(1)). However, it enables the State of govern any economic, political or secular activity of the religion and to make any law for social welfare, reform or throwing open of Hindu religious institutions of a public character to all classes (Art. 25(2). The State would allow every religious denomination to establish and maintain the institutions for religious or charitable purposes (Art. 26), but it will not allow any religion to compel any one to pay any tax for the promotion of that religion (Art. 27). The State will not allow to impart religious instruction in any educational institution maintained out of its fund (Art. 28). It will not deny admission to any one only on the ground of religion, race or caste (Art. 29(2)). All the religious or linguistic minorities shall have the right to establish and administer educational institutions of their choice. (Art. 30 (1)).

It is the duty of the citizens "to promote harmony and the spirit of common brotherhood amongst all the people of India transcending religious, linguistic or sectional diversities." (Art. 51A(e)) and "to value and preserve the rich heritage of our composite culture." (Art. 51A(f)).

The State shall not discriminate against any citizen on grounds only of religion, race, Caste etc. (Art. 15(1)) and it will try to secure for all the citizens a uniform civil code (Art. 44). All these provisions, however, reflect the secularistic character of the Indian Constitution.

(3) It is true that the Constitution of India is a living organism growing with the aspirations of the age and taking the country ahead with humanitarian values including love and compassion, common brotherhood, scientific temper, and the spirit of inquiry. It has compassionate heart and judicious mind. Its humanitarian values transcend the artificial barriers of caste, creed and religion. As against the cruel and inhuman traditional practices of the past, its humanitarian and compassionate nature conspicuously appears to be very kind, reasonable and unique.

It has endowed with certain fundamental rights, including the right to equality, right to freedom, right to education, right against exploitation, right to freedom of religion and right to Constitutional remedies to all the people without any discrimination on grounds of religion, race, caste, sex or place of birth. It has provided for making any special provision in favour of women, children, the Scheduled Castes, Scheduled Tribes, backward classes, minorities, destitutes, bonded labourers and workers.

It has specifically directed the state "to promote the welfare of the people by securing and protecting as effectively as it may a social order in which justice, social economic and political, shall inform all the institutions of the national life. It has assured that the operation of the economic system does not result in the concentration of wealth and means of production to the common detriment." It is the mandate of the constitution to the state to secure that, "The operation of the legal system promote justice."

All these principles enshrined in the Constitution are really compassionatory especially to the disadvantaged sections of the society. It is not unjust and prejudicial to any person unlike the Traditional Law. It promises to each and evey one to give him what he deserves for or what is due to him on the basis of equal opportunity. It is humanitarian in nature and compassionate in approach towards the individual and social problems.

However, it is but a self-evident fact that constitutional values have not yet fully rooted in our composite culture. There seems to be some conflict between caste, religious and parochial values to one side and constitutional values to the other. Whether the remnants of Traditional, Parochial and feudal values will triumph over the sublime constitutional values is a question which is more concerned to the socially conscious mind.

It is the ultimate responsibility of the State to put in operation all those values enshrined in the Constitution in the real perspective.

They should not keep any value-oriented aspect of the Constitution dormant. It is said that, "what charcterizes the law is that it is enforced[26(a)], if it is not enforced in its true letter and spirit it is of no avail. It requires a strong political will to enforce those modern values in the pursuit of happiness of the people.

4.3 Arguments against and for the Constitution

The Constitution is not only value based and Supreme, but a suitable document to the Indian Socio-Political situation. However, the anti-constitutionalists are wantonly challenging to its validity, supremacy and legitimacy. Who are those persons who are challenging the constitution ? Why do they challenge it ? What are their arguments against the constitution ? What harm that challenge is to do to our body Politic ? what is the remedy on this problem ? These are certain pertinent questions which need to be addressed.

Who are the persons challenging to the Constitution is a pertinent question. Evidently the persons challenging the constitutional legitimacy are those fundamentalist, capitalists and obscurantists whose vested interests are persumably in jeopardy. Those who adore and admire Manu in their hearts of hearts are the real enemies of the Constitution. It seems that they have no faith in the new social order envisaged in the Preamble of the Constitution. They want to implicity revive the old decadent social model given by Manu. Their challenge is not only to the structure the constitution embodies, but to the culture which it aims to bring about and infuse the same in our body Politic.

(1) What are their arguments against the constitution ? They argue that the Constituent Assembly formed to frame the constitution was not a fully representative body. The members were indirectly elected by the state legislatures, who were elected by communal and limited franchise in British India and the representatives of the Princely States. Firstly, as it was constituted in 1946, there were 296 members belonging to various political parties and communities. However, out of the total 296 members, 73 members of Muslim League boycotted the Constituent Assembly. Thus there remained only 223 members in the Assembly. After partition, it was reorganized. Thus on 31st December 1947 there were total 299 members out of which 229 were from various provinces and 70 were from various Indian States which merged in India. "Although the Constituent Assembly was not elected through Universal Franchise, utmost care was taken to make it representative of all the diverse view points and Political ideologies.[27]

Thus the Constituent Assembly was a representative and Sovereign body which derived its authority from, "We, the People of India." The Constitution was framed by the most eminent and brilliant men who were in Public Life in those days. Therefore, there is no force in the argument, that the Constitution was not framed by the representatives of the people. Had there been elections on adult franchise basis most probably the same persons or a few others would have been elected.

(2) It is generally said that the Constitution has been copied verbatim from the Government of India Act, 1935. This charge can be rebutted in the words of Prof.S.P. Sathe. This charge may be true so far as the structure of the state is concerned, but so far as its 'essence' is concerned, it differs from the said Act. "The first difference is that it speaks in the name of the People of India. The second difference is that it contains a bill or rights, which includes the right to equality, personal liberty, freedom of religion, rights of the minorities and the right to constitutional remedies for the enforcement of fundamental rights. In the Directive principles of State Policy in Part IV, the Constitution envisions profound social and economic change to be ushered into through state intervention."[28] Moreover, some of the provisions are said to have been copied from the foreign constitutions; for instance, the Directive principles of state policy from Ireland, the provision of residuary power of the Union from Canada, Fundamental Rights and Judicial review from the U.S.A. and Parliamentary system from the U.K. According to M.S. Golwalkar Guruji, "Our constitution is a cumbersome and heterageneous piecing together of various articles from various constitutions of western countries. It has absolutely nothing which can be called our own."[28(a)] However, taking some thing good from others cannot be a demerit of any constitution. On the contrary, one should appreciate the founding fathers' knowledge of world constitutions and their spirit of 'borrowing' the ideals from others. It is true that the Constitution makers had not shown any love for the old Traditional Socio-Political model enshrined in the Shastras and Puranas.

(3) It is also argued that the Drafting Committee headed by the legal luminary and the real nationalist like Dr. Babasaheb Ambedkar was merely a 'Drifting' Committee; which was swayed by the Congress Leaders while framing the Constitution. Though the Drafting Committee was expected to take into account the opinions of the members of the Constituent Assembly, Dr. Babasaheb Ambedkar, the Chairman of the Drafting Committee exerted a great influence being a man of higher learning, wisdom and intelligence

par excellence. He could very wisely mould the resolutions and opinions of the Constituent Assembly members in a suitable manner without disturbing the democratic process. Dr. Pattabhi Sitaramayya liked to call Dr.Babasaheb Ambedkar "a steam-rollar intellect he brought to bear upon this magnificient and tremendous task, irresistable, indomitable, unconquerable, levelling down all palms and short poppies : whatever he felt to be right he stood by, regardless of consequences.[29]

While refuting this charge levelled by Mr. Naziruddin Ahmad, one of the members of the Constituent Assembly, Dr. Babasaheb Ambedkar himself said in a befitting manner, that, "there is a difference between drift without mastery and drift with mastery. If the Drafting Committee was drifting, it was never without mastery over the situation. It was not merely angling with the off chance of catching a fish. It was searching in known waters to find the fish it was after. To be in search of something better is not the same as drifting.

"The Drafting Committee would have been guilty of gross dereliction of duty and of a false sense of dignity if it had not shown the honesty and the courage to withdraw the amendments which it thought faulty and substitute what it thought was better. If it is a mistake, I am glad the Drafting Committee did not fight shy of admitting such mistakes and coming forward to correct them."[30]

(4) It seems on the Constituent Assembly Debates that it was not a mere gathering of 'yes-men' observing party discipline. There were some intellectual 'rebels' also. The deliberations seem to be very lively and illuminating. How stupendous and difficult this task was could be gathered from the chairman of the Drafting Committee himself who said that, "The Draft Constitution, as prepared by the Constitutional Advisor as a Text for the Drafting Committee to work upon consisted of 243 articles and 13 schedules. The first Draft Constitution as presented by the Drafting Committing to the Constituent Assembly contained 315 articles and 8 Schedules. At the end of the consideration stage, the number of articles in the Draft Constitution increased to 386. This final form, the Draft Constitution contains 395 articles and 8 schedules. The total number of amendments to the Draft Constitution tabled was approximately 7635. Of them the total number of amendments actually moved in the house were 2,473.[31]

In the words of Shri R.K. Sidhwa, "Accepting the preamble without a change or single comma or punctuation, several articles have been changed. We were fighting our battles in this Constitution Hall, to put our views and we have fought our battle very well, and

I am glad that the Drafting Committee have taken our battles in the right spirit.[32]

(5) Since the very beginning of the commencement of the Constitution, the critic of social equality are against the provisions of protective discrimination meant for the hitherto underprivileged and oppressed strata of the society. Firstly the scheme of community wise reservation being implemented by the then Madras Government came under attack. The Supreme Court in Champakam Dorairajan Vs. State of Madras and in Venkatramana Vs. State of Madras struck down the communitywise quota system respectively in educational institutions and employment for the backward classes.[33] The Supreme Court observed that, the state was at liberty to achieve the objective enshrined in Article 46, but the action of the state should not contravene or infringe any provision under the fundamental rights. Therefore, the Government felt the need of taking on its agenda, the first amendment to the Constitution in 1951. The first Amendment Act, 1951 added, inter alia, clause 4 to Article 15 of the Constitution to overcome the decision of the Supreme Court in the above said cases. Yet the challenges came in spates later on, some time in the form of litigations and some time in the form of agitations which pierced our body politic. The enemies of social justice do not want even to spare a meagre quota for the backward classes in the education and in the employment. On the contrary they are enjoying the implied or hidden reservation rooted in the traditional social structure at the cost of the weak and meak backward classes.

(6) Another area of challenge has been the power of Government to acquire the private property for the purpose of public utility. The first challenge came in the form of Chiranjit Lal Vs. Union of India in 1950 itself.[34] The next challenge came in the form of Kameshwar Singh Vs. State of Bihar in 1951[35], which resulted in invalidation of the agrarian reforms measures. Therefore, the Parliament had to add Article 31A and 31B and incorporate 13 such laws in the Ninth Schedule so as to be immune from 'legal attack' on the ground of violation of fundamental right to property through first Amendment Act, 1951. The Major Challenge came in Golaknath case in 1967.[36] Bank Nationalization case in 1970.[36(a)] The Privy Purses case in 1971[37], Keshavanad Bharti case 1973[37(a)] and Minerva Mills Vs.Union of India, in 1980.[38] In all these cases the fundamental right to property obviously was invoked. Consequently, the parliament had to struck off the fundamental right to property in the year 1978, Under 44th Amendment Act. It withdrew the right to property as a fundamental right and made it only a Constitutional

Right under Article 300A. Under Article 300A an individual can be deprived of his property only by authority of law made by the Parliament or State legislature or a rule having force of law; and not by an executive order. When the right to property was a fundamental right a few were enjoying it. Now even in its absence also those people are enjoying the right to property as the constitutional right. The real property is with the propertied class. Presently, no property can be acquired unless there is authority of Law, the property is taken for public purpose and just compensation is fixed. Thus the propertied class would not lose any thing, as there is no substantial change in his right to property.

(7) We have adopted a socialistic pattern of society and planned economic development. However, the major plan allocation and its benefits were derived by the land lords and the capitalists. The land reformation Acts remained in the Ninth Schedule of the Constitution unimplemented fully. The industrialists got very easy infrastructure facilities, loans and concessions from the national physical and financial resources. Till the sixth plan period even one percent of the total allocation was not made especially for the economic development of the Scheduled Castes and the Scheduled Tribes. However, due to constitutional constraints envisaged especially under Article 38, 39, 41, 46 and 47, the concept of having a special component plan was introduced in 1979 with a view to achieving overall development of the scheduled castes. As well as the Tribal Sub-Plan was introduced for the over all development of the Scheduled Tribes. In addition to SCP and TSP the Special Central Assistance (SCA) has been introduced through which assistance is given to the backward classes indirectly through various financing corporations. However, due to want of proper planning, under-utilization of allocation, and misuse of funds the target is not achieved. This type of programme for the socio-economic development of the backward classes became a cause of jeolousy and heart burning on the part of the so called caste people. In order to get scrapped all these welfare measures, they are bent upon reviewing the Constitution itself.

(8) Their another contention is the minorites got something undue under the constitution. 'Minority' means a numerically smaller group having its own language, religion or culture distinct from the majority in the state. The fact is the minorities got the right to conserve their culture under Article 29(1) and establish and administer the educational institution of their own interest under Article 30(1).

The right to establish and administer the educational institutions of their choice conferred under Article 30(1) is not absolute in the sense the state shall have the right to impose reasonable conditions regulating the administration. Thus, as a condition for granting aid or recognition to an institution coming under Article 30(1), "Regulation made in the true interests of efficiency of instruction discipline, health, sanitation, morality, public order and the like may undoubtedly be imposed. Such regulations are not restrictions on the substance of the right which is guaranteed; they secure the proper functioning of the institutions, in matters of education."[39]

(9) Another cause of contention is Article 370 pertaining to the special status of Jammu and Kashmir. Under the Constitution Order of 1954, the jurisdiction of the Parliament has been extended to all the subjects mentioned in the Union list. The Governor and the High Court Judges of J&K are appointed by the President of India. The jurisdiction of the Election Commission, Supreme Court, Comptroller and Auditor General of India have been extended to J & K. In the words of Madhu Limaye, "the existence or non-existence of Article 370, the use or non-use of a separate flag by J & K, the fact of a separate constitution being or not being in force, makes no substantial difference to its status. It is, therefore, purely an emotional issue."[40]

(10) Another cause of contention is the problem of Uniform Civil Code, which could of course, be decided by mutual understanding and rational approach. The Muslims are being governed by their own personal law which is related to muslim marriage, divorce, succession etc. So for as criminal law, contract and civil law, industrial law, administrative law etc. are concerned, the common law is applicable. Therefore it is absolutely immaterial whether they are governed by their personal law or uniform law. However, there is a provision under Article-44 of the Directive Principles of state policy that, "The state shall endeavour to secure for the citizens a uniform civil code throughout the Territory of India." There is no unanimity on this issue. We have accepted the Policy of secularism in our polity. Therefore, we have to be more liberal, tolerant and rational in the religious matter. However, the secular nature of Indian Constitution is being subjected to ridicule. The anti-constitutionalists are not content with performing Hindu rituals and worships, preaching and propogating communal inequality, superstitions and blind faith. They have not only put dynamite to the historic Babari Masjid (1992) but to the secular principle itself. The Buddhist shrine at Buddha Gaya is being

converted into a Hindu Temple. The same persons are now bent upon converting our secular Republic into a Hindu theocratic State.

(11) Even after the commencement of the Constitution for several decades objections are being raised to the quasi-federal structure of the Government; Parlimentary System, emergency powers, importance of directive principles etc. It is all a foul play to keep something in heart and something on lips. In order to wield such a vast country having different languages, cultures, history and aspirations, it was but necessary to have neither a unitary government nor a federal government. We have struck the balance between the two and evolved a dual government system. At the centre there is a national Union Government and at the States, there are State Governments. We have made distribution of powers into three lists, union list, state list and concurrent list. However, the residuary powers are with the Union Government. Our Constitution is Supreme and inviolable. The Supreme Court is to interpret the laws and guard the Constitution. It is because of these features our Constitution is called federal.

On the otherhand it is described as quasi-federal due to certain factors which take it to unitary form. We have formed various states for administrative convenience taking into account linguistic and cultural factors. All the people are the citizens of Union of India. Our Judicial system is based on hierarchical system. Our constitution provides for the All India Services common to the Union and the States. The authorities for conducting election and accounts and audit are also common. During emergency the federal nature of our Constitution could be converted into a unitary government. Our constitution is neither very rigid nor flexible, but it can be amended with the changing situation.

(12) We have adopted Parliamentary System of Government. The President of India is indirectly elected. Our Parliament is Supreme but its laws are subject to review by the Supreme Court. The executive authority vests with the Prime-Minister who is the leader of the majority party in the Parliament. He forms his ministry but they are collectively responsible to the Parliament. However, the anti-constitutionalist want to replace the parliamenary system by the Presidential form of Government.[41] It seems that they would like to change the present form of government into Hindu Theocratic State on the model of 'Ramrajya' or 'Chakravarti Rajya' of ancient times.

(13) Their opposition to emergency powers, especially the power of the Union Government to dissolve the State Governments on the ground of failure of constitutional machinery in the States,

envisaged under Article 356 of the Constitution, is based on wrong notion and fear that the Union Government would misuse this power for its political gain. This cannot be ture. This power of Union government is subject to 'checks and balances'. It is, however, difficult to usurp the power in the name of failure of constitutional machinery in the States. This provision of emergency powers enables the state to invoke such powers to contain with critical situation.

(14) The Directive Principles of state policy are not enforceable by the Court, "but the principles therein laid down are nevertheless fundamental in the governance of the country and it shall be the duty of the state to apply these principles in making laws " (Art. 37). Thus the state is "duty" bound to bring about a new social order "in which Justice, Social, Economic and Political, shall inform all the institutions of the national life." Therefore, the Union government as well as the State Governments have made some efforts to implement the Directive principles. They had passed the laws to abolish Zamindari and Privy Purses, passed the land ceiling Acts, Tenancy Laws, Untouchabiity Offences Act, SC/ST Prevention of Atrocities Acts, Traffic in Human beings abolition Act etc. Altogether 284 land reforms Acts have been brought under Ninth Schedule of the Constitution, so as to immune them from Judicial review. But it is difficult to know how honestly these Acts are in implementation. Although Zamindari is abolished, landlordism is in continuation in its place. Privy Purses were abolished, but new princes are coming up. In the name of globalization, privatization is coming up. A good number of people are suffering from increasing poverty, unemployment and mal-administration. In such as adverse situation, the common people got the weapon of Constitution to wage a war for the establishment and consolidation of "Sovereign Socialist, Secular, Democratic, Republic."

(15) It is true that no constitution is final and infallible. It has been amended as and when it became necessary under Article 368 of the Constitution. Thus till now 93 amendments are made to the constitution. The honourable Chairman of the Drafting Committee, Dr.Babasaheb Ambedkar had very categorically said that the Constituent Assembly has, "not only refrained from putting a seal of finality and infallibility upon this Constitution by denying to the people the right to amend the constitution as in Canada, or by making the amendment of the constitution subject to the fulfilment of extra-oridinary terms and canditions as in America or Australia; but has provided a most facile procedure for amending the constitution."[42]

He was of the view that "the principles embroiled in the Constitution are the views of the present generation."[43] and as such they need not be binding on the ensuing generations. In order to substantiate his thoughts, he referred to Jefferson, the great American Constitutionalist who said that, "We may consider each generation as a distinct nation, with a right, by the will of the majority, to bind themselves, but none to bind the succeeding generation, more than the inhabitants of another country."[44] Thus, he gave to the nation the Constitution which is novel in this sense that is partly flexible and partly rigid.[45] It is really a noteworthy quality of our Constitution.

Although we had to amend the Constitution several times, it virtually continues in its basic structure. In the words of D.C.Ahir, "However, the large number of amendments need not frighten us. Most of the amendments so far made relate either to the details of the administration which became necessary as a result of the eventual evaluation of the political system in the country or to the temporary and transitional matters. Of course, some of them were necessary because of the practical difficulties experienced in the working of certain provisions of the Constitution. In sum, the changes so far made by and large relate to form and not to content and, in spite of numerous additions, alterations and omissions made in it, the Constitution of India still remains, in essence, the same document."[46]

(16) Judicial system assumes a great importance in any State. Before the advent of Britishers, Canonical Law was in force. In the civil matter the Hindus were governed by the code of Manu and the Muslims were governed by the Quranic Principles. In the criminal matter both the comunities were governed by the Muslim law. In the administration of justice, there was no equality before law nor there was equal protection of law.

The Britishers brought in a new legal and Judicial System. They had declared Suttee System to be illegal in 1829. In 1843 slavery was made illegal. In 1850 the Caste Disabilities Removal Act was passed. It legalized the widow-remarriage of Hindus. The Indian Penal Code was passed in 1860. Thereafter, the whole legal and judical system was renewed and reorganized.

The Hindu traditionalists most probably thought that the new legal system which continued under the Constitution of India gave a great locolt to the traditional social order. In the Indian Society the concept of fundamental right was a revolutionary step. The concept of Constitutionalism was opposed to their vested interests. Social Justice, Socilism, Secularism, Personal Liberty and abolition of caste, inequality and untouchability were but strange to Indian situation. The judiciary was made guardian of such a Constitution which was totally opposed to their vested interests. Therefore, in order to protect their own communal interests they opposed to the policy of reservation, land reforms, social reform legislation, gender equality and directive principles of state policy. Firstly they used the doctrine of "judicial review", then took the undue advantage of the theory of 'basic structure' and now they are bent upon unduly resorting to 'constitutional review.'

4.4 Failure of the Government

(1) It is true that we could not be successful on almost all the fronts. It need not be proved by adducing statisical data. It is true that we could not establish that 'social order' in which justice social, economic and political could inform all the institutions of our national life. We have to search in our hearts that whether we have implemented the Constitution in its letter and spirit. Whether we had national moral character in discharging our own duty towards our fellow brothers and sisters and the whole nation. We have to investigate in reality whether it was the fault of the Constitution or of the politicans. If the Constitution proved to be failure in securing justice, social, economic and political to all the people, what should be done ? Once Dr.Babasaheb Ambedkar himself, while retorting to the then Home Minister Katju said that, "Sir, my friends tell me that I made the Constitution. But I am quite prepared to say that I shall be the first person to burn it out. I do not want it. It does not suit anybody."[47] However, people forgot the very spirit behind his bold statement. It was a hint given in good faith to the people who suffered injustice would go against the Government for securing their just rights. Though the underprivileged people could not derive any substantial benefit under the Constitution, they have shown their utmost faith in the constitution, of course only with the fond hope that there is possibility of getting justice only under the present Constitution of Indian Republic. It was the first occasion in the life of common masses that they had seen the charter of rights in the form of the preamble, fundamental rights and other provisions of the Constitution. Their hopes and aspirations were naturally raised after commencement of the Constitution and still they hope that their future would be bright under this Constitution; provided it is properly implemented. On the contrary surprisingly enough, those who have derived utmost benefits under the Constitution are pleading for change of Constitution ? This shows that their greed or lust for more and more benefit has remained unsatiable. They do not want

to share any benefit or pleasure with the underprivileged sections of the society. Some of the persons think that the failure of the Government is but failure of the Constitution. In this respect it is worth while to remember what his excellency the then president of India Shri K.R. Narayanan said while addressing joint session of Parliament on 27th January 2000, that, "It is after deep thought and considerable debate that the founding fathers adopted the Philosophy and the form of Government for India. Speaking on the draft of the Constitution Dr. Ambedkar claimed that, "It is workable, it is flexible and it is strong enough to hold the country together both in peace time and war time. Indeed if I may say so, if things go wrong under the new Constitution, the reason will not be that we had a bad Constitution. What we will have to say is that, "Man is Vile." Today when there is so much talk about revising the Constitution or even writing a new Constitution, we have to consider whether it is the Constitution that has failed us or whether it is we who have failed the Constitution."[48]

(2) In a bid to review the Constitution, the then Bharatiya Janta Party Government under the leadership of Atal Bihari Bajpai, formed the Constitution - Review Committee under the Chairmanship of the former Chief Justice of India, Shri M.N. Venkatachalayya alongwith other ten members on 13th February 2000. The review committee submitted its interim draft report on 15th Feb.2002. It was finally submitted to the Government of India on 31st March 2002. It is however not known as to what happened to it.[49]

The Bharatiya Janta Party Government was loudly stating it was brought to Power due to its promises to review the Constitution. Thus the people had allegedly gave a mandate to them to review the Constitution. Even though, it formed the Constitution Review Committee and started the reviewing work, it was defeated in the general elections held in the month of May 2004. Was it not logically then negative mandate to the B.J.P.?

(3) If the whole nation agrees to the proposal of framing a new constitution, which was not possible, whether the proposer would have been able to frame a Constitution fully acceptable to the whole nation ? The next question which is intrinsically linked with the previous question? In this respect, what Babasaheb Ambedkar observed in 1945, seems to be very much relevant. He said, "The problem of solving the Indian deadlock is not easy. India has not so far succeeded in evolving order out of her confusion. It is not she had no opportunities to do so. In fact, there have been quite a number. The first opportunity came in 1927, when Lord Birkenhed gave a challenge to Indians asking them to produce a constitution

for India. That challenge was taken up. A committee was formed to frame a Constitution. A Constitution was, however not accepted by Indians and was buried without remorse. A second opportunity presented itself to Indians in 1930, when they assembled at the Round Table Conference. Then again Indians failed to play their part and write out their own constitution. A third attempt is the one recently made by the Sapru Committee. The proposals of this committee too have fallen flat."[50] It was Dr.Babasaheb Ambedkar who could frame the present Constitution giving full accommodation to views and values of the Constituent Assembly, which worked during 1946 to 1949. Whether such efforts would be possible in the present situation ? Whether the doctrine of Basic Structure would not come in the way of new constitution makers ? Whether the constitution which is being contemplated, would be able to satisfy all the sections of the society and interests of the nation as such?

(4) The ruling congress party, previously and even now, by its wrong and inefficient handling of certain issues gave and still giving indirectly undue provocation to the fundamentalists to argue against the Constitution. The inefficiency and impropriety of the political parties are wrongly attributed to the Constitution. However, the fundamentalists and their protagonists are conveniently forgetting what Dr. Babasaheb Ambedkar said in the Constituent Assembly on 25th November 1949. He said : "However good a constitution may be, it is sure to turn out to be bad because who are called to work it, happen to be a bad lot. However bad a constitution may be, it may turn out to be good if those who are called to work it, happen to be a good lot. The working of a constitution does not depend wholly upon the nature of the constitution. The constitution can provide only the organs of state such as the legislature, the executive and the judiciary. The factors on which the working of those organs of the state depend are the people and the political parties, they will set up as their instruments to carry out their wishes and their politics."[51]

4.5 A Common Conspiracy

(1) Almost all the fundamentalists, communalists and feudalists have joined their hands in waging a war of propaganda against the Constitution. It seems that they do not want this Constitution of "Sovereign, Socialist, Secular, Democratic Republic" of India to remain in operation. Thus the struggle between the progressive and traditional forces, irrespective of their party affiliations and ideologies has been going on persistently. Thus it is the war between

two diametrically opposit ideologies. Actually it needs rational approach to deal with the national problems, if any in their real perspective and to solve them by resorting to amending and not reviewing or changing the Constitution.

(2) What harm the challenge to the constitution is to do to our body politic and what is the remedy on this issue are the two interlinked and very pertinent questions. The challenge to the Constitution will, of course, lead to confusion, chaos and communal disharmony. Therefore, it is necessary to give a serious thought to this problem. In order to overcome this crisis, it is necessary to organize a strong "People's Movement" in defence of the Constitution. In the words of Upendra Baxi, "the answer is shift, going through, exemplary retoration of responsible politics. To this end, a political education programme to propogate the constitutional values and vision is imperative."[52]

Conclusion

Thus, the Constitution is the Supreme Law of the Land. It is inviolable, fundamental and mandatory. It is based on certain sublime values. It is most suitable to the Indian Socio-Political situation. It is not fully rigid. It is flexible and amendable according to the changing situation and need of the hour. It is a product of the collective conscience and wisdom of the founding fathers of the constitution. It is committed to give justice : social, economic and political taking into consideration the needs and aspirations of the people. Its commitment to social welfare, scientific temper and international peace, is a unique feature of our Constitution. It gives importance to national unity and international peace and security. In the era of Scientific and Technological advancement, globalization and search for human identity, our Constitution is most suitable document. It is the only hope of suffering backward classes and they will certainly guard it at any cost.

References

1. Iyer Krishna J. Review of the Constitution : issues and perspectives, an article published in Review of the Constitution of India p. 2 National Centre for Advocacy Studies Pune (2000).
2. Dahl Robert : Modern Political Analysis. p. 99. Prentice Hall of India, New Delhi, 1965.
3. Johnson Harry M.Sociology : A systematic Introduction p. 49. Allied Publishers, New Delhi, 1970.

4. Evan William M. (Ed) : Law and Sociology. p. 107, Art. by Thomas A. Cowan entitled, what law can do for social science. Free Press, MacMillan, New York, 1962.
5. Constituent Assembly Debats, Vol. I. p. 59.
6. Gajendragadkar P.B. : Law, Liberty and Social Justice p. 78. Asia Pub. House, New York, 1965.
7. Iyer V.R. Krishna : Some Half Hidden Aspects of Indian Social Justice. p. 36. Eastern Book Comp. Lucknow, 1979.
8. Dr. Babasaheb Ambedkar : Writing and Speeches Vol. 7. p. 379 Govt. of Maharashtra; 1990.
9. *Ibid*. p. 249, 266.
10. Manusmriti : Chapter : VIII : 3. Na Stri Swatantramarhati.
11. As quoted by Dr. Babasaheb Ambedkar : DBAWS : Vol. 17 (iii). Govt. of Maharashtra, 2003.
12. Mill J.S. Representative Government. p. 42. Form Book, New York, 1958.
13. DBAWS : Vol.17 (iii) p. 475 (2003).
14. Ghurye G.S. Social Tensions in Ind: p. 502. Popular Prakashan, Bombay, 1968.
15. The Encyclopaedia of Social Sciences.
16. Fredrick Carl J. : Constitutional Government and Democracy. p. 8. Oxford & IBH Publishing Co. Calcutta. (1966).
17. Barnes, Cartes and Skidmore : The World of Politics. p. 75. St. Martins Press, New York. (1980).
18. DBAWS : Vol. 13, p. 1216.
19. Basu Durga Das. Constitutional Law of India. p. 2, 1978.
20. DBAWS Vol. 13 p. 1215 (1994).
21. Rajurkar N.G. and Kurundkar Narhar : Jawaharlal Nehru : The Thinker and the Statesman. p. 62. Manthan Pub. Rohtak (1985)
22. DBAWS Vol. 13 p. 1216.
23. DBAWS.Vol. 1. p. 394.
24. CAD.Vol. 7, p. 831/832.
25. Sharma M.P. : the Government of Indian Republic : p. 37. Kitab Mahal, Allahabad. (1968).
26. Luthera V.P. The Concept of the Secular State and India. p. 15. Oxford Press, London : (1964).
26a. Stein Pater and Shand John. Legal Values in Western Society. p. 26. University Press : Edinburgh. (1974).
27. Iyer Krishna; Sathe S.P.(Ed) Review of the Constitution of India. p. 11. National Centre for Advocacy Studies, Pune. (2000)
28. *Ibid*. p. 10.
28a. Golwalkar M.S. Bunch of Thoughts. p. 314 Jagaran Prakashan, Kempegowda Nagar, Bangalore. (2nd, 1980).

29. CAD X pp. 946 (25-11-1949).
30. *Ibid.* p. 973.
31. *Ibid.* p. 972.
32. CAD Vol.X. 17-11-1949. p. 623.
33. AIR 1951 SC 226.
34. AIR 1951 SC 42.
35. State of Bihar V. Kameshwar. AIR 1952 SC 889.
36. Golak Nath V. State of Punjab AIR 1967 SC 1943.

36a. AIR 1970 SC 564.

37. Madhav Rao Scindia V. Union of India. AIR 1971 SC 530.
38. Minerva Mills Ltd. V. Union of India. AIR 1980 SC 1789.
39. Sidhrajbhai V. State of Gujarat. AIR 1963 SC 540, 545.
40. Limaya Madhu : Contemporary Indian Politics p. 86. Radiant Publishers, New Delhi. (1987)
41. For details see "Have we outgrown the Constitution ? an article by Shanti Bhushan, the former Law Minister of India. The Sunday Times of India. October 27, 1996.
42. CAD Vol. X, 25th November 1949. pp. 972-981.
43. *Ibid.*
44. *Ibid.*
45. "Review of the Constitution : Past, Present and Future" by S.P. Sathe published in Review of the Constitution of India. p. 14. National Centre for Advocacy Studies Pune. (2000).
46. Ahir D.C. Dr. Ambedkar and Indian Constitution. p. 174. Low Price Publications, Delhi, 1997.
47. Keer Dhanajay : Dr. Ambedkar : Life and Mission p. 449. Popular Prakashan, Mumbai (1971).
48. President K.R. Narayan's address to the Joint Session of the Parliament, on 27th January 2000, on the occasion of 50th Anniversary of the Republic of India.
49. For details see, Reconstitution of the Constitution of India by Kanahailal Sharma. Deep and Deep Pub.Rajouri Garden, New Delhi (2002).
50. DBAWS Vol.1, p. 378
51. CAD Vol. X, 25th Nov. 1949.
52. Main Stream : Jan. 30, 1993 : (XXXI)

29. [illegible] 1967 [illegible]
30. Ibid.
31. Ibid. [illegible]
32. CAD Vol. X, [illegible] 1949, p. 968.
33. AIR [illegible]
34. AIR [illegible]
35. State of Bihar V. Kameshwar, AIR 1952 [illegible]
36. Golak Nath V. State of Punjab AIR 1967 SC 1643.
36a AIR 1973 SC 1461
37. Madhav Rao Scindia V. Union of India AIR 1971 SC 530.
38. Minerva Mills Ltd. V. Union of India AIR 1980 SC 1789.
39. [illegible] V. State of Gujarat AIR 1963 SC [illegible]
40. [illegible] Contemporary [illegible] p. 66. Radiant Publishers, New Delhi, 1987.
41. [illegible] the [illegible] the Constitution [illegible] Tata [illegible] India, [illegible] 1976.
[illegible] Vol. X, [illegible]

44. Ibid.
[illegible] Constitution [illegible] Reports [illegible] Parliament [illegible] Law [illegible] 1993.
45. [illegible] Constitution [illegible] 1997.
46. [illegible] Dr. Ambedkar [illegible] Bombay, 1991.
[illegible] R. [illegible] Parliament, [illegible] the Constitution [illegible] University [illegible]
48. [illegible] the [illegible] of the Constitution of India, [illegible] New Delhi, 2002.
[illegible] Vol. [illegible]
51. CAD Vol. X, [illegible]
52. [illegible] 1949 [illegible]

5

Scheduled Castes, Scheduled Tribes and Backward Classes

Our Constitution has pledged to secure justice to all the people, with special reference to the Backward Classes. The Backward Classes, however include three categories. They are (1) the scheduled castes (2) the scheduled tribes, and (3) the other backward classes.

It is proposed to discuss as to how these categories are respectively specified in the schedules and how such schedules are modified as and when required. It is also proposed to discuss whether there is any scope for sub-categorization of castes or classes included in the said schedules.

5.1 Specification

(a) So far as the Scheduled Castes are concerned the Constitution under its Article 341(1) states that, "The president may with respect to any state (or Union Territory), and where it is a state, after consultation with the Governor thereof, by Public notification, specify the castes, races or tribes or parts of or groups within castes, races or tribes which shall for the purpose of this Constitution bc deemed to be Scheduled Castes in relation to that state (or Union Territory, as the case may be)."

The President of India, empowered under Article 341(1) of the Constitution, promulgated 'The Constitution (Scheduled Castes) Order, 1950 (C.O.19 in August 1950). It was obviously based on the 1935 list. However, the four Sikh Castes, Mazhabis, Ramdasis, Kabirpantis and Sikligars were included in the list of Scheduled Castes for Punjab in 1950 as an exception although Hinduism was a major criterion for such inclusion.

What could be the reasonable basis for the classification of certain castes as Scheduled Castes ? In the absence of constitutional provision regarding the criterion in that respect, it would be worth while to look into its history and its purpose for finding out the reasonable criterion. An inquiry into the history of the list of Scheduled Castes specified and enclosed as the Ninth Schedule to the Government of India Act, 1935 reveals that the basis of enlisting certain castes as Scheduled Castes was the stigma of untouchability traditionally imposed on certain castes. The present list of Scheduled Castes is but the modified version of the list specified in 1935. In the opinion of Shri V.I. Muniswamy Pillai, a member of the Constituent Assembly, it was untouchability, "which brought out the special name of Scheduled Castes".[1] In the opinion of the first commissioner for SC and ST, 'the Hutton's 1931 census criteria on the basis of which the list of Scheduled Castes was prepared in 1935 appears to hold good for urposes of specifying the Scheduled Castes.'[2] In the opinion of Dr.P.T.Borale "The untouchables are not mentioned, under our Constitution as untouchability stands abolished under Article 17 of our Constitution, after examining the relevant provisions of the Constitution, we have come to the conclusion that only the Scheduled Castes are known to be the historically known untouchables and they are referred to as the Scheduled Castes under the Constitution."[3] According to Prof. Marc Galanter, "The Scheduled Castes have been chosen primarily by the criterion of low social and ritual standing."[4]

There could be an argument that due to anti-untouchability law and other measures like protective discrimination policy, untouchability may come to an end, in that situation there would not be any need of protective discrimination. However the fact is anti-untouchability movement is in vogue since beginning of the 19th Century. We have passed the Untouchability Offences Act or the Protection of Civil Rights Act in 1955 itself, but the age old practice of untouchability is still in existence. The cases under the said Act are on rising every year. It seems that it would be very difficult to do away with untouchability at least in near future. Another important thing is the so called untouchables have suffered a lot in the past because of which they could not get human identity as such and still they are suffering a lot. In view of this prevailing criterion of untouchability the list of Scheduled Castes as a beneficiary group under the Constitution is very much pertinent and relevant.

The Constitution (SC) order, 1950 specifically provides for a criterion of religion in negative terms. It states that "no person professing a religion different from Hinduism or Sikhism or Buddhism shall be deemed a member of a Scheduled Caste." Sikhism was introduced in 1956 and Buddhism was introduced in 1990 in the said order. There was a long standing demand of the Scheduled Castes converts to Buddhism that they should be included in the list of the beneficiaries on par with the Scheduled Castes. The said genuine demand was conceded by the Government as late as 1990. It is true that untouchability is a concomitant of Hinduism but it cannot be so of other religions although it might have intrudent in them. Therefore a convert need not prove that still he suffers untouchability in the new envioronment for getting the benefits under the special provisions of the Constitution. Untouchability being abolished by the Constitution, does not exist as a valid social custom even in Hindu religion. Although most of the ex-untouchables who are in Hinduism or converted suffer more or less untouchability but the past suffering is more relevant than the present in this respect. It is because of their suffering in the past, they became socially, and economically weak and unable to develop at their own in the present. Therefore all of them who were subjected to untouchability in the past need a special treatment for their development.

How caste could be a criterion for inclusion in the list of Scheduled Castes in a secularist country like India ? However, "one has to remember that those privileges were given not on account of caste or religion, but to improve the socio-economic backwardness of some identifiable groups who were subjected to untouchability."[5] It need not be construed, as Prof. Marc Galanter observes, "in the ordinary sense, but in the sense of a 'Identifiable' group or community which suffered a low social and ritual status[6] in the Hindu Social Order". If the "Caste" is construed in its Traditional sense, the provision under Article 341 would be contradictory to the provisions under Article 14, 15 and 16. Of course, the makers of the Constitution must have not contemplated such an absurdity to prevail in the Constitution. (See Chapter-II)

Thus, the President, empowered under Article 341(1) of the Constitution has duly specified certain castes by Public notification for the purpose of this Constitution as Scheduled Castes in relation to state or union territory as the case may be; as under :-

(1) The Constitution (Scheduled Castes) order, 1950.
(2) The Constitution (Scheduled Castes) (Part C States) Order, 1951.
(3) The Constitution (Scheduled Castes) (Union Territories) Order, 1951.

(4) The Scheduled Castes and Scheduled Tribes lists (modification) Order, 1956.
(5) The Constitution (Jammu and Kashmir) (Scheduled Castes) Order, 1956.
(6) The Constitution (Dadra Nagar Haveli) Scheduled Castes, Order, 1962.
(7) The Constitution (Pondicherry) Scheduled Castes, Order 1964.
(8) The Constitution (Sikkim) Scheduled Castes, Order, 1978.

(b) So far as the Scheduled Tribes are concerned, the Constitution under its Article 342(1) states, that, "the President may with respect to any state (or Union Territory) and where it is a state, after consultation with the Governor thereof, by Public notification, specify the Tribes or Tribal communites or parts of or groups within Tribes or Tribal Communities which shall for the purpose of this Constitution be deemed to be Scheduled Tribes in relation to that state (or Union Territory as the case may be)."

The President, empowered under Article 342(1) of the Constitution promulgated the Constitution (Scheduled Tribes) order, 1950 in September 1950, Firstly, the list of "Backward Tribes" was promulgated in 1936 for all the provinces except Punjab and Bengal. In order to protect their interest the then Govt. earmarked the area wherein they were largely concentrated as "Backward Areas". Under the present constitution they are identified as Scheduled Tribes for each state and the areas of their concentration as the Scheduled Arreas as stated in the fifth schedule to the Constitution.

What could be the reasonable criterion on the basis of which the Tribes are Scheduled ? According to Prof. Marc Galanter, those groups are "distinguished by Tribal Characteristics" and by their spatial and cultural isolation from the bulk of the Population."[7] Thus they are spatially and culturally isolated from rest of the society. Their abode, language, rituals and festivals, food habits and drinks, their Tribal faith and ways of worships, dress and means of livelihood and dependency on forest, poor standard of living, housing and aloofness, medicines and propitiation are obviously different from the bulk of the society. The criterion of religion is not relevant in their case. It was, however, proposed by the Joint Committee on the SC and ST Orders Amendment Bill in 1969, that no person who has given up Tribal faith or faiths and has embraced either Christianity or Islam shall be deemed a member of Scheduled Tribes.[8] The said proposal was not acceptable to the Government as it meant "unconstitutional discrimination" on the ground of religion. The Patna High Court also observed in Kartik Oran Vs. David Munzni (1964) that conversion did not extinguish membership in the tribe. "... it appears to me that Christian Orans are orans inspite of their conversion and are entitled to the rights and privilages of the tribals."[9] However due to ignorance, poverty and illiteracy the tribes became physically and psychologically meak, weak, desperate and vulnerable. They are easily identifiable as Tribals on the basis of their Tribalism. They really need special treatment to remove their backwardness and improve their social and economic condition. Therefore they are brought under the category of Scheduled Tribes so that they may be able to take benefit under the special provisions of the Constitution.

The President empowered under Article 342(1) of the Constitution has specified them as under :

(1) The Constitution (Scheduled Tribes) order, 1950.
(2) The Constitution (Scheduled Tribes) (Union Territories) Order, 1951.
(3) The Constitution (Scheduled Tribes) (Andaman Nicobar Island) Scheduled Tribes, Order, 1959.
(4) The Constitution (Dadra and Nagar Haveli) Scheduled Tribes, Order, 1962.
(5) The Constitution (Uttar Pradesh) Scheduled Tribes Order, 1967.
(6) The Constitution (Nagaland) Scheduled Tribes, Order, 1970.
(7) The Constitution (Sikkim) Scheduled Castes, Order, 1978.
(8) The Constitution (Jammu and Kashmir) Scheduled Tribes, Order 1989.

(c) So far as the Backward Classes are concerned no such provision is made. However, the Constitution under its Article 340, provides that -

"(1) The President may by order appoint a commision consisting of such persons as he thinks fit to investigate the conditions of socially and educationally backward classes, within the Territory of India and the difficulties under which they labour and to make recommendations as to the steps that should be taken by the Union or any State to remove such difficulties and to improve their condition and as to the grants that should be made for the purpose by the Union or any State and the conditions subject to which such grants should be made, and the order appointing such Commision shall define the procedure to be followed by the commission.

(2) A Commission so appointed shall investigate the matters referred to them and present to the president a report setting out the facts as found by them and making such recommendations as they think proper.

(3) The President shall cause a copy of the report so presented together with a memorandum explaining the action taken thereon to be laid before each house of Parliament."

Accordingly the Backward Classes Commission under the Chairmanship of Shri B.P. Mandal was appointed in 1979, which submitted its Report in 1980. It could duly identify altogether 3744 Castes throughout India as socially and economically backward and recommended for 27% reservation for them in the civil posts and services under the Union of India. Eventually the Government of India accepted the said report and issued the Office Memorandum to that effect on 13th August 1990. However, the Governments decision was challenged through several writ petitions filed in the Supreme Court; known as Indra Sawhney Case.[10] In this case the honourable Court upheld 27% reservation for OBCs in civil posts and services under the Union of India, subject to exclusion of the so called "Creamy Layer". In the said decision the Supreme had also directed that a statutory commission be setup to deal with the matter of inclusion or exclusion of the castes in the list of Backward Classes. Accrordingly, the National Commission for Backward Classes Act was enacted in April 1993.

As per Section 2 of the NCBC Act, "Backward Classes" means such backward classes of citizens, other than the Scheduled Castes and Scheduled Tribes, as may be specified by the Central Government in the lists for the purpose of providing reservations in appointments to the OBCs, "under the Government of India and any local or other authority..." With the Amendment of Article 15 of the Constitution in January 2006 and the enactment of the Central Educational Institutions (Reservation in Admissions) Act 2007 the list of backward classes became relevant for admission in the Central Educational Institutions also."[11]

The first central list of SEBCs was issued vide Resolution dated 10-09-1993 of the then Ministry of Social Welfare in respect of 14 states. The list for another 7 states and 4 UTs was issued vide Notification dated 19-10-1994 and 24-5-1995.[12]

5.2 Inclusion or Exclusion of Any Caste/Tribe

Under Article 341(1) and 342(1) of the Constitution, the President alone is empowered to specify any Caste or Tribe, as the case may be in the respective list. Subject to consultation with the Governor concerned. However, the president is not empowered to vary such lists in his own discretion.

The Constitution, under its Articles 341(2) and Article 342(2) empowers the Parliament alone to either include in or exclude from

TABLE 5.1
Statewise Number of Caste / Tribes Notified as Backward Classes

Sr. No.	*State / UT*	*State / UT Formed / Recognised in the Year*	*Number of Entries (Including Castes, Sub-Castes etc.*		
			SC	*ST*	*OBC*
1.	Andhra Pradesh	1956	60	33	106
2.	Arunachal Pradesh	1987	--	12	--
3.	Assam	1950	16	14	27
4.	Bihar	1950	23	30	131
5.	Chhattisgarh	2000	43	46	74
6.	Goa	1987	05	05	16
7.	Gujarat	1960	36	29	100
8.	Haryana	1966	37	-	73
9.	Himachal Pradesh	1971	57	08	50
10.	Jammu & Kashmir	1950	13	-	21
11.	Jharkhand	2000	22	30	131
12.	Karnataka	1956	101	49	183

(Table Contd.)

(Contd. Table 5.1)

Sr. No.	State/UT	State/UT Formed/ Recognised in the Year	Number of Entries (Including Castes, Sub-Castes etc.		
			SC	ST	OBC
13.	Kerala	1956	53	35	82
14.	Madhya Pradesh	1956	48	46	74
15.	Maharashtra	1960	59	47	216
16.	Manipur	1972	07	29	04
17.	Meghalaya	1972	16	14	--
18.	Mizoram	1987	16	14	--
19.	Nagaland	1963	--	05	--
20.	Orissa	1950	93	62	193
21.	Punjab	1966	38	--	65
22.	Rajasthan	1956	59	12	65
23.	Sikkim	1975	04	02	10
24.	Tamil Nadu	1956	76	36	180

(Table Contd.)

(Contd. Table 5.1)

Sr. No.	*State / UT*	*State / UT Formed / Recognised in the Year*	*Number of Entries (Including Castes, Sub-Castes etc.*		
			SC	*ST*	*OBC*
25.	Tripura	1972	34	19	43
26.	Uttarakhand	2000	65	05	01
27.	Uttar Pradesh	1950	66	05	75
28.	West Bengal	1950	60	38	57
1.	Andaman Nikobar	1950	--	06	01
2.	Chandigarh	1966	36	--	59
3.	Dadra & Nagar Haveli	1961	04	07	10
4.	Delhi	1956	36	--	54
5.	Daman & Diu	1987	05	--	20
6.	Lakshadweep	1956	--	--	--
7.	Puducherry	1963	16	--	47
	Total :		**1204**	**638**	**2168**

the list of Scheduled Castes or the Scheduled Tribes as the case may be any Caste or Tribe related to any State list.

(a) The Parliament has introduced certain modifications by law in the Sc/ST orders. Those Acts were -
   (1) The Scheduled Castes and Scheduled Tribes Orders (Amendment) Act, 1956 (63 of 1956).
   (2) The Scheduled Castes and Scheduled Tribes Orders (Amendment) Act, 1976 (Act 108 of 1976).
   (3) The Constitution SC/ST Orders Amendment Act, 1986 (Act 34 of 1986).
   (4) The Constitution SC/ST Orders Amendment Act, 1986 (Act 69 of 1986).
   (5) The SC/ST Orders (Amendment) Act, 1987 (Act 18 of 1987).
   (6) The Constitution SC/ST Amendment Act, 1991 (Act 39 of 1991).
   (7) The SC/ST Orders (Amendment Act, 2000 (Act 28 of 2000)
   (8) The SC/ST Orders (Amendment Act, 2000 (Act 29 of 2000)
   (9) The SC/ST Orders (Amendment Act, 2000 (Act 25 of 2002)
   (10) The Constitution SC / ST Orders (Amendment) Act, 2002 (Act 30 of 2002).
   (11) The Constitution SC / ST Orders (Amendment) Act, 2002 (Act 32 of 2002).
   (12) The Constitution SC / ST Orders (Amendment) Act, 2002 (Act 61 of 2002).
   (13) The Constitution SC / ST Orders (Amendment) Act, 2003 (Act 10 of 2003).

(b) The statewise number of Castes / Tribes notified by Union Government so far as Scheduled Castes, Scheduled Tribes and Backward Classes are shown in the following Table. See Table No. 5:1.

5.3 Procedure of Specification and Modification

On perusal of Article 341 and 342, it appears that the Constitution does not specifically lay down the criteria as such on the basis of which certain Castes are designated as Scheduled Castes or the Scheduled Tribes as the case may be. It merely laid down the procedure and not the criteria.

(a) Article 341(1) as well as Article 342(1) provide that the President may -

(1) after consultation with the Governor of concerned state.

(2) by public notification.
(3) specify the Castes / Tribes etc.
(4) for the purpose of the Constitution be deemed to be Scheduled Castes or Scheduled Tribes as the case may be.
(5) in relation to that state.

Thus, the Head of the State, i.e. President of the Union of India is empowered to specify the Castes or Tribes as Scheduled Castes or Scheduled Tribes. It is stated very specifically and explicitly that, "but as aforesaid a notification issued under the said clause shall not be varied by any subsequent notification." It is the privilege of Parliament alone to include any Caste / Tribe in the list of Scheduled Castes or in the list of Scheduled Tribes as the case may be. It implies that no other authorities including the state legislatures are competent to introduce any change in the SC. Order or ST. Order.

In State of Maharashtra Vs. Milind and others the Supreme Court[13] held that, "the Scheduled Tribes order must be read as it is. It is not even permissible to say that a Tribe, Sub-Tribe, Part of or group of any Tribe or Tribal community is synonymous to the one mentioned in the Scheduled Tribes order if they are not so specifically mentioned in it."

"It is not at all permissible to hold any enquiry or let in any evidence to decide or declare that any Tribe or Tribal community or part of or group within any Tribe or Tribal community is included in the general name even though it is not specifically mentioned in the concerned Entry in the Constitution (Scheduled Tribes) Order, 1950."

"It is not open to State Governments or Courts or Tribunals or any other authority to modify, amend or alter the list of Scheduled Tribes specified in the notification issued under clause (1) of Article 342."

The notification "can be amended only by law to be made by the Parliament."

This ratio decidendi would be equally applicable to the Scheduled Caste order 1950 also.

According to Article 341(1) and 342(1) the Castes or Tribes are respectively listed as SC or STs in relation to a particular state or Union Territory, as the case may be. When any person belonging to either SC or ST migrates to any other state, he is not treated so due to area restrictions. It has been, however clarified by the Ministry of Home-Affairs, Govt of India in 1977 that the inter-state area restrictions were deliberately imposed so that the person belonging to a specific caste residing in a specific area qualified to be designated so, should only get the benefit under the Constitutional safeguards. The basic principle behind this, presumably is the people belonging to the same caste but living in different states would not necessarily suffer from the same disabilities. Consequently, it became difficult for the genuine beneficiary to obtain the Caste/Tribe status in that state or in the state of his origin due to migration.

However, any discrimination based on the ground of 'Place of Birth' or 'Residence' is prohibited under Article 15(1), 15(2) and Article 16(2) of the Constitution. Every body is permitted to move freely through out the Territory of India" (Article 19(1)(d) and "reside and settle in any part of the Territory of India (Article 19(1)(e).

In view of these rights how could the principle of area restriction be interpreted ?

However, 'The Scheduled Castes and Scheduled Tribes (Amendment) Act, 1976 "eliminated most intra-state area restrictions, adding about 2.5 Million to the Scheduled Castes population and over 3 million to the Scheduled Tribes."[13(a)] However, the problem of area-restriction was not fully solved.

It is a fact that the Constitution itself has made it mandatory on the part of President to specify such Castes or Tribes as Scheduled Castes or Scheduled Tribes, as the case may be , "in relation to that state or Union Territory," wherein they ordinarily reside. The SC order 1950 framed in pursuance of the Constitutional provision provides two criteria - Territory and Religion. The criterion of Territory has present relevance whereas the criterion of religion has past relevance of SC order appended to the Act of 1935. Both the criteria are however, upheld by the apex court in several cases. So far as the S.T. order 1950 is concerned there is only one criterion of Territory and not of religion.

In Union of India Vs. Dudh Nath Prasad, the Supreme Court[14] observed that, "A person can be said to be ordinarily residing at a particular place if he has intention to stay at that place for a considerable long time; it would not include a flying visit or a short or a casual presence at that place."

(b) The list of Scheduled Castes and Tribes could not remain in their prestine form due to certain reasons. They were modified rationally and made more broad based with inclusion, exclusion or transferring some castes or Tribes in the respective lists. The causes of modication of the lists could be as under :

(1) Due to partition of India into two nations, some parts of Punjab and Bengal were Transferred to Pakistan; which resulted into migration and immigration of population in

both the countries. This must have reflected in the SC/ST lists.

(2) On the eve of independence near about six hundred princely states were joined to India during 1947 to 1949. Therefore it was necessary to make some modication in the SC/ST lists.

(3) Due to reorganization of states on linguistic basis in 1956, there was reshuffling of population on large scale. Therefore, the President had to underake modification of SC/ST lists in 1956 under the modification order, 1956.

(4) In order to include in or exclude from the SC/ST lists, certain Castes and Tribes the Parliament enacted the SC and ST orders (Amendment) Act, 1956. (No. LXIII of 1956).

(5) In a bid to rationalize the SC/ST lists the Parliament has passed the SC/ST lists (Amendment Act, 1976 and made certain changes in the said lists. This Act has removed certain 'intra-state area restrictions' which resulted in increase of SC/ST population to the extent of 2.5 million Scheduled Castes and over 3 million Scheduled Tribes.

(c) So far as Backward Classes are concerned the state-wise central list contains altogether 1963 Castes.[15] All of them are based on the criteria of social, educational and economic backwardness. Religion is no bar for them. The list consists of almost all the backward Castes belonging to Hindu, Muslim and Christian Communities. They are known as Backward Classes, (BCs) other Backward Classed (OBCs) and Socially and Educationally Backward Classes. (SEBCs).

The Government of India formed 'National Commission for Backward Classes' in 1993. The commission is to give advice to the Central Government in respect of inclusion in or exclusion from the list of Backward Classes.

Presently, several castes are persistently demanding inclusion of their Caste in the OBC list. The Jat Caste, which is more resourceful and dominant caste in some of the northern states, has been included in the Central B.C. list owing to their demand to that effect, on Oct., 27, 1999. They are included in U.P. State B.C. list on March 10, 2000. The inclusion of Jats in Central B.C. list for Rajasthan, however caused a reasonable apprehension in the mind of the Gujjars who were already included in the BC list, that the Jats would usurp the prospective benefits of BCs due to their dominant position in the social milieu.

Consequently the Gujjars started their agitation for inducting their Caste in the Scheduled Tribes to safeguard their interests by getting apart from the Jats in BC Category. This however had further repurcussions on the Mina Community. The Mina, a more politicised Tribe is already in the S.T. list in Rajasthan. The Minas thought that inclusion of Gujjars in the S.T. would geopardise their position in S.T. Hence they started agitation against inclusion of Gujjars in the S.T. list. Eventually, Gujjar's slackened their agitation only on the assurance of quota in the general category.[16]

Presently, the Marathas in Maharashtra, who were once against Mandal proposals, are demanding that their Caste be included in the BC Category. Maratha is comparatively a major and dominant caste enjoying hegemonic power almost in every field of social life in Maharashtra[17] except a very Tiny Minority of them. Some of them have already got entry in BC list under the nomenclature of 'Kunbi', but they are unsatisfied over this listing. If their demand is accepted, it would allegedly adversly affect other socially and educationally backward castes.

The Schedules or lists of some Castes or Tribes or Classes are, however based on some rational criteria. Hence no inclusion in the respective lists could be made without increasing the quota fixed for any category and without assigning reasonable grounds.

5.4 Denotified Tribes and Nomadic Tribes

(a) The Denotified Tribes or Vimukta Jatis are the former criminal Tribes. Previously, under the Criminal Tribes Act, 1871 a large section of our society was degraded and segregated as 'Criminal Tribes'. They were constrained to live on criminal avocation. They were subjected "to constant vigilant watch by the administrators and their movements were closely observed." and markedly restricted. After independence, a committee, under the Chairmanship of Ananthsayanam Ayyangar was formed in 1949. After detailed study of the working of the Criminal Tribes Act, throughout the country, it submitted its report in 1950, in which it made several recommendations including the repealing of the Act of 1871 and undertaking poverty amelioration programme.[18] Accordingly the Government has repealed the Criminal Tribes Act, 1871 with effect from 31 August 1952 by the Criminal Tribes (Repeal) Act, 1952. However, "to keep effective control over the so called hardened criminals," Habitual Offenders Act, 1952 was passed and it is still in implementation. Thus, altogether 153 Tribes were liberated from the criminal bondage.

The population of the ex-criminal Tribes or Denotified Tribes in the year 1955 was approximately 35 Lakh in India; of whom 17 Lakh, i.e, half of them lived in Uttar Pradesh alone and next comes Maharashtra where more than 6 Lakh people lived. In almost all the states they are either included in the Scheduled Castes or Scheduled Tribes, except the state of Maharashtra, Madhya Pradesh and Tamil Nadu, where they are in the separate category of Denotified Tribes. Some of the DNTs are included in OBC list also.

It is difficult to state as to why did they adopt criminal avocation. However it could be said that most probably they might be warriors or soldiers but having lost their jobs, they turned into criminals. They were constrained to adopt the said avocation only under the 'compelling situations'. It is also true that, "These groups of people failed to adjust themselves with changing situations and the normal social order and traditions, either because of clash of

TABLE 5.2
Ex-Criminal Tribes

Sr.No.	*State*	*Population*	*Percentage*
1.	Andhra Pradesh	2,02,242	0.98
2.	Bihar	13,311	0.03
3.	Bombay	6,23,809	1.73
4.	Madras	3,93,198	1.10
5.	Orissa	74,762	0.51
6.	Punjab	76,564	0.60
7.	Uttar Pradesh	16,68,845	2.64
8.	West Bengal	2,598	0.01
9.	Hyderabad	69,202	0.37
10.	Madhya Bharat	76,722	0.96
11.	Mysore	2,10,321	2.13
12.	Pepsu	3,453	0.98
13.	Rajasthan	55,440	0.43
14.	Saurashtra	2,302	0.05
15.	Ajmer	1,152	0.16
16.	Bhopal	1,500	0.18
17.	Kutch	500	0.08
18.	Vindhya Pradesh	983	0.03
	Total :	**34,76,904**	

(Compiled on the basis of RCSCST 1955 Part-I Section X).

culture or because of conflicts, which in course of time, brought corresponding social disorganization among them. This state of affiars gradually brought total degeneration, throwing these people into the vortex of anti-social activities."[19]

(b) The Nomadic Tribes are the most vulerable and neglected people. They are nomatic in the sense they have no permanent house of their own in any village or town. Nomadic Tribes pre a collection of diverse Tribals/Castes of different professions, especially degrading and fetching low income. They are socially, educationally and economically backward. They have in them a Jat (Council) Panchayat.[20] to settle their internal problems. They are very much stick to their caste rules and superstitious beliefs. They are but subjected to exploitation by the so called high castes and landlords. Their honour is not protected.

They lead a sub-standard life.[21] Neither modern amenity nor any facility reached upto them. Most of them are illiterate and ignorant. Some people among them are taking lead to bring a new social awakening among them. However, due to unsympathetic attitude of the casteist Government machinery, they are still in the pre-social state.

They are categorized separately as Nomatic Tribes for the purpose of getting certain educational and economic facilities under the Constitution in some states. It is learnt that there are nearabout six hundred Tribes or Castes in India who are called Nomadic Tribs. In most of the states they are included in OBCs. In Maharashtra, Madhya Pradesh and Tamil Nadu, they are still treated as Nomadic Tribes. So far as Maharashtra's list of Nomadic Tribes is concerned, there seems to be considerable dissatisfaction over the inclusion of Dhangar and Vanjari, Castes. It is alleged that those castes are comparatively better placed than the other nomadic tribes in the list. They can not be comparable with the nomadic tribes on any count.[22]

(c) Consequent upon the increasing demands from the DNT/NT communities for their socio-economic development, the Government of India, through its ministry of Social Justice and Empowerment had Constituted "the National Commission for Denotified, Nomadic and Semi-nomadic Tribes" under the Chairmanship of Balkrishna Renake which asumed its work with effect from 6th Feb. 2006. After due inquiry into the matter, the commission submitted its report on 30th June 2008. It is, however under consideration of the ministry till now.

The National Commission for Denotified, Nomadic and Semi-Nomadic Tribes had made several valuable suggestions for improving the socio-economic condition of the said disadvantaged communities. Its first and foremost suggestion is to identify those communities on certain rational basis and statewise lists be prepared so that benefit could be given to the real sufferers. It has suggested that an Advisory Committee at the state level/U.T. level be constituted under the chairmanship of the Chief-Minister incuding the prominent anthropologists, socialogists and activists. Such committee be established at District level also under the chairmanship of the District Magistrate including the police officers and community leaders and activists. They should meet regularly and formulate the plan of development of those communities and take the review of the situation. The commission suggested that the special component plan for the economic development of the NT/DNTS be formulated on the line of SC/ST Sub-Plans. The commission suggested that the NT/DNTs be provided with educational and medical facilities. It has also suggested that the Scheduled Castes and Scheduled Tribes (Prevention of Atrocities) Act, 1989 be made applicable to them so that they may regain confidence and lead a dignified and fearless life. They Commission suggested that they may be given constitutional status on the same lines as given to the Scheduled Castes and the Scheduled Tribes. Accordingly, the constitution may be amended by making addition of Article 342A on the lines of Article 341 and 342 of the constitution and suggested that all social, economic and political facilities ought to be given to those communities for their overall development so that they may be able to live a honourable life.

The commission has rightly thought that the NT and DNTs are human beings and they should be given equal status and equal share in all walks of life. We must remember that we can not afford to leave those nomadic Tribes in the present uncivilized condition for a longer time.

5.5 An attempt to descheduling of some Castes / Tribes

(a) The ministry of law, Government of India had constituted a committee, known as "Advisory Committee on the Revision of the list of Scheduled Castes and Scheduled Tribes "under the Chairmanship of B.N. Lokur, Secretary, Ministry of Law in June 1965". The main task before the committee was to undertake adjusting the lists "in a rational and scientific manner," the committee reported "promptly" on Aug. 25, 1965, within a short period of two months only.

The committee, advised inclusion of 9 castes, all small and the deletion of 171 castes on different reasons. It found that 38 castes altogether "do not suffer from untouchability".[23] So far as the list of Scheduled Tribes was concerned, it advised to include 19 more Tribes and delete 131 Tribes.

The committee advised to delete the following major castes from the SC list:

(1) Andhra Pradesh	:	Mala
(2) Assam	:	Jhalo-Malo, Jalia Khaibarta, Dhupi/ Dhobi.
(3) Bihar	:	Chamar, Dhobi
(4) Gujarat	:	Vankar, Dhed.
(5) Kerala	:	Vannan, Mannan, Perumannan, Velan.
(6) Madhya Pradesh	:	Chamar, Jatav, Satnami, Mahar, Mehra
(7) Madras (TN.)	:	Mannan, Velan, Vannan
(8) Maharashtra	:	Mahar
(9) Mysore (Karnataka)	:	Bhovi
(10) Orissa	:	Dhoba, Dhobi
(11) Punjab	:	Chamar
(12) Uttar Pradesh	:	Chamar, Dhobi
(13) West Bengal	:	Dhoba / Dhobi, Rajbanshi, Namasudra, Sunri[24]

The Committee put its conclusion in the following words : "we feel that the time has come when the question of descheduling of relatively advanced communities should receive serious and urgent consideration."[25]

The question is, had the committee inquired into the matter properly ? The matter was before the consideration of the committee only for two months. How did the committee complete the inquiry in respect of SC/STs of the whole country within a short period of two months ? What was the criterion on the basis of which it advised to delete certain castes, that too without survey. How could they become relatively advanced communities" within a short period of commencement of the constitution. After reorganisation of the states on linguistic basis, the (S.C.) orders were finally issued, the Untouchability Offence Act, 1955 (PCRA 1955) was brought in operation in 1955. How could the committee conclude that almost 38 major untouchables castes "do not suffer from untouchability."

It ought to be taken into account that, the Government of India in the Department of Social Welfare had Constituted the Committee under the Chairmanship of Shri L. Elayaperumal on April 27, 1965 "to examine the question of untouchability as also the problems of economic uplift and educational development of the Scheduled Castes."[26] The said committee, however, after due inquiry submitted its factual report to the Government of India, on 30th January 1969, the committee took almost three years and eight months to complete its work.

The committee stated very explicitly that, "it is necessary to see that there is a distinction between untouhability as a "touch-me-notism" and untouchability as a mental attitude manifesting itself in social discrimination. The two are quite different. It may be that untouchability as a touch-me-notism may be gradually vanishing in towns, although there yet no clear evidence that it is happening in any appreciable degree. It is, however, quite cerain that untouchability as a propensity on the part of the Caste Hindus to discriminate against the Scheduled Castes is not vanishing either in town or in villages. In the villages both the types of untouchability are still prevalent in acute form."[27] This fact is applicable to the present society also.

There is, of course substantial difference of facts between the Lokur Committee report (1969) so far as status of untouchability is concerned. The later is a studied observation whereas the former seems to be based on no such study, but on assumption.

One more question is, as to why some of the Castes, which are major and leading Castes were advised to be deleted by the Lokur Committee ? the elites and leaders belonging to those castes were active in Dalit liberation movement. Some of the individuals were comparatively well to do. However, an individual is known by his Caste and not by his individual status. Moreover, such elites of lower castes are treated with prejudice, hatred and jeolousy. It seems that there is an anger against those castes and they want to weaken the Dalit movement by eliminating certain castes or tribes from their respective lists.

It is, of course true that the suggestions of the Lokur Committee were not accepted by the Government and its report had no effect on the SC/ST Lists.

(b) It should be noted that the SC/ST Orders Amendment Act, 1976, provided for the removal of area restrictions except in cases where it was considered necessary.

Accordingly, the Registrar General has notified the revised population of Scheduled Castes and Scheduled Tribes in respect of the concerned states / union territories where area restrictions were removed. Consequently, there was increase of approximately 25 Lakh in the population of SC and 31 Lakh in the population of ST in the total population of the respective communities in the census of 1971.[28]

(c) The architect of the Constitution of India, Dr. Babasaheb Ambedkar, after referring to the Criminal Tribes, the aboriginal Tribes and the untouchables in his famous book, " the untouchables" (1948) said very categorically that, "the existence of these classes in an abomination, the Hindu Civilization, gauged in the light of these social products, could hardly be called civilization. It is a diabolical contrivance to suppress and enslave humanity. Its proper name would be Infamy. What else can be said of a civilization which has produced a mass of people who are taught to accept crime as an approved means of earning their livelihood, another mass of people who are left to live in full bloom of their primitive barba rism in the midst of civilization and a third mass of people who are treated as an entity beyond human intercourse and whose mere touch is enough to cause pollution ?"[29]

Thus, it is certainly "a diabolical contrivance to suppress and enslave humanity". It is a deep rooted caste prejudice which has enslaved the humanity. It is but a unique system of exploitation and oppression of all sorts. Al though we have enacted and adopted the Constitution based on a new social order of liberty, equality and fraternity in 1950 it self, caste prejudices are still in vogue. Even today "the peculiar social psychology' comes in the way of social unity and integrity of the nation. They do not want to share any benefit with those suppressed communities. Therefore they oppose to the policy of reservations in the field of education and the services.

5.6 Sub-Categorization

The problem of sub-categorization of the Scheduled Castes with the ulterior motive of 'divide and rule,' Policy is becoming conspicuously significant. It is becoming complicated and creating a great cleavage among the ex-untouchables. It has erupted in Andhra-Pradesh, Punjab and Tamil Nadu, and its poision may spread to almost through out India; not only amongst the Scheduled Castes but even amongst the Scheduled Tribes and the other Backward Classes.

In support of sub-categorization the Government of Andhra Pradesh took an awaful lead in passing, the Scheduled Castes (Rationalization of Reservations) Act, 2000. It was instantly challenged by E.V. Chinnaiah and others by an Appeal No. 6758 before the Hon'ble Supreme Court. The Hon'ble Supreme Court, however gave a very landmark decision on 5th November 2004, stating that the scheme of sub-categorisation is ultra vires of the Constitution (AIR 2005 SC 162). Even then in derogation of the decision of the apex court, the moves for sub-categorization are going on in Andhra Pradesh itself. Such moves are taking root in some other sates also.[30] It is, of course a great challenge to the whole Judicial System and the Constitution of India. Therefore, it is proposed to discuss as to what is Sub-Categorisation, why Sub-Categorisation, is Sub-Categorisation legal and Constitutional, is it rational, and logical and has it any beneficial value.

(1) What is Sub-Categorisation is a pertinent question.

(a) Sub-Categorization is also known by sub-classification or micro-classification. Classification means grouping of persons on the basis of common characteristics like region, occupation, education, culture and language and socio-economic status for some purpose to be achieved.

(b) "The Scheduled Castes" is a Schedule of certain castes, classified so on the basis of their low social status in the caste hierarchy. The said classification was made and enclosed as the Ninth Scheduled to the Government of India Act, 1935. The purpose for which the list of Scheduled Castes was specified in 1935 was, obviously to identify those castes or sub-castes who were supposed to get representation in the legislature on reserved seats and representation in the public services and educational facilities as provided in the Poona Pact, 1932.

(c) The criterion on the basis of which the castes and Sub-Caste were brought under one Schedule was, of course "untouchability" which they suffered from time immemorable. According to Dr. Babasaheb Ambedkar the "Broken Men" who professed Buddhism and opposed to Brahmanism, were boycotted and subjected to untouchability. Due to beef eating, poverty and illiteracy they lost their high cultural status and Buddhist Identity.[31] All of them were deliberately divided into several Castes and Sub-Castes, as such they lost their common brotherhood and even became inimical to each other. The number of such low status castes who were outside the pale of four varnas was 429 in 1935.

(d) The present list of the Scheduled Castes is but a modified version of the list prepared in 1935. In the opinion of Shri V.I. Muniswamy Pillai, a member of the Constituent Assembly it was untouchability "which brought out the special name of Scheduled Castes.[32] In the opinion of first Commissioner for SC and ST, the Hutton's 1931 Census Criteria on the basis of which the list of Scheduled Castes was prepared in 1935 "appears to hold good for purposes of specifying the Scheduled Castes.[33] According to Prof. Marc Galanter, "The Scheduled Castes have been chosen primarily by the criterion of low social and ritual standing.[34]

(e) As per Article 366 (24) of the Constitution of India, "Scheduled Castes" means such Castes, race or Tribes or parts of or groups within such Castes, races or Tribes as are deemed under Article 341 to be Scheduled Castes for the purpose of this Constitution. In exercise of the powers vested by Article 341(1) of the Constitution, the President after due consultation with the Governors or Rajpramukhs of the States concerned had issued the Constitution (Scheduled Castes) Order, 1950 specifying the consolidated list of Scheduled Castes. It consists of near about 900 castes as at present. There is one criterion of categorisation and one schedule of the Castes. Thus, "the castes once included in the Presidential list form a class by themselves." There is no scope for further categorisation or sub-categorisation on any ground whatsoever.

(2) The next question is as to why sub-categorisation is demanded by some section of the Scheduled Castes and supported by the caste Hindus.

(a) It is being stated that, "some particular groups within the Scheduled Castes have cornered all the benefits at the cost of others in the said list". This statement made by the pro-categorisationists should have been proved by adducing sufficient data and facts in corroboration of their statement. The National Commission for Scheduled Castes formed under Article 338 should have undertaken the indepth study in this matter. Therefore there is no substance in their statement. The onus of proof lies on their part, but they have failed in doing so.

(b) In the case of Andhra Pradesh for instance, where it was alleged that the Malas grabbed "all the benefits", the position was made clear in the petition submitted by the Late P.V. Rao, on behalf of Mala Mahandu on 28-05-1998 to the Chairman, National Commission for SC/ST. He states :-

"To say the Malas have grabbed the major share is not based on facts. As per the data supplied by the government of Andhra Pradesh to the Commissioner, the representation of Scheduled Castes in group 'A' is 3.98%

and in group 'B' it is 5.36 per cent; still about 11 per cent backlog exists. The proportionate representation of Malas is not complete. Then how did they have grabbed the major share." The position is same almost in every state. There is no substance in saying that the Malas in Andhra Pradesh, the Mahars in Maharashtra and Jatavas in U.P. had grabbed all the benefits under Article 15(4) and 16(4) of the Constitution. Even some of the intellectuals also are liberally subscribing to the theory of 'cornering' all the benefits by some of the castes among the Scheduled Castes which is absolutely wrong.

(c) There seems to be a covert reason behind the "grabbing" Theory. It seems that the Brahmanic forces have planned to divide the Scheduled Castes and continue to dominate and exploit them. It is true that the Scheduled Castes, especially the Ambedkarites amongst them are comparatively more politicised, as such they are spearheading the struggle for secuirng social justice to all the exploited brethren. With mass conversion to Buddhism their struggle became more virulent against all orthodox, obscurantists and feudalist elements in the society. They stood firmly against all the anti-reservation agitations in Bihar, U.P. Gujarat and Maharashtra. Thus they have conspicuously come to prominence.

(d) In Maharashtra, the Ambedkarite movement has successfully spread even at the grass root level under the staunch leadership of RPI and militant Dalit Pathers. In Uttar Pradesh, the Ambedkarite movement has spread almost through out the State under the leadership of RPI leaders and later under the successful leadership of BSP led by Kanshiram and Mayavati. The majority of nomadics in Maharashtra are entering into the Buddhist stream under the leadership of Laxman Mane. In Andhra Pradesh the Ambedkarite movement is becoming predominant. Thus Ambedkarite Movement is fastly spreading almost through out the country. Thus the increasing influence of Ambedkarite movement through out the country created an apprehension in the minds of Brahmanic forces. The Ambedkarite forces which are for the establishment of egalitarian society are naturally supposed to be arch enemies of Brahmanic forces. It is submitted that in their bid to curb the Ambedkarite movement and to protect their vested interests, they are constrained to revive their old Manusmriti based divide and rule policy in the name of 'Sub-Categorization' among the Scheduled Castes.

(e) The first experiment of divide and rule Policy was made in Andhra Pradesh, but became utterly unsuccessful due to intervention of judicial wisdom. The Government of Andhra-Pradesh passed 'the Andhra Pradesh Scheduled Castes (Rationalization of Reservation) Act, 2000 and 15% reservation meant for them under Art. 15(4) and 16(4) of the Constitution was apportioned amongst the 4 Sub-Groups. They were Group A 1%, Group B 7%, Group C 6% and Group D 1%. The Malas and Madigas, the two major ex-untouchable Castes were respectively put into Group B, (7%) and Group C (6%) alongwith other castes among all the 59 castes of the Scheduled Castes in Andhra Pradesh. The said Act was challenged by E.V. Chinnaiah, before the Hon'ble Supreme Court in which the court declared the Sub-Categorization as null and void on 5th November 2004.[35] Thus the legal battle is over on this issue; but the intra-caste struggle is in vogue. Even it is spreading to other states.

Thus the overt reason of Sub-Caterization is to Pollute the minds of the Scheduled Castes with vicious 'sub-caste' feeling, and the covert reason is mainly responsible for Sub-Caste feuds.

(3) Is Sub-Classification Constitutional is an important question. This question has been viewed by the Supreme Court from procedural point of view and substantial point of view.

(a) Firstly, Article 341 provides that the President may with respect to any state or union territory after consultation with the Governor thereof by Public Notification, specify the Castes, races or tribes or parts of or groups within castes, races or tribes which shall for the purposes of this Constitution be deemed to be Scheduled Castes in relation to that state or Union Territory. Thus there can be only one list of Scheduled Castes for that state.

Article 341(2) provides that, "Parliament may by Law include in or exclude from the list of Scheduled Castes specified in a notification issued under clause (1) any caste, race or tribe or part of or group within any caste, race or tribe, but save as aforesaid a notification issued under the said clause shall not be varied by any subsequent notification."

Thus, the Parliament only by law include in or exclude from the list any caste or sub-caste. This is the only procedure prescribed for making any change in the list of Scheduled Caste. Of Course, "There is no provision either to sub-divide, sub-classify or sub-group these castes which are found in the Presidential List of Scheduled Castes." (E.V. Chinnaiah V. Andhra Pradesh 5-11-2004) (Para 13)

(b) It was argued that, while making Sub-Categorization, there was no inclusion in or exclusion from the list of the Scheduled Castes, what is prohibited under Article 341(2) is not done at all. So there is nothing unconstitutional in the Sub-Categorisation. The argument prima facie seems to be very much sound, but it is not so.
Under Article 341(2) what is important is, "but save as aforesaid a notification issued under the said clause shall not be varied by any subsequent notification." The important point is the notification "shall not be varied" and empowering parliament to include in or exclude from the list any castes or sub-caste is an exception. The notification issued under Article 341(1) shall not be "varied" is the substantial point. "Orders once issued under clause (1) of the said Article can not be varied by subsequent order or notification even by the President except by law made by Parliament."[36]
(State of Maharashtra V. Milind Civil Appeal No. 2294 of 1986 as decided on November 28, 2000 by the Supreme Court). In Sub-Categorization the list is "varied", even without the initiative of Parliament which is unconstitutional. There is strict constitutional limitation on any authority to make any variation in the list of the Scheduled Castes. Therefore, Article 341 needs to be properly interpreted in its real perspective. Thus, any variation in the list of the Scheduled Castes notified under Article 341(1) is absolutely unconstitutional.

(c) It ought to be borne in mind what Dr. Babasaheb Ambedkar, the Chairman of the Drafting Committee said in the Constituent Assembly on 11th October 1949, that, "(b) all the scheduled castes in any province or state shall be deemed to be a single community."[37] This "explanation" was accepted by the Constituent Assembly. When it is a single community, it can not be divided on any ground.

(d) The Sub-Categorisation of the Scheduled Castes without any statistical base and objective research or scientific survey would be absolutely wrong. There is National Commission for Scheduled Castes constituted under Article 338(1) of the Constitution. It is manned by a chairperson, vice-chairperson and three other members. It shall be the duty of the Commission to investigate and monitor all matters relating to the safeguards provided for the Scheduled Castes and to evaluate the working of such safeguards.

According to clause 9 of the said Article, "The Union and every State Government shall consult the Commission on all major policy matters affecting Scheduled Castes." Thus, while taking any important decision affecting the safeguards under the Constitution and other states it shall be incumbant on the part of union or the state, as the case may be to take into account the recommendations of the said Commission and "shall consult the Commission." In order to investigate and report on the working of various safeguards meant for the Scheduled Castes as well as the safeguards meant for the Scheduled Tribes and other Backward Classes separate national commissions i.e. National Commission for Scheduled Castes (338(1)), National Commission for Scheduled Tribes (338 A (1) and National Commission for Backward Classes (340(1)) are appointed.

(e) There is no direct reference as to welfare of the Scheduled Castes in the Union list or State list or Concurrent list. It was, however not necessary also in view of the Provision of Article 15(4) and 16(4) and Article 17 of the Constitution in Fundamental Rights Chapter where "the State" primordially the Union Government is responsible for the implementation of those provisions. The President is to specify the Castes and Sub-castes in the list of the Scheduled Castes and the Parliament only is empowered to include in or exclude from the list any caste or sub-caste. The period of the political rights could be extended only by the Parliament. All these provisions obviously indicate that so far as availing "Equality of opportunity and equal protection of the laws" is concerned, the Union Government is responsible. The State Governments shall implement the policies and the safeguards for the Scheduled Castes under the aid and advice of the Union Government.

(f) In the words of S.N. Mandal," in addition to a number of specific provisions for safeguarding the rights and interests of SCs and STs there is a separate part in the Constitution with special provisions relating to these classes clearly demonstrate the intention of the constitution makers to treat this matter as a "reserved" subject for the Centre to administer, of Course through the States. To take the Plea subsequently that the welfare of SCs and STs is the responsibility of the State Governments and that their problems form part of the law and order question which is a state subject is to make a mockery of the Constitutional provisions for the protection of these people."[38] This indicates how great importance is given to the welfare of the Schedulede Castes and the Scheduled Tribes in the Constitution.

(g) From the substantial point of view it can be said that any attempt to tinker with the list of Scheduled Castes is beyond the legislative competence of the State Legislatures. It has been observed by the Hon'ble Supreme Court in E.V. Chinnaiah V. Andhra Pradesh (2004) that "one of the proven methods of examining the legislative competence of an enactment is by the application of doctrine of pith and substance. In this process, it is necessary for the courts to go into and examine the true character of the enactment; its object, its scope and effect to find out whether the enactment in question is genuinely referable to the field of legislation alloted to the State under the Constitutional Scheme." The Court applied the doctrine of Pith and Substance to the Andhra Pradesh (Rationalization of Reservations) Act, 2000 and declared that the said Act did not fulfil that criterion.

(h) The next point is whether the enactment creats sub-classification of the Scheduled Castes so as to violate Article 14 of the Constitution. "Under the States reservation policy the backward class consists of other Backward Class, Scheduled Castes and Scheduled Tribes. Therefore, there is already a classification for the purpose of reservation." In that situation there can not be re-classification or sub-classification for the same purpose of reservation. In the State of Jammu and Kashmir V. Triloki Nath (1974)/SCC 19, the Hon'ble Supreme Court rightly observed that, "Classification must be Truly founded on substantial differences which distinguish persons grouped together from those left out of the group and such differential attributes must bear a just and rational relation to the object sought to be achieved." (Quoted in the case)

(4)a. The next point is whether Sub-Classification is reasonable and logical. What is not legal and constitutional is not reasonable.

The classification of the Scheduled Castes is done on the basis of their low social and ritual status which they suffered out of "untouchability". Now on what ground sub-classification could be made ? They had already exhausted that basic ground. "Equality is for equals. That is to say that those who are similarly circumstanced are entitled to an equal tratment."[39] All the ex-untouchables are similarly circumstanced and equal in status; as such they ought to get equal opportunity. While piloting the draft article 341 in the Constituent Assembly Dr. Babasaheb Ambedkar, the Hon'ble Chairman of the Drafting Committee observed that, "once a notification has been issued by the president, which, undoubtedly, he will be issuing in consultation with and on the advice of the Government of each State, thereafter, if any elimination was to be made from the list so notified or any addition was to be made, that must be made by Parliament and not by the President. The object is to eliminate any kind of political factors having a play in the matter of the disturbances in the Schedule so published by the President."[40]

(b) Presently the Sub-Categorisation of the Scheduled Castes is being sought and not of other lists, such as list of the Scheduled Tribes and Other Backward Classes.[40(a)] If the same reason and logic is applied, which is being applied in respect of the Scheduled Castes they also would be subjected to divisions and Sub-Categorisation.

(c) It is alleged that some of the Castes under the Schedule are 'cornering' the benefits of the safeguards. This has not been proved; but it is made plank on which the demand of Sub-Categorisation is being unreasonably justified. In this regard, the Hon'ble Supreme Court in E.V. Chinnah's case stated that, "If benefits of reservation are not percolating to them equitably, measures should be taken to see that they are given such adequate or additional Training so as to enable them to compete with the others but the same would not mean that in the process of rationalizing the reservation to the Scheduled Castes the constitutional mandate of Article 14, 15 and 16 could be violated."

In Vasant Kumar Case, Justice Chinnappa Reddy has rightly observed that, "a few of seats and posts reserved for backward classes are snatched away by the more fortunate among them is not to say that reservation is not necessary. This is bound to happen in a competitive society such so ours. Are not the unreserved seats and posts snatched away, in the same way by the top creamy layer of society itself ? Seats reserved for the backward classes are taken away by the top layers amongst them on the same principle of merit on which the unreserved seats are taken away by the top layers of society."[41]

(d) The Hon'ble Supreme Court in the same case has very rightly observed that "Reservation must be considered from the social objective angle, having regard to the Constitutional Scheme, and not as a political issue and, thus adequate representation must be given to the members of the Scheduled Castes as a group and not to two or more groups of persons or members of castes." Thus all the Scheduled Castes are and ought to be treated as one homogeneous group and their progress as a whole group ought to be our target.

(5) Although the Supreme Court had invalidated the scheme of Sub-Categorization in Andhra Pradesh in its Landmark decision on 05-11-2004, The Andhra Pradesh Assembly at its meeting held on 10-12-2004 resolved to recommend to the Government of India to take up the matter in Parliament.

(a) In view of the said resolution the Government of India had constituted the National Commission under the Leadership of Justice Usha Mehra on 21st May 2007; to examine various facets of the issue of Sub-Categorization in Andhra Pradesh and make suitable recommendations on the future course of action. Justice Usha Mehra visited several places and persons to collect opinion of the people and discussed the matter with several authorities and representatives of the people in Andhra Pradesh. Eventually the said commission submitted its report to the Ministry of Social Justice and Empowerment, Government of India, on 1st May 2008.

(b) The said commission, however, came to the conclusion that the Scheduled Castes are not homogeneous group in view of their traditional occupations and rituals, separate habitation, endogamy, separate dining and caste status and socio-economic status. The commission, eventually concluded that Madigas, Malas, Rellis and Adi-Andhras among the Scheduled Castes be Sub-Categorized for securing the benefits of special safeguards under the Constitution.

(c) It is an acknowledged fact that the criterion for listing some of the castes as Scheduled Castes was "untouchability". If so what could be the criterion for Sub-Categorisation? Sub-Categorization would be obviously based on caste or sub-caste, which is absolutely unlawful. Caste is Constitutionally not a permissible ground on which any benefit could be drawn under the Constitution.

(d) Caste "A" is not respnsible for depriving Caste "B" from the special safeguards. It is the so called Hindu Social System which has been responsible for depriving the so called unoutchable castes from all the benefits. If the protagonists of Sub-Categorisation really want equitable distribution of the benefits may come under one banner and launch a strong movement for distribution of all the benefits of education, administration, property and power in equal terms among all the people of this country. Are they really prepared for that ?

(e) It is difficult to apply the scheme of Sub-Categorisation at the national level. The posts and services under the Union under reservation would be meant for approximately eleven hundred castes and subcastes in the country. If so how the quota would be fixed ? If it is taken at national level is it not against the constitutional mandate under Article 14, 15(4), 16(4) and Article 341 of the Constitution ?

(f) Whether Sub-Categorisation has any beneficial value is a main question. Generally there is total reservation of 15% in the educational institutions and in the public services. In the event of Sub-Categorisation some castes would be brought into a separate sub-group. No doubt the number of such castes in those sub-groups would be reduced; but the number of seats in the re-fixed quota would also be reduced. Again there would be fierce competition for the re-fixed seats for that sub-group. Is there any guarantee that no caste would wrest more benefits in the new situation ?

(6) Dr. S.N. Busi, who had submitted his memorandum to the said National Commission on the issue of Sub-Categorisation of Scheduled Castes in Andhra Pradesh, on 27-06-2007 stated very rightly that, "In its judgement in E.V. Chinnaiah Vs. State of Andhra Pradesh and others (C.A. No. 6758/2000), the Hon'ble Supreme Court of India has made it very clear that the Scheduled Castes mentioned in the presidential order of 1950 shall be considered as one single homogenous group / class for the purpose of extending the helping hand under Articles 15(4) and 16(4) of the Constitution of India. Hence, it is impermissible to resort to sub-categorisation or micro-

classification. The act of sub-categorization/ micro-classification invites wrath of the quality clause under Article 14 Ibid. In view, thereof, even if Article 341 of the Constitution is amended so as to authorize the Parliament to sub-categorize the Scheduled Castes, it would still be held unconstitutional, for such an amendment can not stand the test of equality under Article 14 Ibd. In this connection, it may be noted that Article 14 cannot be amended as it amounts tampering with the basic structure of the Constitution." (Para 13 of the Memorandum)

Thus, the plea of sub-categorization is neither legal and constitutional, nor it is logical and beneficial. It is against the principle of equality, as such it is contradictory to basic structure of the constitution.

Conclusion

As the Constitution provides, the President may specify the Scheduled Castes and the Schedules Tribes; and the Parliament may include in or exclude from the schedules any Caste or Tribes as the case may be. Although no specific criterion is prescribed for such classification, such Castes or Tribes are identified on the basis of their social and ritual low standing and their Tribal status. The Constitution orders promulgated by the President cannot be varied either on the pretext of rationalization of the Schedules or Sub-Categorization of Castes and Tribes. The 'classification' of certain Castes and Tribes is, however meant for their social, educational and economic upliftment.

References

1. Constituent Assembly Debates Vol. IX p. 1638, 17th Sept.1949.
2. Report of The Commissioner for Scheduled Castes and the Scheduled Tribes, 1952. p. 11.
3. Borale P.T. Segregation and De-segregations, p. 65. Manak Tala & Sons Pvt. Ltd. Bombay, 1968.
4. Galanter Marc : Competing Equalities. p. 135. Oxford University Press, Delhi. (1984).
5. Kshirsagar R.K. A Legal view of the problem of S.C. Converts to Buddhism. p. 3.
   Buddha Jyoti Prakashan, Aurangabad. (1989).
6. Galanter Marc : Competing Equalities. p. 135.
7. *Ibid*. p. 147.
8. RC SC ST 1969-70, p. 13.
9. AIR 1964 Pat 201.

10. AIR 1993 SC 477, 579. (Para 117).
11. Annual Report : 2009-2010 : p. 87 Ministry of Social Justice and Empowerment, Govt. of India.
12. Annual Report : 2009-2010. p. 88.
13. AIR 2001 SC 393, 409.
13a. Galanter Marc : Competing Equalities : p. 139.
14. (2000) 2 SCC 20.
15. Annual Report, 2009 to 2010 p. 253, Ministry of Social Justice, New Delhi.
16. See OBC Che Rajkaran: by Uttam Kamble : p. 10. Lokvanmaya Griha, Prabha Devi, Mumbai (2008).
17. However, their demand was not conceded by the justice Ramesh Bapat State Backward Classes Commission in its Report submitted on 16th July 2008 to the Govt. of Maharashtra.
18. Article by P.K. Bhoumik, "Ex-Criminal Tribes of India," in National Museum, Calcutta;1972.
19. *Ibid.*
20. For details see, "Jat Panchayat" by Dr. Narayan Bhosale. Taichi Prakashan, Shivaji Nagar, Pune (2008).
21. For details see, "Bhatakya - Vimuktanche Antrang" by Ramnath Chavan. (1989).
22. An Article by Asaram Guruji published in Lokmat (Aurangabad) dated 14-07-1993.
23. Article by Lelah Dushkin, "Scheduled Caste Politics" in the Untouchables in Contemporary India," p. 221. Edited by Michael Mahar. The University of Arizona Press, Arizona, U.S.A. (1972).
24. *Ibid.* p. 222.
25. *Ibid.* p. 221.
26. Report of the Committee on Untouchability. p. XIX. Dept. of Social Welfare, Govt. of India. (1969).
27. *Ibid.* p. 2.
28. RC SC ST 1975-1977 Part.1 p. 16.
29. Dr. Babasaheb Ambedkar : Writings and Speaches. Vol.7 p. Preface, 339. Education Department, Government of Maharashtra. (1990)
30. The Govt. of Punjab has alloted the quota of fifty percent to Balmikis and Mazabhi Sikhs from among the reserved quota meant for The Scheduled Castes in the State Services. (Act 33 of 2006). Even the Govt. of Tamil Nadu made the provision of special quota for Arunthathiar among the Scheduled Castes. (G.O. No. 61 of 2009).
31. See, DBAWS Vol. 7 Part. 2.
32. CAD Dated 17th Sept. 1949.Vol. IX p. 1938.
33. RC SC ST 1952 p. 11.
34. Galanter Marc, Competing Equalities. p. 135.

35. E.V. Chinnaiah Vs. State of A.P. (2005) 1 Sec. 394.
36. State of Maharashtra Vs. Milind and others. AIR 2001 SC 393.
37. CAD Vol. X, p. 103, 104, Vol. 13, p. 1084.
38. See S.N. Mandal's article, "Scheduled Castes and Scheduled Tribes : Center's role and responsibility," Indian Express : December 9, 1985.
39. Triloki Nath V. State of J & K (1974) 1 SCC 19 as quoted in the Judgement.
40. CAD Vol. 9 p. 1637 quoted.
40(a). It is learnt that such categorization exists for B.C.s in Andhra Pradesh.
41. 1985 Supp. SCC 714.

6

New Economic System and The Backward Classes

The economic development of a nation, however depends on material factors, like natural resources capital formation, agricultural and industrial production, conditions of Trade and Commerce, infrastructural facilities as well as on non-material factors like man power, and technical know-how. All these factors are properly mobilized with a certain objective in a given economic system. The economic system, in turn depends on the socio-political system, generally designed and developed by the Constitution and the contemporary Government.

We have adopted neither capitalist system nor the communist system. We have, obviously adopted the mixed economy with socialist leaning. However, with the advent of new economic policy, we are slowly moving towards capitalist system with all its concomitants and implications.

Under the new economic policy characterized by globalization, liberalization and privatization, Indian economy has sustained a great change. Therefore, it is proposed to know as to what is the essence of constitutional foundation of the economic policy, what is economic policy and the new economic policy, what are its effects on the people in general and the backward classes in particular.

6.1 Constitutional Foundation of Economic Policy

The Constitution under its Preamble, the Fundament Rights (Part III), The Director Principles of State Policy (Part IV) and the Fundamental Duties (Part IVA) has laid down the basic philosophy of Indian Polity.

Under preamble of the Constitution, we have resolved to Constitute India, into a Sovereign socialist secular Democratic Republic and to secure to all its citizens, inter alia, "Justice : Social, Economic and Political."

Our Constitution under its 'Directive Principles of State Policy' provides as under -

Art. 38(1)

The State shall strive to promote the welfare of the people by securing and protecting as effectively as it may a social order in which justice, social, economic and political, shall inform all the institutions of the national life.

Art. 38(2)

The State shall, in particular, strive to minimize the inequalities in income, and endeavour to eliminate inequalities in status, facilities and opportunities, not only amongst individuals but also amongst groups of people residing in different areas or engaged in different vocations.

Art. 39

The state shall in particular, direct its policy towards securing-

(a) That the citizens, men and women equally have the right to an adequate means of livelihood;

(b) That the ownership and control of the material resources of the community are so distributed as best to subserve the common good;

(c) That the operation of the economic system does not result in the concentration of wealth and means of production to the common detriment;

(d) That there is equal pay for equal work for both men and women;

(e) That the health and strength of workers, men and women, and the tender age of children are not abused and that citizens are not forced by economic necessity to enter avocations unsuited to their age or strength.

(f) That children are given opportunities and facilities to develop in a healthy manner and in conditions of freedom and dignity and that childhood and youth are protected against exploitation and against moral and material abandonment."

Art. 46

The state shall promote with special care the educational and economic interests of the weaker sections of the people and, in particular, of the Scheduled Castes and the Scheduled Tribes, and shall protect them from social injustice and all forms of exploitation.

Article 275 provides for grants-in-aid to the State Governments for the purpose of promoting the welfare of the Scheduled Tribes in that state.

Under the first Constitution Amendment Act, 1951, the Ninth Schedule was added to the Constitution, so as to keep away certain land reforms laws from the parliamentary reach. Under the provisons of 44th Amendment Act, 1978, the fundamental right to property was abolished and brought under Article 300A. The Mandal Commission Report was approved by the then Prime-Minister Shri V.P. Singh in August 1990.

Thus, the Constitution of India, which is the Supreme Law of the land has definitely contemplated the economic policy suitable to transform India into Welfare State. The State is expected to assume a role not merely of a police state, but of a welfare state giving freedom from want and fear to all the people. The economic policy cannot be inconsistent with the constitutional directive, which "We, the People of India"[1] have deliberately accepted.

6.2 Economic Policy

(1) In pursuance of our economic objectives as specified in the Constitution of India, we have adopted mixed economic system for achievement of those objectives. We have not accepted the laisseze fair capitalism nor communistic socialism. Thus, we have three economic sectors – (1) Public sector, exclusively managed and controlled by the State. (2) Joint sector managed and controlled by the State and private enterprise; and (3) Private sector, which is fully managed by the private enterprise subject to regulations by the State. We have also developed co-operative sector which is managed by the members of the respective society.

(2) In order to achieve planned and equitable development of all the people and of all the regions, so that they would be able to subserve the national interests, we have introduced planning system in our economic life. For that purpose, we take into account our potential national economic resources and devise the planned way of utilization of all those resources. Till now we have implemented ten five years plans and the eleventh plan is in operation.

(3) We have set an objective of socialistic pattern of society. Under the leadership of Pandit Jawahar Lal Nehru, the ruling national congress resolved to accept the ideal of socialistic

pattern of society in its Avadi Session in January 1955. Again it confirmed its faith in "a Socialist State" in its Jaipur Session in November 1963. Under the Prime-Ministership of Indira Gandhi, the philosophy of socialism has got its due place in the Preamble in 1976.'

(4) We had set up a Legal System in support of the Constitutional objective. We have envisaged a new social order based on justice, liberty, equality and fraternity. We have passed several land reforms Acts including Land Tenancy Acts, Land Ceiling Acts, Inam Abolition Acts; Taxation Laws including Income Tax Act, Wealth Tax Act etc. We have passed the Bank Nationalization Act, Privy Purses Abolition Act, Industrial Disputes Act, Factories Act, Workmens. Compensation Act, Minimum Wages Act, Consumers Protection Act and Insurance Act. We have passed the Protection of Civil-Rights Act, the SC/ST prevention of Atrocities Act, The Protection of Human Rights Act, the Bonded Labour Abolition Act; etc. We have been implementing reservation policy and other safeguards for the Weaker Sections of the Society.

6.3 Land Reforms Policy

(1) Agriculture is the Backbone of Indian Economy. It is also a source of income, prestige, pride and power to the individual land owners. Hence, there is a tendency in our country to hold as much land as possible.

However, total land is not properly used. "Out of total land area of 304 million hectares, net area sown is only 143 million hectares or 47 percent."[2] Still some portion of the forest land, barren land and grazing land which could be cultivable need to be utilized.

In order to free the land from the land lords, land reforms laws have been passed. However, due to inter-relationship between caste, property and power, we couldnot be successful in freeing, land and agricultural labourers. The laws aimed to provide for security of tenure, to fix rents and conditions of Tenancy became unsuccessful.

The laws passed by various State Governments in respect of land reforms were brought under Ninth Schedule of the Constitution, so as to keep them immune from the judicial review.[3]

Indian economy has been primordially caste economy. Land was owned by land owners, necessarily belonging to high caste feudals, it was cultivated by Petty Tenants on petty share in crops. There was the priestly class artisam class and a class of menial servants. All of them were dependent on land. Their status, profession and duties were according to Caste System.

(2) Land Tenure Systems

Before independence there were three types of Land Tenure Systems existing in different parts of our Country. In the Zamindari System, the land actually owned by the hereditary land lords and they were responsible to collect the revenue from the Tenants and pay to the State. In the Mahalwari System, the whole village was treated as a unit and the headman was responsible to collect the land revenue from the Tenants. In the Ryotwari System the land revenue was paid to the state by the individual cultivators. In all the three systems the tenants were actual cultivators of the land and they were exploited by the land lords or the intermediaries. The worst sufferers under all the three systems were the small farmers, land less labourers and the village artisans or workers who belonged to the weaker sections of the society. In order to do away with these unjust systems and to give justice to the common people in accordance with the socialistic objectives of the Constitution, the Land reforms laws were enacted by almost all the State Governments as the matter relating of land and revenue belonged to the state list.

(a) Abolition of Zamindari

In order to protect the right to property of the individuals and to facilitate its acquisition, as and when necessary for the public purposes, the Constitution had initially provided under Article. 31(1) that, "No person shall be deprived of his property save by authority of law; (2) "No property movable or immovable..... shall be taken possession of or acquired for public purposes.... unless the law provides for compensation for the property taken possession of or acquired and either fixes the amount of the compensation or specifies the principles on which and the maner in which, the compensation is to be determined and given."[3(a)]

The said Article stated under clause (4) and (6) that such law having assented to or certified by the President shall not be called in question in any court on the ground that it contravenes Clause (2) of Article 31 as referred to above.

Thus, Article 31(1) had provided protection against the executive authority, but not against the legislative appropriation of property. The state under Article 31(2) was permitted to acquire the property of an individual if the acquisition or requisition is for public purpose and after payment of compensation. Accordingly, certain state laws passed at the time of commencement of the Constitution had abolished Zamindari System prevailing in our Country since a long back.

Consequently, certain laws passed by the State Governments in this respect were challenged by some persons having vested interests in such property. Firstly, the Bihar Land Reforms Act, 1950 was challenged in Kameshwar Singh V. State of Bihar in the Patna High Court.[4] The Patna High Court declared the said Act unconstitutional on the ground of equality provision (Article 14) of the Constitution and not under the property right clause (Article 31)[5]. However in Suryapal Singh V.U.P. Govt.(1951) the Allahabad High Court found the Uttar Pradesh Zamindari Abolition and Land Reforms Act 1950 valid in all respects. In Maloji Rao V. State of Madhya Bharat (1953)[6], the Nagpur High Court found that the Madhya-Pradesh Abolition of proprietary Rights Act, 1950 to be valid.

In order to thwart the legal complications in future the 1st Constitution Amendment Act, 1951 was passed on 18-06-1951; through which two new Articles, 31A and 31 B were inserted after Article 31. The object of Article 31A was to bring about necessary changes in the agricultural economy and to facilitate agrarian reforms. It was specifically stated that no law providing for the acquisition or recquisition of any estate shall be deemed to be violative of Article 14 or Article 19 of the Constitution. Article 31B is to be read with Ninth Schedule to the Constitution, in which 13 Zamindari abolition acts were included so as to keep them above judicial review.

However, the 1st Constitution Amendment Act 1951 was challenged in Shankari Prasad V. Union of India.[7] It was held by the Supreme Court that, the amendment passed by the Parliament according to the procedure laid down in Article 368 would be valid even if it curtailed any of the fundamental rights conferred by Part III of the Constitution. This view was based on the ground that "such an Act would not come under the expression 'Law' in Article 13(2), as such expression is only applicable to a legislative measure and not to a Constituent measure."

Later, in Dwarkadas Shriniwas Vs. Sholapur Spinning and Weaving Company,[8] it was held by the Supreme Court that, the Central enactment by which the said company was taken over by the Government was invalid, and thus infringed the fundamental right of the company. In Bella Bannerjee Vs. State of West Bengal.[9] the Supreme Court observed that what is determined as compensation must be equivalent to what the owner had deprived of.

Consequently, the 4th Constitution Amendment Act, 1955 was brought into operation. It provided that "No law acquiring property compulsorily for a state would be questioned in any court on the ground of inadequacy of compensation."[10] It added 7 more state laws to the 9th Scheduled of the Constitution.

The landlords very much insisted on compensation means, "full compensation", equivalent to market value." The 4th Constitution Amendment, of course specifically mentioned that the agricultural reforms laws would not be challenged on the ground of 'inadequacy of compensation.' However, the validity of this amendment was also successfully challenged in K.K. Kochini Vs. State of Madras (1960)[11] and Karimbil V. State of Kerala (1962).[12]

Again this judicial impediment constrained the Parliament to pass the 17th Constitution Amendment Act, 1964 (20-06-1964). It enlarged the definition of 'estates' contained in Article 31A(2) a so as to cover any Jagir, Inam or Muafi and any land held under ryotwari settlement and any wasteland, pasture, forest land and sites of building etc. It added Entries 21-64 to the 9th Schedule of the Constitution. It aimed to save various land Reforms Acts and protect the farmer cultivating the land personally.

Later, the Constitutionality of this amendment was challenged in Sajjan Singh Vs. State of Rajasthan (1965)[13] but it was affirmed by the Supreme Court. However, this view was over ruled in Golaknath Vs. State of Punjab (1967)[14] and in Cooper Vs. Union of India (1970)[15] (Bank Nationalization Case) and Madhav Rao Scindhia Vs. Union of India (1971)[16] Privy Purses Case. It was held in these cases that the Parliament had no power to abridge or abrogate fundamental rights. The court, observed that the fundamental rights occupied a Transcendental position in the Constitutional Scheme.

In order to nullify the effects of the decisions in the aforesaid cases, the Parliament enacted the Constitution 24th, 25th, 26th and 29th Amendments. The Constitution 24th Amendment Act, 1971 amended Article 368 to nulling the effect of Golaknath's case, by expressly providing that the Parliament had power to amend every part of the Constitution, including the fundamental rights. The Constitution 25th Amendment Act, 1971 substituted "amount" in place of Compensation in Article 31(2); so as to avoid the burden of paying compensation at the rate of market value in cases of acquisition of property. It introduced Article 31C which stated that no law giving effect to directive principles contained in Articles 39(b) and 39(c) would be deemed to be void on the ground of inconsistancy with Article 14, Article 19 or Article 31. The Constitution 26th Amendment Act, 1971 nullified the effect of Privy Purses Case and the Constitution 29th Amendment Act, 1972 added items 65-66 to the 9th Schedule.

Again all these Amendments were challenged in Keshavananda Bharati V. State of Kerala Case (1973).[17] The Supreme Court, however upheld the Constitutionality of these

Amendments but struck down the second part of Article 31C; that is, "no law containing a declaration that it is for giving effect to such policy shall be called in question in any court on the ground that it does not give effect to such policy." It is because the exclusion of this part enables the Courts to enquire into the question about the existence of any rational nexus between the law and object intended to be achieved."[18]

In this case a new doctrine of 'Basic Structure' of the Constitution has come up by majority of the Judges of the Supreme Court. Accordingly the 'basic structure' is inviolable.

It included :-

(1) The Supremacy of the Constitution.
(2) Republican and Democratic form of Government and Sovereignty of the Country.
(3) Secular and federal character of the Constituion.
(4) Demarcation of power between the legislature, the executive and the Judiciary.
(5) The dignity of the individual secured by the various freedoms and basic rights in Part III and the mandate to build a welfare state contained in Part IV.
(6) The unity and the integrity of the nation. (Para 599).

Further, it observed that, "the entire discussion from the point of view of the meaning of the expression" "amendment" as employed in Article 368 and the limitations which arise by implications lead to the result that the amending power under Article 368 is neither narrow nor unlimited." (Para 600)

"On the careful consideration of the various aspects of the case, we are convinced that the Parliament has no power to abrogate or emasculate the basic elements or fundamental features of the Constitution." (Para 682).

"It can also be used to reshape the Constitution within the limits mentioned earlier, to make it an effective instrument for social good." (Para 682)

It was pronounced that judicial review is one of the essential features of the Indian Constitution. Therefore Article 31(c) which stated that any legislative declaration that, Particular law as made to implement the directives in Article 39(b) (c) shall not be open to question in a court, is itself unconstitutional.

Later, the Parliament passed the 42nd Constitution Amendment Act, 1976. It was a comprehensive amendment based on the recommendations of the Swaran Singh Committee. It assigned a supreme position to the directive principles as compared to the fundamental rights. It had amended Article 31(c) and inserted 31D. Accordingly, the Article 31(c) reads as follows :

"Notwithstanding anything contained in Artcle 13, no law giving effect to the Policy of the State towards securing all or any of the principles laid down in Part IV shall be deemed to be void on the ground that it is inconsistent with, or takes away or abridges any of the rights conferred by Article 14, Article 19 or Article 31."

Article 31D has no relation to property. It was related to the freedom of expression and association. However, Article 31D was repealed, among others, by the 43rd Amendment Act, 1977.

Later on, the Parliament passed the 44th Constitution Amendment Act, 1979. The purpose of this Amendment was to do away with the effect of the 42nd Amendment. The 44th Amendment obviously omitted Article 19(1) F and Article 31' related to right to property from Part III, fundamental right; and inserted a new Article 300 A in the Constitution'.

The 44th Amendment, however amended Article 30 relating to right of minorities and inserted Clause (1A) which reads : "In making any law providing for the compulsory acquisition of any property of an educational institution established and administered by a minority, referred to in Clause (1), the state shall ensure that the amount fixed by or determined under such law for the acquisition of such property is such as would not restrict or abrogate the right guaranteed under that clause."

The new Article 300A relating to right to property under Chapter IV of Part XII reads as under : "No Person shall be deprived of his property save by authority of Law." This right is now an ordinary but Constitutional right and not fundamental right.

In the Minerva Mills V. Union (1980) the Supreme Court has observed that the Constitution is founded on the bedrock of the balance between Part III and Part IV. To give absolute primacy to one over the other is to disturb the harmony of the Constitution which is the essential feature of the basic structure. The goals set out in Part IV have to be achieved without the abrogation of the means provided for by Part III. To destroy the guarantees given by Part III in order to achieve the goals of Part IV is plainly to subvert the Constitution.[19]

Thus the main thrust of all these cases was whether, the Directive Principles of State Policy should be given priority over the fundamental rights of the people which are justiciable. Eventually, it has been held that the fundamental rights could be amended but subject to Basic Structure of the Constitution, which included -

(1) Federal Structure, (2) Secularism, (3) Democracy, (4) Limited Power of Parliament to amend the constitution. (5) Harmony and balance between fundamental rights and directive principles;

(6) Fundamental rights. (7) Power of judicial review in certain cases. (8) Independence of Judiciary.

Thus, the Constitution is Supreme, as such the Parliament cannot have unlimited amending power. It may amend the Constitution, but subject to basic structure. In the words of S.P. Sathe, "The basic structure doctrine is a counter majoritarian check on democracy. It saves certain values and institutions from majoritarian tyranny. In a pluralistic nation like India, such counter majoritarian checks are absolutely necessary to provide longevity to democracy."[20]

However the basic structure was not defined in the said cases. In that respect justice Chandrachud pronounced in Indira Gandhi Vs. Rajnarayan (1975) that "...... one has perforce to examine in each individual case the place of the particular feature in the scheme of our Constitution; its object and purpose and the consequences of its denial on the integrity of the Constitution as a fundamental instrument of Country's governance."[21]

We have legally abolished the worst prevailing Zamindari System in our Country for which we had to pay compensation amounting to Rs. 650 crores to the land lords. This has facilitated distribution of 57.7 lakh hectares to landless agriculturists.[22] However, the religious endowments and charitable Inams are still in existence.

(b) Protection to Tenants

Besides, there were some big land owners cultivating their land through the poor-tenants, on lease basis. In 1953-54 the percentage of area leased out varied from 11 to 26 percent. They were being exploited by the land owners and they were not able to bring out the yield to the optimum level. Therefore, it became necessary to regulate the rents, to give security of tenure and to give right of ownership to tenants.

From, first five year plan period tenancy laws were being enacted by various state Governments. The legislation provided for (1) conferring of the right of occupancy on all tenants subject to the owner's right to resume a limited area for personal cultivation. (2) the resumption for personal cultivation to be permitted upto three family holdings. (3) the tenants of the non-resumable area were authorised to purchase the land for the price to be determined in terms of multiple of the rental value of the land. (4) the maximum rates of rent were fixed to the extent of 1/4 to 1/5 of the gross produce in most of the states.

However, there were certain loopholes in the said legislation. It was still permissible to eject the tenants on certain grounds. There is provision regarding "voluntary surrender" of tenancy. the tenants could be easily succumbed to pressures and promises for voluntary surrender of their right to ownership. the term personal cultivation has been so defined to cover cultivation through hired labour. Most of the tenants being from weaker sections of the society were neither in the knowledge of provisions in detail of law, nor they had courage to assert their legal right.

It is however learnt that, "the process of abolition of intermediary tenures which covered more than 40% of area, with few exceptions was completed in the country by 1960 and over two crores cultivators were reported to have come into direct contact with the Government. Only a few minor Inams and Jagirs exist and necessary steps are being taken to remove the last remnants of the feudal system."[22(a)]

So far as conferment of ownership rights to the tenants is concerned, "out of 20 states, such measures have been taken up only in 12 states, viz. Assam, Bihar, Gujarat, Karnataka, Andhra Pradesh, Haryana, Manipur, Maharashtra, Orissa, Tamil Nadu, Tripura and Punjab. No such measures exist in the other 8 states. In four states out of 12 states where provisions to confer ownership right exists, it is noticed that these provisions have not been legally enforced as yet. These states are Assam, Bihar, Manipur and Tripura."[22(b)]

Following Table shows the number of Tenants who have been Conferred Ownership till 1980.

TABLE 6.1

Sr.No.	*States*	*Conferment of Ownership Right*	
		No. of Tenants	*Land Area involved*
1.	Gujarat	11.86 lakhs	24.10 La.ha.
2.	Orissa	36.278	35.709 acres
3.	Karnataka	3.15 lakhs	12.37 La. acres
4.	Maharashtra	11.92 lakhs	13.80 La. acres
5.	Haryana	12.300	23.500 acres

(*Source* : RCSCST, 1979-1980, p. 24).

(c) Ceiling on Holdings

Almost al the State Governments have passed land ceiling Acts, so as to restrict the land lord to hold more than, what is

TABLE 6.2
Ceiling Limits on Land Holdings

(In hectares)

Sr. No.	*State*	*Irrigated with two crops*	*Irrigated with one crop*	*Dry Land*
1.	Andhra Pradesh	4.05 to 7.28	6.07 to 10.93	14.16 to 21.85
2.	Assam	6.74	6.74	6.74
3.	Bihar	6.07 to 7.28	10.12	12.14 to 18.21
4.	Gujarat	4.05 to 7.28	6.07 to 10.93	8.09 to 21.85
5.	Haryana	7.25	10.9	21.8
6.	Himachal Pradesh	4.05	6.07	12.14 to 28.33
7.	Jammu & Kashmir	3.6 to 5.06	--	5.95 to 9.20
8.	Karnataka	4.05 to 8.10	10.12 to 12.14	21.85
9.	Kerala	4.86 to 6.07	4.86 to 6.07	4.86 to 6.07

(Table Contd.)

(Contd. Table 6.2)

Sr. No.	*State*	*Irrigated with two crops*	*Irrigated with one crop*	*Dry Land*
10.	Madhya Pradesh	7.28	10.93	21.85
11.	Maharashtra	7.28	10.93	21.85
12.	Manipur	5.00	5.00	6.00
13.	Orissa	4.05	6.07	12.14 to 18.21
14.	Punjab	7.00	11.00	20.50
15.	Rajasthan	7.28	10.93	21.85 to 70.82
16.	Tamil Nadu	4.86	12.14	24.28
17.	Sikkim	5.06	--	20.23
18.	Tripura	4.00	4.00	12.00
19.	Uttar Pradesh	7.30	10.95	18.25
20.	West Bengal	5.00	5.00	7.00

Source : Ministry of Agriculture, Agricultural Statistics at a Glance (2002), p. 250.

TABLE 6.3

Extent of land distributed among Scheduled Castes and Scheduled Tribes under Land Ceiling Laws as on 18-12-1980

(In Acres)

S.No.	*State / U.T.*	*Total*	*Scheduled Castes*	*Percentage of Total*	*Scheduled Tribes*	*Percentage to Total*
1.	Andhra Pradesh	2,69,337	1,26,935	47.30	48.298	18.00
2.	Assam	3,12,802	24,196	7.74	30.298	9.69
3.	Bihar	1,31,000	53,800	44.07	15.200	11.60
4.	Gujarat	3,664	2,527	68.97	184.00	5.02
5.	Haryana	9,313	4,658	50.02	Nil	Nil
6.	Himachal Pradesh	4,773	3,401	71.25	28.00	0.69
7.	Jammu & Kashmir	--	--	--	--	--
8.	Karnataka	44,540	22,990	51.62	3,197	7.18
9.	Kerala	49,835	17,460	38.04	4,395	8.82
10.	Madhya Pradesh	76,892	19,240	25.02	37,671	48.99

(Table Contd.)

(Contd. Table 6.3)

S.No.	State / U.T.	Total	Scheduled Castes	Percentage of Total	Scheduled Tribes	Percentage to Total
11.	Maharashtra	2,80,315	91,853	32.77	51.640	10.42
12.	Manipur	Nil	Nil	Nil	Nil	Nil
13.	Orissa	99,606	30,657	30.78	43,145	43.32
14.	Punjab	5,161	2,339	45.32	Nil	Nil
15.	Rajasthan	1,21,665	42,664	35.07	14,279	11.74
16.	Tamil Nadu	50,821	15,074	29.66	11	0.02
17.	Tripura	938	195	20.79	182	19.40
18.	Uttar Pradesh	2,23,251	1,33,669	39.87	Nil	Nil
19.	West Bengal	52,397	N.A.	N.A.	N.A.	N.A.
20.	Dadra & Nagar Haveli	3,192	28	0.88	3,164	99.12
21.	Delhi	Nil	Nil	Nil	Nil	Nil
22.	Pondicherry	837	595	71.09	Nil	Nil
	Total	**17,39,339**	**5,92,281**	**34.05**	**2,51,690**	**14.47**

(RCSCST. 1979-1980. p. 60).

TABLE 6.4
No. of Beneficiaries Scheduled Castes and Scheduled Tribes under Land Ceiling Acts as on 18.12.1980

S.No.	State / U.T.	Total Number of Beneficiaries	Scheduled Castes	Percentage	Scheduled Tribes	Percentage
1.	Andhra Pradesh	1,84,274	91,070	49.42	28,194	15.30
2.	Assam	2,53,811	20,798	8.19	17,859	7.04
3.	Bihar	1,38,299	75,000	54.23	15,500	11.21
4.	Gujarat	826	575	69.61	31	3.75
5.	Haryana	2,992	1,514	50.60	Nil	Nil
6.	Himachal Pradesh	6,921	4,793	69.25	N.A	N.A
7.	Jammu & Kashmir	Nil	Nil	Nil	Nil	Nil
8.	Karnataka	8,565	4,444	51.89	611	7.13
9.	Kerala	78,609	30,718	39.08	5,267	6.70
10.	Madhya Pradesh	30,633	8,709	28.43	13,027	42.53

(Table Contd.)

(Contd. Table 6.4)

S.No.	*State / U.T.*	*Total Number of Beneficiaries*	*Scheduled Castes*	*Percentage*	*Scheduled Tribes*	*Percentage*
11.	Maharashtra	76,581	24,229	31.64	15,575	20.34
12.	Manipur	Nil	Nil	Nil	Nil	Nil
13.	Orissa	75,523	25,204	33.37	29,701	39.33
14.	Punjab	2,717	1,276	46.96	Nil	Nil
15.	Rajasthan	26,017	10,658	40.97	3,921	15.07
16.	Tamil Nadu	30,339	12,815	42.24	13	0.04
17.	Tripura	800	170	21.25	155	19.38
18.	Uttar Pradesh	1,81,339	1,33,698	73.73	Included in SC	Nil
19.	West Bengal	1,16,374	52,225	44.88	22,985	19.75
20.	Dadra & Nagar Haveli	1,412	13	0.92	1,399	--
21.	Delhi	Nil	Nil	Nil	Nil	Nil
22.	Pondicherry	960	716	74.58	Nil	Nil
	Total	**12,16,992**	**4,98,625**	**40.97**	**1,54,271**	**12.68**

(RCSCST. 1979-1980. p. 61).

TABLE 6.5

Average Size of Land Holdings Distributed (In Acres) under Land Ceiling Acts as on 18-12-1980

S.No.	*State / U.T.*	*General*	*Scheduled Castes*	*Scheduled Tribes*
1.	Andhra Pradesh	1.46	1.39	1.71
2.	Assam	1.23	1.16	1.70
3.	Bihar	0.95	0.72	0.98
4.	Gujarat	4.44	4.39	5.26
5.	Haryana	3.11	3.00	Nil
6.	Himachal Pradesh	0.69	0.71	N.A.
7.	Jammu & Kashmir	Nil	Nil	Nil
8	Karnataka	5.20	5.17	5.23
9.	Kerala	0.63	0.57	0.83
10.	Madhya Pradesh	2.51	2.21	2.89

(Table Contd.)

(Contd. Table 6.5)

S.No.	*State / U.T.*	*General*	*Scheduled Castes*	*Scheduled Tribes*
11.	Maharashtra	3.66	3.79	3.32
12.	Manipur	Nil	Nil	Nil
13.	Orissa	1.32	1.22	1.45
14.	Punjab	1.90	1.83	Nil
15.	Rajasthan	4.68	4.00	3.64
16.	Tamil Nadu	1.68	1.18	0.85
17.	Tripura	1.17	1.15	1.17
18.	Uttar Pradesh	1.23	1.01	Nil
19.	West Bengal	0.45	N.A.	N.A.
20.	Dadra & Nagar Haveli	2.26	2.15	2.26
21.	Delhi	Nil	Nil	Nil
22.	Pondicherry	0.87	0.83	--
	Total :	**1.43**	**1.33**	**1.92**

(RCSCST. 1979-1980. p. 62).

required for a family and to distribute the surplus land to the landless agricultural labourers. The following table shows the upper limit on land holdings for each family.

Accordingly one can retain that much portion of land which is generally required for one's livelihood. But the laws are not properly implemented. Landlordism is openly prevailing irrespective of land ceiling laws, law implementing machinery and leaders and unions. In the words of Benedict Costa, "India is a country of Small Scale farming, with average size of the farm holding being 6.4 acres. About 62 per cent of the cultivators farm less than 5 acres, 31 per cent farm from 5 to 20 acres, 6 percent farm from 20 to 50 acres, and one per cent farm more than 50 acres."[23] Shri B.D. Sharma the then Commissioner for SC and ST cites two glaring examples of the village landlords one in Palamau district of Bihar who holds about 4000 to 5000 acres of land, and other is in Pulimamidi near Hyderabad in A.P. who also holds about 5000 acres of land.[24] Probably there could be many more such examples. There seems to be an inherent tendency of grabbing land by this or that way and accumulating the same at the cost of the poor cultivators and landless labourers. According to Rudra datta and Sundaram, "Out of the total area of 4.3 million acres declared as surplus, only 3 million was acquired till December 1983, out of which only 2.1 million acres (or 46 per cent) were distributed."[25] There were as many as 1.6 million land ceiling cases pending in the courts all over the country, till the end of 1984.[26]

(d) Benefit of Land ceiling Legislation

In order to avert accumulation of land with a few land Lords and to distribute surplus land to the landless agriculturists, it became necessary to pass land ceilings laws. They are brought under 9th Schedule of the Constitution, so as to avoid any litigation on the ground of their validity. Whcthor they have proved to be of any avail to the poor landless SC and STs is a pertinent question. However, due to certain exemptions and flaws in the respective state laws and improper implementation, the land ceiling laws were not proved to be of much benefit. The Report of the Commission for Scheduled Castes and Scheduled Tribes (1979-1980) enlighten on this point.

What is the share of the Scheduled Castes and Scheduled Tribes in the land holdings is the main question. Prof. Munagekar, after referring to National Sample Survey Organization report states that, in the year 1987-88, 20.4 per cent Scheduled Castes had no land and in the year 1993-94 18.1 per cent people had no land. In case of Scheduled Tribes 12.6 percent people had no land in the year 1987-88 and the percentage of landless people increased upto 13.3 in 1993-94.[27]

The majority of the land owners from amongst the SC, ST owned marginal land below one hectare or so. The landless labourers and marginal farmers work on the land of landlords.

They are paid minimum wages. They are largely indebted and work as bonded labour. The bounded labour Abolition Act has been passed in 1976, but it is not properly implemented. Most of the people survive below poverty line. In the year 1993-94 so far as SCs are concerned in the rural area 48.11 percent and in the urban area 49.48 percent and so far as STs are concerned 51.94 percent in rural area and 41.14 percent in urban area were living below poverty line.[28] See Table 6.3, 6.4, and 6.5.

6.4 Scheduled Caste Sub-Plan and Tribal Sub-Plan

(a) In order to achieve overall socio-economic development of the people, the Government of India, with the help of the planning commission under the chairmanship of the Prime-Minister, formulated the five year plans virtually from the commencement of the Constitution itself. However, the Government of India realised the drawbacks in the process of Planning in as much as it related to the SC/STs, at the end of fifth five year plan. The fact was there was no allocation of plan outlays / especially for the development of the weaker sections in proportion to their population and their requirements.

The following table shows the percentage share of Backward Classes sector out of the plan outlays upto sixth plan period.

TABLE 6.6

in Crores

Plan Period	*Total Public Sector Outlay*	*Backward Classes Sector Outlay*	*Percentage*
I Plan	2378	39	1.6
II Plan	4800	90	1.8
III Plan	7500	114	1.5
IV Plan	15902	171	1.0
V Plan	39303	228	0.6
VI Plan	97600	960	0.9
Total :	**167383**	**1602**	**0.9**

(*Source* : RCSCST 1979-80, Second, p. 65).

The Commission for SC, ST also noted that, "barely 1% of the total public sector outlays was earmarked under Backward Classes

Sector during various plan periods whereas the population of Scheduled Castes and Scheduled Tribes was 14.67% and 6.80% respectively. Even this meagre outlay of 1% was not wholly meant for Scheduled Castes and Scheduled Tribes and included in it a provision of other Backward Classes also as defined by the Planning Commission, with the result that the actual allocations available for Scheduled Castes and Scheduled Tribes were less than even 1%." Therefore, the commission felt that, "during the VI Five year plan a radical approach, matched with adequate funds should be evolved."[28(a)]

Therefore, the government had decided to adopt a new strategy of formulation of plan outlays taking into account the proportion of SC and ST population in the total population and the special needs of those people in different areas. It was decided to bring out the weaker sections living below poverty line to the general level by adopting the special component plan now it is known as SCSP (Scheduled Caste Sub-Plan) for the economic development of the Scheduled Castes from 1979-1980 and the Tribal Sub-Plan for the development of the Scheduled Tribes, from the 1974-78. These plans, however, formed the special part of the plan outlays from the sixth plan period (1980-85) onwards.

In order to achieve the objectives of the The Scheduled Caste Sub-Plan and the Tribal Sub-Plan, it was decided (1) to make proper allocation of outlays for different sectors of the economy taking into account the proportion of the weaker sections in the total population and the needs of the target groups for their composite upliftment, (2) to give special emphasis on agriculture based allied activities like animal husbandry, dairy, forestry, cooperations and small scale industries, and (3) to formulate such schemes which would give direct benefit exclusively to the Scheduled Castes and Tribes individuals and families to the maximum possible extent.

Under Article 275 (1) of the Constitution of India grants from the Consolidated fund of India each year for promoting the welfare of the Scheduled Tribes are provided by the Ministry of Tribal Affairs to all Tribal sub-plan states (22) and (4) Tribal majority states of the Country (total 26 states). The grants are sanctioned to the states on the basis of the percentage of ST population in the state concerned.

Although the SCSP and TSPs are formulated, respectively for the development of the SCs and STs, they are not properly implemented. Even the allocations made for certain purposes are being diverted for other irrelevant purposes. In order to avoid such misuse of Public money the Planning Commission had appointed a

Task Force under the Chairmanship of Dr. Narendra Jadhav for enlisting suggestions on the matter. The said committee in its meeting held on 2nd Sept. 2010 had suggested to the Government to make a law forbidding such misuse; but in vain.[28(b)] Sometime the amount is not fully utilized and such unutilized amount is not carried forward for the next year. It is submitted that every care should be taken to utilize the allocation made under the said Sub-Plans.

(b) In addition to the allocation of outlays under the special component plans at the various state level, the Special Central Assistance is given to the financing corporations for the implementation of the centrally sponsored schemes. The assistance is given to contribute towards the equity capital of the corporations which is shared between the centre and the states on 49:51 basis. It is an additive to the states special component plans. The SCA funds are being utilized for the schemes of margin money, subsidy and training.

(c) In order to undertake income generating schemes under the special component plan, one has to contribute the margin money, which lacks with the Scheduled Caste members, they are unable to get co.ordination among different agencies and they have no knowledge of inputs like raw materials and improved technical knowledge. Therefore the financial corporations are established to cater as catalysts to the needs of the Scheduled Castes. These corporations are expected :

(1) to mobilize at the State level sufficient finance both from the Commercial banking sector and the co-operative sector.

(2) to formulate suitable and viable family oriented schemes for the Scheduled Castes in different areas and occupational groups in the state.

(3) to play a catalystic role in providing financial and non-financial inputs. For that purpose necessary linkages with various credit and marketing institutions and Technological departments have to be established. Thus, the main functions of the SC Development Corporations are mobilisation of institutional credit for the economic development schemes of the Scheduled Castes entrepreneurs by functioning as catalysts, promoters and guarantors.

(d) There are Tribal Development Co-operative Corporations in some of the states. They are expected to serve the Tribal Community by advancing loans for agricultural produce, exploiting forest wealth, sale of consumer goods, grant of loans for new occupations, traders etc.

TABLE 6.7

Special Central Assistance to Scheduled Caste Component Plan Released to States / UTS During 2007-08, 2008-09 and 2009-10

(Rs. in Lakhs)

S.No.	States / UTs	2007-08 Actual Release	2007-08 Beneficiaries Assisted	2008-09 Actual Release	2008-09 Beneficiaries Assisted	2009-10 Actual Release	2009-10 Beneficiaries Assisted
1	2	3	4	5	6	7	8
1.	Arunachal Pradesh	4476.42	196735	5167.85	217205	3668.5	--
2.	Assam	972.70	9557	1089.04	3219	12.1	--
3.	Bihar	1268.76	--	4009.15	--	1916.9	--
4.	Chhattisgarh	294.30	--	547.21	--	220.8	--
5.	Gujarat	1111.40	--	959.52	--	932.9	--
6.	Goa	0.00	--	0.00	--	0.00	--
7.	Haryana	1443.53	16643	1213.48	12926	1152.7	8397
8.	Himachal Pradesh	1035.64	20936	517.08	24943	453.8	7744
9.	Jammu & Kashmir	161.61	--	230.48	--	173.2	--

(Table Contd.)

(Contd. Table 6.7)

S.No.	States / UTs	2007-08		2008-09		2009-10	
		Actual Release	Beneficiaries Assisted	Actual Release	Beneficiaries Assisted	Actual Release	Beneficiaries Assisted
1	2	3	4	5	6	7	8
10.	Jharkhand	0.00	--	574.94	--	0.00	--
11.	Karnataka	2723.09	15913	3605.30	18374	2464.4	--
12.	Kerala	312.72	--	813.12	--	763.2	--
13.	Madhya Pradesh	3822.66	12500	4806.42	--	2532.4	--
14.	Maharashtra	3398.55	19053	4222.80	--	2880.7	11633
15.	Manipur	0.00	--	0.00	--	0.00	--
16.	Orissa	2453.49	14528	2832.14	20283	1010.5	--
17.	Punjab	375.85	12006	1004.07	6996	1075.9	--
18.	Rajasthan	3988.14	22532	3331.86	37341	2433.1	--
19.	Sikkim	52.40	--	40.06	20	22.60	--

(Table Contd.)

(Contd. Table 6.7)

S.No.	States / UTs	2007-08		2008-09		2009-10	
		Actual Release	*Beneficiaries Assisted*	*Actual Release*	*Beneficiaries Assisted*	*Actual Release*	*Beneficiaries Assisted*
1	*2*	*3*	*4*	*5*	*6*	*7*	*8*
20.	Tamil Nadu	4897.99	49985	6002.81	43845	3930.4	1459
21.	Tripura	424.90	--	311.42	2592	355.60	--
22.	Uttar Pradesh	11023.37	119499	14351.57	65140	8898.6	60244
23.	Uttarakhand	594.24	1503	0	3142	0.0	2009
24.	West Bengal	5158.23	--	4503.80	--	3262.3	--
25.	Chandigarh	25.00	--	25.00	--	18.8	--
26.	Delhi	0.0	--	0.0	--	0.0	--
27.	Pondicherry	125.00	608	0	278	0.0	451
	Total All India	**50139.99**	**511998**	**60159.12**	**456304**	**38179**	**91937**

Source : Ministry of Social Justice and Empowerment : Govt. of India, Annual Report : 2009-10, p. 242.

TABLE 6.8
Funds Released under SCA to TSP during 2002-03 to 2009-10 (As on 31-12-09)

(Rs. in Lakh)

S.No.	Name of State / U.T.	2002-03	2003-04	2004-05	2005-06	2006-07	2007-08	2008-09	2009-10 As on (31/12/09)
1.	Andhra Pradesh	2732.80	2459.52	2459.52	2751.14	3344.33	3712.99	4176.75	1930.00
2.	Assam	3058.99	2753.09	2064.82	3066.59	3601.59	3220.27	3755.65	2883.00
3.	Bihar	556.56	500.90	250.45	543.57	656.00	715.50	0.00	870.94
4.	Chhattisgarh	4626.18	4405.12	5397.76	4641.08	5477.04	5893.78	6829.20	6322.88
5.	Goa	0.00	0.00	0.00	0.00	110.00	133.00	0.00	0.00
6.	Gujarat	3930.91	3743.09	3537.82	3963.52	4882.13	5419.14	4571.435	2800.00
7.	Himachal Pradesh	643.53	612.79	750.87	825.90	1022.14	1133.43	1276.00	1179.40
8.	Jharkhand	5870.24	5283.22	5283.22	5896.10	7041.25	7711.12	2198.25	0.00
9.	J & K	971.94	925.50	874.75	901.28	1088.00	956.24	676.00	0.00
10.	Karnataka	771.33	694.19	899.97	1029.06	1242.00	1372.00	1544.00	1647.96

(Table Contd.)

(Contd. Table 6.8)

S.No.	*Name of State / U.T.*	*2002-03*	*2003-04*	*2004-05*	*2005-06*	*2006-07*	*2007-08*	*2008-09*	*2009-10 As on (31/12/09)*
11.	Kerala	273.70	260.62	319.35	274.03	318.13	352.36	396.25	366.10
12.	Madhya Pradesh	8733.22	7458.93	9139.70	8186.01	10126.02	9129.39	12644.25	8722.00
13.	Maharashtra	3823.83	3351.45	3351.45	3351.45	3888.00	4293.00	2500.00	895.91
14.	Manipur	731.96	725.55	685.76	685.76	796.00	879.00	989.00	527.795
15.	Orissa	6495.30	6184.94	7578.63	6516.82	7695.87	8543.41	10110.50	8885.55
16.	Rajasthan	3649.56	3284.60	3284.60	3490.91	4214.00	4654.00	5236.00	3400.00
17.	Sikkim	108.02	102.86	126.04	109.49	135.52	280.36	315.00	291.38
18.	Tamil Nadu	323.32	290.99	377.25	323.70	375.55	142.59	469.00	108.00
19.	Tripura	1041.03	991.29	1214.66	1045.03	1240.34	1318.28	1548.00	1431.29
20.	Uttar Pradesh	32.10	30.57	37.45	33.63	0.00	425.36	644.25	0.00
21.	Uttarakhand	92.91	88.47	83.62	83.62	50.00	0.00	0.00	50.00
22.	West Bengal	2202.57	1982.31	1982.31	1982.31	2270.00	2894.59	3255.75	2654.34
	Grand Total :	**49700.00**	**46130.00**	**49700.00**	**49701.00**	**59573.91**	**63179.81**	**63135.29**	**44966.545**

Source : Ministry of Tribal Affairs, Govt. of India Report (2009-10), p. 96.

TABLE 6.9
Funds Released under Article 275(1) of the Constitution during X Plan and XI Plan

(Rs. in Lakh)

S.No.	Name of State / U.T.	2002-03	2003-04	2004-05	2005-06	2006-07	2007-08	2008-09	2009-10 As on (31/12/09)
1.	Andhra Pradesh	2160.30	1785.00	2300.46	3112.31	2830.31	2453.03	1863.44	1946.20
2.	Arunachal Pradesh	300.00	200.00	273.72	384.06	322.52	544.29	308.68	0.00
3.	Assam	1023.40	668.87	1155.00	1381.41	1514.17	1192.63	1444.88	1240.77
4.	Bihar	209.00	209.00	229.90	0.00	293.00	319.20	0.00	95.00
5.	Chhattisgarh	2689.50	2089.00	2858.56	3479.69	4131.86	3090.44	3211.43	2834.80
6.	Goa	0.00	0.00	0.00	0.00	62.00	68.45	7.00	0.00
7.	Gujarat	2250.00	2280.00	2515.00	5660.96	3964.38	3652.68	2372.77	58.00
8.	Himachal Pradesh	80.00	80.00	109.36	133.88	330.33	165.43	148.32	180.00
9.	Jharkhand	2808.00	2208.00	2428.80	400.00	3244.15	3060.27	1852.43	3730.00
10.	J & K	318.00	367.00	398.70	361.29	427.00	286.61	193.66	0.00
11.	Karnataka	904.35	797.00	957.88	1519.35	1526.87	1458.05	1496.37	1823.00

(Table Contd.)

(Contd. Table 6.9)

S.No.	Name of State / U.T.	2002-03	2003-04	2004-05	2005-06	2006-07	2007-08	2008-09	2009-10 As on (31/12/09)
12.	Kerala	588.00	158.00	161.56	0.00	497.19	101.52	159.42	134.92
13.	Madhya Pradesh	4052.32	3821.58	5173.57	6420.27	6052.44	5973.00	6466.80	6435.00
14.	Maharashtra	2925.00	2672.00	2939.20	3459.20	2508.35	3610.310	2441.46	2000.00
15.	Manipur	424.55	230.00	253.00	0.00	411.00	311.96	324.44	352.50
16.	Meghalaya	555.00	50.55	759.50	0.00	0.00	773.02	155.33	0.00
17.	Mizoram	240.00	240.00	488.41	422.62	384.17	409.79	403.57	441.00
18.	Nagaland	0.00	0.00	529.58	700.93	812.22	866.170	200.00	576.59
19.	Orissa	3641.60	2830.00	4346.98	4445.48	4029.11	4176.84	4219.73	7026.00
20.	Rajasthan	2224.48	2070.00	2200.00	2240.48	3160.00	3168.91	3107.04	1500.00
21.	Sikkim	83.00	33.00	45.20	143.92	50.99	101.50	65.00	149.20
22.	Tamil Nadu	210.00	250.00	287.40	619.57	477.62	0.00	291.39	342.00
23.	Tripura	665.50	313.00	428.30	412.28	570.32	485.04	434.88	780.00
24.	Uttar Pradesh	27.00	27.00	36.82	0.00	0.00	499.12	391.28	0.00
25.	Uttarakhand	78.00	128.00	135.80	0.00	249.00	107.81	20.00	120.00
	West Bengal	1543.00	1763.00	1987.30	2702.30	2151.00	2151.620	2489.09	2320.00
	Grand Total	**30000.00**	**25270.00**	**33000.00**	**38000.00**	**40000.00**	**39027.69**	**33978.41**	**34084.98**

Source : Ministry of Tribal Affairs, Govt. of India Report (2009-10), p. 97.

(e) There is one National Backward Classes Finance and Development Corporation (NBCFDC) since 1992. Its authorised share capital is Rs.700 Crore. The Corporation provides additional source of finance to backward classes for economically viable schemes and projects. It provides term loan and margin money loan to the extent of 85% and 40% respectively. It provides education loan for pursuing professional or technical education to the extent of Rs.1.25 lakh to Rs. 5 lakh per studnet. It provides micro finance loans to the self-help groups to the exent of Rs.25,000 per beneficiary. It provides loans to the Special Schemes of the women, under New Swarnima and Mahila Samruddhi Yojana.[29] See Table No. 6:7, 6: 8 and 6:9.

6.5 Industrial Policy

(1) The Government of India declared its industrial policy firstly in 1948, secondly in 1956, thirdly in 1977 and fourthly in 1980. Accordingly they have defined small scale industries, and large scale industries and decided to undertake effective operational management and promote regional balances. The top public sector industries, including steel, coal, textile, cement, were started on large scale.

(2) The public sector industries run by the Union Government were in profit to some extent but the performance of industries run by the State Governments was not satisfactory. There were twenty large industrial houses in India till 1986 with total assets to the tune of Rs. 23,156 Crores.[30] On the other hand, the large industries including Engineering, Cotton, Chemicals, Sugar, Jute, Rubber, Cement etc., were becoming sick progressively. From 1980 to 1986 total 1,47,740 industrial units were sick with a huge amount of outstanding Bank Credit of Rs. 4,874 Crores.[31]

(3) In all the large industries the owners and managers were high caste persons, none of them belonged to Dalits. This reveals that they utterly failed in proving their merit and efficiency; and mismanaged the huge bank credit and other infrastructure.

In this background India had to accept the New Economic Policy in 1991.

6.6 New Economic Policy

India was moving ahead, though slowly, with socialistic agenda till 1985. When Rajiv Gandhi became Prime-Minister of India in 1985, he outlined the new economic policy of the Government.

The main Constituents of the new economic policy were as under :

(1) Expanding the role of Private Sector

It was felt necessary to expand the role of private sector in industrial activities like power-generation, transport, fertilizers, steel and Patroleum. It wanted to introduce the element of competition in Public sector as well as private sector to achieve more production.

(2) Modernization of Industries

It was decided to bring in new sophiscated technology to achieve target oriented production within a given time and relaxation in MRTP.

(3) Policy of Liberalization in Trade of Goods and Services

Liberalization includes opening up of economy to foreign direct investment by providing facilities to foreign companies; allowing Indian companies to enter into foreign collaboration in India and encouraging to set up joint ventures abroad and delicensing.

(4) Import-export mobilization

It was decided to allow the companies to determine their own exchange rate in the 'international market without official intervention.'

(5) Long Term Fiscal Policy

It was proposed to bring in additional resources for financing the anti-poverty programme. It was also proposed to revise the tax structure and to increase the share of direct taxes in total tax revenue.

(6) Curtailment of Non-Plan Expenditure

It was decided to curtail the non-plan expenditure including (a) defence expenditure (b) interest payment and (c) food and fertilizer - subsidies, (d) social welfare mesures etc.

(7) Reform of Indirect Taxes

It was proposed to merge various excise duties into a single basic rate. The loss of duty on input would be recovered through higher excise taxation on final products known as VAT. It was announced to take strict action against the income tax evaders and smugglers.

TABLE 6.10
Foreign Direct Investment inflows
(Countrywise)

Country	*U.S. Millions* 2007-08	2006-07	2005-06	2004-05
Mauritius	9518	3780	1363	820
USA	950	706	346	469
Japan	457	80	86	122
Germany	486	116	45	143
UK	508	1809	261	84
Netherlands	601	559	50	196
Total (Incl. Others)	**19427**	**9307**	**3359**	**2320**

Statistical Outlines of India : 2009-10.
Tata Services Ltd. Mumbai (2010) p.166.

Later on, under the leadership of P.V. Narasimha Rao, a major change in the economic strategy was occured in July 1991. India accepted the new economic policy based on globalisation, liberalisation and privatisation.

Thus, there occured a major shift from the socialistic pattern of society visualised by Pandit Nehru to the capitalistic pattern of society under the leadership of Prime Minister P.V. Narasimha Rao.

The matter of common Trade and Tariff Policy was under consideration of World Nations from 1946 itself. They reached to interim agreement in 1948. Finally, the proposals submitted by Dunkel in 1986 were brought before the Uruguya Round on 20th December 1991, and the proposals were finally approved on 15th December 1993. India approved the (GA TT) in March 1994. It was renamed with certain additional provisions as World Trade Oranization (WTO) on Jan.1, 1995.

The Major thrust of WTO is on free market and open competition, increase in production through modern technology, no restrictions on import or exports, reduction in the share of Government in Public Sector, Transfer of ownership and management in public sector and curtailment of subsidies. This would certainly cause a major turn from our previous economic system.

Even when the new economic policy was on envil, the National Convention of SC and ST Parliamentarian and Legislators stated on 16th June 1992 in New Delhi that "the new economic policy had been formulated without either consulting the SC and ST opinion or taking into account its impact on these communities." It further stated that, "the new economic policy is based on "Market-Friendliness" but the market has never been friendly to the SCs and STs". Thus, they resolved inter alia against the new economic policy. It was reportedly attended by 350 Sc/ST Parliamentarians and legislators in the country.[32] However, their resolution had no effect on the economic policy of our country.

6.7 Aspects of New Economic Policy

In view of the new economic Policy, The Government of India formulated new policies and plans in respect of industries, agriculture, foreign trade, education, five year plan and services.

(a) New Industrial Policy, 1991

The major changes in the matters relating to industries are as under :

(1) Abolition of Industrial Licensing

In pursuance of the New Industrial Policy, it was decided to remove the barrier of licensing in a phase manner. Till now almost all the industries are delicensed. Presently licensing is compulsory for only six industries. They are alcohol, cigarettes, hazardous chemicals, electronics aerospace and defence equipment, drugs and pharmaceuticals and industrial explosives.

(2) Public Sector Curtailed

The 1956 resolution had reserved 17 industreis for the Public sector. Presently only three industreis are reserved exclusively for the public sector. They are atomic energy, certain minerals and rail transport.

(3) MRTP Limit removed

Under the Monopolies and Restrictive Trade Practices Act all firms with assets above a certain size (Rs.100 Crores since 1985) were classified as MRTP firms. Such firms were permitted to enter selected industries only. Now such limits of assets is removed. The Act was accordingly amended.

(4) Foreign Direct Investment Allowed

Presently foreign direct investment is allowed in all sectors including services sector, subject to specified ceilings.

(b) National Agriculture Policy, 2000

The main features of the National Agriculture Policy, 2000 are as under :

(1) It is proposed to increase private sector participation through contract farming and land leasing arrangements.

(2) The Policy hopes to achieve sustainable development of agriculture, create gainful employment and raise standard of living.

(3) The policy envisages to evolve a 'National Livestock Breeding Strategy' to meet the requirement of milk, meat, eggs and livestock products.

(4) Plant varieties would be protected by law to encourage research and breeding of new varieties. Therefore, the Parliament has passed the 'Protection of plant varieties and farmers Act in 2001.'

(5) It is proposed to provide a frame work for the long term reform of agricultural trade with the objective of providing market access, regulating domestic support and export subsidies.

(6) Rural electrification would be given high priority.
(7) Progressive institutionalization of rural and farm credit would be continued for providing timely and adequate credit to farmers.
(8) In order to bring Patent Legislation in line with the requirement of WTO, it was amended once in 1999 and second in 2002; and later in 2005. Under trade related intellectual property rights [TRIPs] Agreement, methods of agriculture, horticulture and bio-technological process are patentable.

6.8 Impact of New Econommic Policy

It is necessary to critically evaluate impact of the new economic policy in general, but it is beyond the purview of the present study. However, it is proposed to gaze succinctly its effects on Indian economy.

(1) Under the influence of GATT/WTO India allowed Foreign Direct Investment (FDI) to a great extent. We have allowed foreign multinational companies to operate their business in India in the field of agriculture and allied activites, mining and quarrying, processing and manufacturing, construction, commerce, trade, finance and insurance. The following table gives the investment inflows from some of the major countries. See Table No. 6: 10.
(2) India introduced the policy of disinvestment and withdrawing from public sector enterprise and giving boost to privatization. The following table indicates the effect of disinvestment policy.

TABLE 6.11

Disinvestment in Public Sector Undertakings

(Rs. in Crores)

Year	*Realization*	*Cumulative*
2000-2001	1,071	20,354
2001-2002	5,658	26,012
2002-2003	3,348	29,360
2003-2004	15,548	44,908
2004-2005	2,765	47,673

Statistical Outline of India, p. 124.

(3) Due to privatization a good number of employees were constrained to opt for voluntary retirement scheme (VRS). In the year 2003, there was reduction of 18505 lakh employees in public sector undertakings and 8421 lakh employees in Private Sector undertakings.

(4) Due to certain inconceivable reasons, a huge number of industrial units became sick or unfit to profitably operate. Industrial sickness has infested in almost all the industries including engineering, iron and steel, cotton and textiles, chemicals, sugar, jute textiles, rubber, cement and others. The following table shows the magnitude of industrial sickness.

TABLE 6.12
Magnitude of Industrial Sickness

End of Year	*Large Medium*	*Small*	*Total*
March 2001	3,317	2,49,630	2,52,947
March 2002	3,261	1,77,336	1,80,597
March 2003	3,396	1,67,980	1,71,376
March 2004	5,650	1,38,811	1,44,461
March 2005	5,658	1,38,041	1,43,699
March 2006	4,729	1,26,824	1,31,553
March 2007	3,992	1,14,132	1,18,124

Statistical Outline of India. p. 67.

TABLE 6.13
Industrial Sickness : Outstanding Bank Credit
(Rs. in Crores)

End of Year	*Large and Medium*	*Small*	*Total*
March 2001	21,270	4,506	25,776
March 2002	21,246	4,819	26,065
March 2003	29,110	5,706	34,816
March 2004	25,742	5,285	31,027
March 2005	36,635	5,380	42,015
March 2006	33,838	4,981	38,819
March 2007	25,066	5,267	30,333

Statistical Outline of India (2009-10), p. 67.

(5) Even after implementation of new economic policy, we could not be able to reduce the ratio of poverty line in our country. According to revised estimates for the year 2004-05. People living below poverty line :
at National Level : 37.2%
at Rural Level : 41.8%,
at Urban Level : 25.7%
(Statistical Outline of India, p. 229)

(6) In view of some of the economic indicators, it could be said that the policy of globalization, privatization and liberalization is not justifiable. If at all it is inevitable, it is necessary to minimize its adverse effects and utilize it for protecting our national intersts.

However, the WTO's insistence on child care, labour welfare modernization of industries, public health and sanitation and protection of environment etc. cannot be ignored.

It is generally argued that, the multinational companies operating in India are responsible for the drain of wealth, but they conveniently forget as to how many Indian capitalists have taken away their assets unauthorisedly to deposit in the foreign banks.

Even increasing defaulcators, fraudulent indebtors dishonest trustees of certain endowments, land grabbers and black markeers are also equally responsible for loss to Indian economy. We have to be alert of their wrong tactics and unfair practices and organize a strong mass movement to defy all of them and protect our national interests.

It seems that there is dearth of skillful, honest efficient and expert management. It seems that it is necessary to take into account what advocate Prakash Ambedkar had suggested. He said very rightly that there outght to be a separate Professional Industrial Management Cadre (like I.A.S. Cadre) to manage the industrial units so that they would be saved from becoming sick units.[32(a)]

6.9 Privatization and Constitutional Safeguards (Under 15(4) and 16(4) and 46 of the Constitution of India) :

(1) The right to education is a sine quo non of the human development. It has been recognized as a fundamental right under Article 21A and 29(2) of the Constitution. It has been recognized so with special reference to the Scheduled Castes, Scheduled Tribes and socially and educationally backward classes under Article 15(4) and 15(5) of the Constitution. It is an important right under Article 41, Article 45 and Article 46 of the Constitution.

In the post-independent period, the government of India formulated its national educational policy firstly in 1968, secondly in 1986 and thridly in 1992 and everytime assured to give quality education to all the students.

Althought there is no direct reference to educational field till now in the GATT/WTO, the spirit of globalization, liberalization and privatization has pierced into the education field also as a matter of Policy.

(a) So far as free and compulsory education to the children below fourteen years is concerned, the parliament made three important changes by the Constitution (86th) Amendment Act, 2002.

(i) Accordingly under Article 21A "The state shall provide free and compulsory education to all children of the age of six to fourteen years in such manner as the state may, by law, determine." The Article however forms a part of fundamental rights. Thus, it is the fundamental obligation of the state to provide free and compulsory education to all the children of the age group of 6 to 14 years.

(ii) It amended Article 45 which stands now as, "The state shall endeavour to provide childhood care and education for all children until they complete the age of six years."

(iii) Under the Fundamental Duties of the citizens, Clause 51A(K) has been added, which states that, "It shall be the duty of every citizen of India, who is a parent or guardian to provide opportunities for education to his child or, as the case may be, ward between the age of six and fourteen years." This article casts a fundamental duty on the parents or guardians of the children. Thus, the State as well as the parents are under obligation to take educational care of the children below fourteen years. The Central Government has made some effort to fulfil its obligation under Article 21A with regard to free education.

It has launched Sarva Shiksha Abhiyan (SSA) to implement the policy of free and compulsory education to the children below fourteen years from the year 2001-2002 for achieving the goal of universalisation of elementary education.

(b) The higher education including technical education, medical education and university education is under the concurrent list[33] and some institutions of national importance, institutions of scientific and technical education and promotion of special studies and research are under The Central list of the Constitution.[34] The matter of admission in the educational institutions is governed by Article 15(4) and (5) and Article 29(2) of the Constitution.

In a Landmark decision in Unni Krishnan V. State of A.P.[35] The Supreme Court pronounced that the right to education flows directly from right to life under Article 21 of the Constitution. However, the state would provide free and compulsory education to all children only upto 14 years under Article 21A of the Constitution.

It has been stated that the right to establish an educational institution and imparting education is not a commercial activity. Such activity can neither be a trade or business nor can it be a profession within the meaning of Article 19(1)(g). Trade or business normally connotes an activity carried on with a profit motive. Education has never been commerce in this country. However, the private educational institutions particularly medical and engineering shall be based on merit; but 50 per cent seats in all professional colleges be filled by candidates prepared to pay a higher fee. The court evolved a scheme in which 50 per cent of the seats, were called "payment seats." The allotment of seats would be based on the basis of inter-se merit and capacity to pay the fees. The appropriate authorities would decide the uniform fee structure. However, in T.M.A. Pai Foundation V. State of Karnataka (2003) some private educational institutions, aided and unaided, filed writ petition to challenge reservations in admission on the ground that those reservations would impede their rights to practice any profession; or occupation. The Supreme Court in the said case observed that, "Education has so far not been regarded as a trade or business where profit is the motive. Even if there is any doubt about whether education is a profession or not, it does appear that education will fall within the meaning of the expression 'occupation'. Article 19(1)(g) uses the four expressions so as to cover all activities of a citizen in respect of which income or profit is generated, and which can consequently be regulated under Article 19(6).[36]

The establishment and running of an educational institution where a large number of persons are employed as teachers or administrative staff, and an activity is carried on that results in the imparting of knowledge to the students, must necessarily be regarded as an occupation, even if there is no element of profit generation. It is difficult to comprehened that, per se, will not fall under any of the four expression in Article 19(1)(g). "Occupation would be an activity of a person undertaken as a means of livelihood or a mission in life."[37]

In this background the Parliament introduced Article 15(5) by the Constitution 93rd Amendment Act, 2005 to enable the state to make special provision for the advancement of the SC, ST and SEBC in relation to a specific subject viz. admission to educational institutions including private educational institutions, whether aided or unaided, with the only exception of the minority educational institutions.

Further, the Parliament has passed the Central Educational Institutions (Reservation in Admission) Act, 2006 (5 of 2007) and provided reservation upto 15% to the SCs, 7 1/2% to the STs and 27% to the OBCs in the Central Educational Institutions. Thus, the said constitutional amendment and the said Act have neutralized the effect of T.A. Pai Foundation decision and privatization in education by legally introducing the policy of reservation in aided and non-aided private educational institutions. In order to get invalidated the said act, the jurisdiction of the Supreme Court was invoked. Thereupon the Hon'ble Supreme Court held the 93rd Constitutional Amendment (2005) as valid and the said Act (5 of 2007) as valid and Constitutional.[38]

Thus the Constitutional provision of reservation in Public or Private educational institutions can not be challenged or withdrawn. So far as increased tuition fees and other fees are concerned, they are reimbursed or borne by the respective government for the backward class students studying in any 'recognized' institution.

We have to develop a suitable regulatory and administrative machnery to exercise control and supervision over the Public as well as private educational institutions and protect the large interests of the nation.

In pursuance of Article 21A the Parliament has passed. "The Right of children to free and compulsory education Act, 2009". It has provided for compulsory education to all the children from sixth and fourteen yeas of age, and it provided for 25% reservation to the disadvantaged classes.[39] It was also challenged in the Supreme Court on the ground of Constitutional validity. However, the Supreme upheld its validity on April 12, 2012 and directed the state to implement it with prospective effect.

(c) In view of the developing privatization in education field, it is necessary to insist on value based education. Our Constitution is the best compendium of social, economic and political values. Our Constitution imposes a duty on all of us to "develop the Scientific Temper, humanism and the spirit of inquiry and reform", our educational philosophy must be wedded to these principles in the real perspective.

Education is an instrument of social change. It is necessary to improve thinking and living standard, so that we may be able to bring about necessary positive changes in the society. Human development is based on quality education imparting modern and scientific education. Mere improving literacy rate is not of any avail.

We have to mobilize more resources for giving standard education. Our present proportion of Public expenditure on education in the GDP is around three percent only. Which needs to be at least doubled. Education ought to be easily accessible to all the persons without any economic hindrance.

(2) The policy of reservation has been made applicable to the Public Sector undertakings from 1964 itself. It is applicable to Autonomous Bodies from 1970 and to the voluntary agencies from 1974. However, it is not made applicable to the Private Sector so far. It ought to be applicable under Article 16(4) of the constitution.

(a) Our nation as a whole is constitutionally committed to social justice, equitable economic development and welfare of all the persons. How private industries or companies could be exception to that commitment ?

The private industries are not fully self-dependent and autonomous entities. They are dependent on financial assistance, requisite land, sufficient water, electricity, market facilities, security, skilled and quality labour, raw material, insurance, managerial and technical knowhow for their successful operations. All this is supplied by or with the positive intervention of the relevant government machinery. Therefore, private industries can not justifiably claim to be independent, private and autonomous. They are subjected to license rules, industrial laws and regulations, laws of taxation and duties. In the same way they would be equally subject to the policy of reservation as the public enterprizes.

(b) As per election manifesto (2004) the UPA Government came out with a proposal to extend reservations to the private sector. It constituted a Group of Ministers under the Chairmanship of Agriculture Minister Sharad Pawar and other Ministers with Meera Kumar, Minister of employment and social justice as the Convenor. The said Group of Ministers Tried to elicite the opinions of some industrialists on the said proposal. Among the industrialists Shri Ratan Tata of the Tata Group, and the Videocon Group responded positively, but others were against it.[40]

(c) According to a survey conducted by the Confederation of Indian Industry, the country's largest industry chamber, in respect of percentage of Scheduled Caste workers in the private industries there is "a sharp mismatch between SCs/STs as a percentage of the total workforce in the private sector and as a percentage of the state's total population."[41]

The following Table reflects the corporate employment for SC/STs has not been proportionate to their population.

TABLE 6.14

S.No.	State	Industry Rank	SC /ST in Industry	SC/St in Population	Gap
1.	Tamil Nadu	1	17.9	20	2.1
2.	Maharashtra	2	05	19.1	14.1
3.	Andhra Pradesh	3	17.1	22.8	5.7
4.	Gujarat	4	09	21.9	12.9
5.	Uttar Pradesh	5	17	21.2	4.2
6.	Punjab	6	21	28.9	7.9
7.	Karnataka	7	8.9	22.8	13.9
8.	Rajasthan	8	14	29.8	15.8
9.	West Bengal	9	20	28.5	8.5
10.	Kerala	10	14.2	10.94	3.26
11.	Haryana	11	19	19.3	0.3
12.	Madhya Pradesh	12	11	35.5	24.5
13.	Delhi	13	15	16.9	1.9
14.	Uttarakhand	17	22	20.9	1.1
15.	Himachal Pradesh	21	12	28.7	16.7
16.	Pondicherry	23	13.2	16.2	3

- Industrialization Rank based on Annual Survey of Industries, 2008-09.
- Share in percentage of Population, based on Census of India 2001.

Thus, Kerala followed by Uttarakhand, Haryana and Tamil Nadu, has the best representation of SC/STs in industry compared to proportion in population. The state of Madhya Pradesh has the largest gap between the representation of SC/STs in industry and their share in population.

(d) In this context, "Most of the industry spokesman have argued that reservation will ruin their competitive edge because of relaxation of merit as the sole criterion for selecting the work force. In other words, they argue that the dilution of merit in the name of reservation will impose a cost (in terms of lower labour productivity) on their industries, which may not be able to compete in the global markets. This is a genuine fear because our past experience in Public Sector Enterprises and even in government departments has shown that those who get secured jobs become indifferent to their duties and responsibilities. This is much more so among persons who enter government service under the reserved category. This allegation against the reserved category employees seems to be very much jaundiced; unfounded and premature.[42] On the other hand, a joint action committee of the federation of SC, ST and other backward castes employees union of states and central government met at Salem in Tamil Nadu on Jan. 31, 2005 and demanded reservations in the private sector as "a fundamental right".[43]

(e) The matter seems to be under consideration of the Union Government. It is however noteworthy that the Uttar Pradesh Government under the leadership of Mayavati has finally decided in August 2007 to implement the Policy of reservation in the private enterprise to the extent of 30% i.e. 10% for SC, 10% for OBC and minorities and 10% for backwards amongst the general category. The industries not responding positively to the said policy would not avail of any benefit or facility from the Government. Thus Uttar Pradesh has got a unique privilege of being the first state in India to extend the policy of reservation to the private sector.[44]

In this respect Prof. Sukhadeo Thorat states that, "In Industrial and Service Sector the discrimination in employment is possibly of high order in certain categories of jobs, if not all. Here is a need to use both categories of legal safeguards in terms of equal employment opportunity act and affirmative action identical to present reservation policy in public sector employment. The equal employment opportunity act will provide legal protection against discrimination in hiring and the reservation with certain fixed share in certain categories of jobs will ensure, fair participation of marginalized groups in industry / tertiary private sector employment. To bring transparency and to monitor the programme administrative mechanism, namely equal employment enforcement office on the pattern of USA and Northern Ireland will be necessary."

"In recent years the UN has also laid down certain provisions and norms for multi-national companies, particularly in employment, to follow in the countries of their location. The Global compact is provided for multi-national companies to observe the equal employment norms and follow the policy of non-discrimination. Indian Government could develop an understanding with multinational companies to follow positive policy on voluntary basis in their employment and other activities."[45]

6.10 Human Development

It is true that we have achieved progress to some extent in all the walks of life. However, we are lagging behind in terms of Human Development. Human development is "a process of widening people's choices as well as raising the level of well being achieved."[46] In order to know the socio-economic development of a country, it is necessary to take into account the reports being published annually by the United Nations Development Programme (UNDP). In the opinion of Misra and Puri, "the concept of human development is wider and richer than what can be caught in any index or set of indicators. However, such indexes are useful in focusing attention and simplifying problems. They have considerable political appeal. They have a stronger impact on the mind and draw public attention more powerfully than a long list of indicators combined with a qualitative discussion."[46(a)]

The Human Development Index generally depends on certain parameters. They are – (1) Life expectancy (2) Educational enrolment and literacy; and (3) Gross National Product. (GNP)

On the basis of these criteria, the UNDP Report for the year 2005 states that among 177 countries, India stands at 127th position.

(1) Life Expentancy

(1) In India life expectancy for 2005-06 was 63.9 for male and 66.9 for female.

(2) **Literacy Rate :** Literacy Rate as per 2001 census was 75.85% for male and 54.16% for female. However, overall general literacy was 65.38% only.

TABLE 6.15

Year	National Income and Per Capita Income (At Market Prices) in Crores			
	Gross National Product (GNP)	*Net National Product (NNP)*	*Per Capita*	
			GNP	*NNP*
2000-2001	20,79,581	18,77,764	20,408	18,428
2004-2005	32,16,849	28,95,620	29,539	26,590
2005-2006	36,80,357	33,10,626	33,276	29,933
2006-2007	42,54,201	38,29,286	38,916	34,129

Statistical Outline of India : 2009-2010, p.16.

(3) Gross National Income and Per Capita Income

According to a survey conducted by the National Sample Survey Oranization (NSSO) in the year 2005-2006, the average expenditure of every Indian in rural areas in a day was only Rs. 21. Every rural Indian was spending Rs. 521 per month, whereas every Urban Indian was spending Rs.1,171 per month.[47] See Table 6.15.

On the other hand there were 800 executives in our country whose income was more than Rs.8 lakh per month during 2009-10. There were some top corporate managers whose income was ranging from 15 crores to 37 crores per year.[48]

Out of 1,21,01,93,422 total population of India 9,30,55,983 persons were slum dwellers. Maharashtra ranking top and Uttar Pradesh was ranking second and Tamil Nadu was on third position.[49] Those people were, of course not getting Urban facilities.

The Test of an ideal economic system in the Indian context is whether it is able to increase the gross national product and make judicious and equitable distribution of the same among the people so as to Minimise social and economic inequalities in the society. Hence, we have to march towards that direction.

General Human Development Index can not be cited as an indicator of human development of the Scheduled Castes, Scheduled Tribes and other Backward Classes. It is appropriate to determine the Particular HDI in respect of all the respective classes referred to above. It is, therefore submitted that the HDI of all those classes living in different regions and different localities ought to be determined for the ready reference of the Policy Planners.

Conclusion

The Constitution of India is the Supreme Law of the Land; as such every rule, regulation, agreement or policy has to be in consonance with the broad Constitutional provisions. We have solemnly resolved to Constitute India into "a Sovereign, Socialist, Secular, Democratic Republic." We have also resolved to secure to all its citizens "justice, social, economic and political" among other things. We can not give up this basic philosophy at any cost. Therefore, it is necessary to remove inconsistencies, if any, between Privatization and Constitutional values for the well being and consolidation of our Republic. There can not be deprivation of fundamental human rights in the name of privatization at all. Therefore, it is necessary on the part of the Union Government and the States / Union Territary Governments to implement the policy of reservation in the expanding area of privatization.

In the process of globalization, there would be more and more competition among the nations for getting power and prestige in the international politics. They have to develop socially, economically and politically so as to be able to stand in the global competition. They can not afford to be weak and no nation aspire to be strong whose people are weak. Hence, it is necessary to bring 'empowerment' to the weaker sections of the people. Privatisation should not culminate into deprivation of certain constitutional benefits to the weaker sections of the society.

References

1. The Constitution 42nd Amendment Act, 1976.
2. Datt Ruddar and Sundaram : Indian Economy. p. 81. S. Chand and Company, Ram Nagar, New Delhi, (26th Edition, 1989).
3. Presently the number of Acts brought under Ninth Scheduled is 284.

3a. This article was repealed by the 44th Constitution Amendment Act, 1978.

4. AIR 1951, Patna 91.
5. AIR 1951, ALL. 674
6. AIR 1953, M.B. (Nagpur) 97.
7. AIR 1951, SC 458.
8. AIR 1954, SC 19
9. AIR 1954, SC 170.
10. While participating in the discussion on the said Amendment Act on 19th March 1955, Dr. Babasaheb Ambedkar, the then Minister of Law said very explicitly that, "we have said "compensastion to be given" and not "paid", so that it is open to the Government at the Centre as well as in the States to acquire property without actually paying componsation " (DBAWS Vol.15, p. 950 Govt. of Maharashtra 1997).
11. AIR 1860 SC 1080.
12. AIR 1962 SC 723.
13. AIR 1965 SC 845.
14. AIR 1970 SC 564.
15. AIR 1970 SC 564.
16. AIR 1971 SC 530.
17. AIR 1973 SC 1461.
18. Sharma B.R. Socio-Economic Justice under Indian Constitution. p. 327. Deep and Deep Publications, Rejouri Garden New Delhi. (1984).

19. AIR 1980 SC 1789.
20. Iyer V.R. Krishna, Sathe S.P. Review of the Constitution of India. p. 19. National Centre for Advocacy Studies Pune. (2000).
21. AIR 1975 SC 2465.
22. Agrawal A.N., Indian Economy P. Wishwa Prakashan, New Delhi. (20th Ed.1994).
22a. RCSCST (1980-81) p. 12.
22b. RCSCST (1979-80) p. 24.
23. Costa Benedict : India's Socialist Princes p. 73. Palyani Publishers, Ludhiana (1973).
24. RCSCST (29th Report) 1987-89. p. 52, 63.
25. Rudra datta and Sundaram : Indian Economy p. 440 (1989).
26. *Ibid*. p. 444.
26a. According to Bipan Chandra, Mukherjee and Mukherjee there were many exemptions like Tea, Coffee and Rubber / Plantations, Orchards, Dairy Farms, Sugar Cane Farms operaed by Sugar Factories, Land held by co-operatives etc. (India since Independence. (Penguin) 2008. p. 540).
27. Munagekar Bhalchandra : Bharatatil Arthik Sudharana Ani Dalit. p. 26. Sugava Prakashan, Pune, (2005).
28. *Ibid*. p. 48.
28a. RC SC ST (1979-80) p. 66.
28b. Gaikwad Pradeep : Samata Prakashan, Nagpur (2011). Magasvargiyanchya Vikas Yojana.
29. For details see Annual Report 2009-2010 Published by Ministry of Social Justice and Empowerment, Govt. of India. (pp. 58, 59, 60, 95 & 97).
30. Datta and Sundaram : *Ibid* p. 356.
31. *Ibid*. p. 596.
32. *The Time of India*, 17-6-1992 & 19-6-1992 (Mumbai.
32a. Gaikwad Ashok (Ed.) Ekach Disha Ekach Dheya. p. 40. Kaushalya Prakashan, Aurangabad (2004).
33. Entry No.25, List III. (Concurrent List).
34. Entry No.63, 64, 65 and 66; List 1, (Union List.)
35. AIR 1993 SC 2178.
36. AIR 2003 SC 533, 535.
37. *Ibid*. p. 535.
38. (2008) Vol. 6 Part 2, SCC p. 445.
39. Section 2(4) & Section of 12 of the Right of Children to free and compulsory education 2001.
40. It is learnt that 55 top private companies including Tata Motors, Godrej Industries, Crompton Greaves, Mahindra and Mahindra, Usha Martin, Tata Ryerson, Tata Steel etc. have decided to make Caste disclosures of their work force in their ensuing annual reports,

so as to facilitate to make reservations in their respective companies. (Indian Express, August 8, 2010)

41. Iyer P.Vaidyanathan. Article : Indian Express, 19-1-2011.
42. Article "Implications of Reservations in Private Sector." by G. Timmaiah : EPW Feb.19-25, 2005, P.749. (Vol. XL No. 8).
43. Article "Reservations and Casteism" by C.P. Bhambhri : EPW Feb. 26-March 4, 2005. (Vol. XL No. 9)
44. Samrat, dated 12-08-2007. (Mumbai)
45. Thorat Sukhadeo : Reservation Policy for Private Sector : why and how. pp. 27, 28 & 29.
    Sugava Prakashan, Sadashiv Peth, Pune (2004)
46. Misra and Puri. Indian Economy p. 28 (Quoted from UNDP Report 1997) Himalaya Pub. House Mumbai. (1983, 2006).

46a. *Ibid.* p. 29.

47. Daily Lokmat 1-2-2008 (Aurangabad).
48. Daily Lokmat 30-05-2011.
49. Indian Express, Mumbai, 19-07-2011.

7

Administrative, Monitoring and Evaluating Machinery

The matter of developmental work relating to all the deprived classes, including the Scheduled Castes, Scheduled Tribes and Other Backward Classes, however forms a major part of the administration. It includes policy formation, policy execution and policy evaluation. It is being done at various levels, and by various agencies of the Government. It is said that the work is judged by its success. It is self-evident fact that the present socio-economic condition of the backward classes is not satisfactory. Therefore, it is imperative to see whether the matter is being properly handled in its real perspective ? It is necesary to know as to what agencies are directly or indirectly involved in coordinatng, monitoring and evaluating various programmes being proposed by the Government and how they are working.

7.1 Ministry or Department

Afer the commencement of the Constitution of India, the Union Government had to shoulder the responsibility of welfare of the weaker sections of the society.

(a) At Union Level

(1) Firstly the ministry of Home Affairs was the nodal ministry for the implementation of various welfare measures in respect of the SC, ST and Backward Classes. From 18th November 1950 to 13th June 1964 the matter related to SC, ST and BCs was under the Ministry of Home Affairs in the Union Government.

(2) From 14th June 1964 to 6th February 1973, the matter was assigned to a newly created Department of Social Security and it was attached to the ministry of Law. In the year 1966, the said Department was reorgnised and renamed as Department of Social Welfare.
Later on, it was attached for some time to the Ministry of Planning, Ministry of Petroleum and Chemicals, Ministry of Law and Ministry of Education.

(3) From February 2, 1973 to 25th November, 1985, the said Department was again attached to the Ministry of Home Affairs. However, it was bifurcated into two divisions, one the Scheduled Castes and Backwards Castes Division, and other, the Tribal Development Division. However, the matters relating to reservation for SC and STs in services and posts in the Government of India and the Central Public undertakings or corporations was dealt with by the Ministry of Personnel and Training, Administrative Reforms and Public Grievances and Pensions.

(4) From 25th November 1985 to 19th March 1998, it was brought under a separate Ministry i.e. Ministry of Welfare by transferring subjects relating to SC, ST, Minorities and other Backward Classes from the Ministry of Home Affairs.

(5) In May 1998, the Ministry of Welfare was renamed as the Ministry of social Justice and Empowerment.

(6) Later, on 1st October 1999 the Tribal Development Division was moved out to form a separate Ministry of Tribal Affairs !

(7) In Jan. 2007, the Minorities Division was moved out of the Ministry of Social Justice and Empowerment and formed a separate Ministry of Minority Affairs.
Thus, the Ministry / Department in question had to make a pathetic journey. Sometime it was a Department, sometime it was a separate ministry. Sometime, it has got a Cabinet Minister. Sometime it was under the charge of State Minister. It was divided into SC/OBC Division and ST Division. Whether all these changes were based on any rational principle ?

(b) At State/U.T. Level

There exists in al most all the state Governments and Union Territory Administration, the Ministry in charge of SC/ST/ OBCs. It is ought to be taken into account that the Constitution especially provides under Article 164 to have a separate

Chart 7.1

(c) Organizational Setup of the Ministry of Social Justice And Empowerment

The Ministry of Social Justice and Empowerment is presently organized as shown in the following chart :

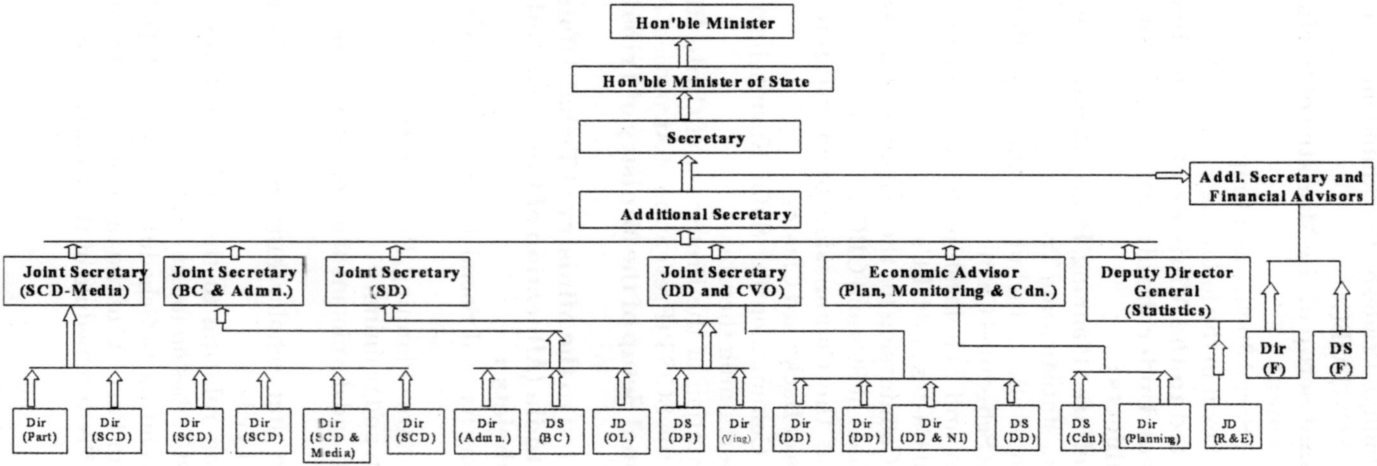

Admn.	- Administration	Parl.	- Parliament
BC	- Backward Class	REM	- Research, Evaluation & Monitoring
Cdn	- Coordination	SD	- Social Defence
CVO	- Chief Vigilance Officer	SCD	- Scheduled Castes Development
Dir	- Director	Vig.	- Vigilance
DP	- Drug Abuse Prevention		
DD	- Disability Development		
DS	- Deputy Secretary		
F	- Finance		
JD	- Joint Director		

Ministry in Madhya Pradesh, Jharkhand and Orissa for the Welfare of the SC/ST/OBCs.[2]

(c) Organizational Setup of the Ministry of Social Justice and Empowerment :

The Ministry of Social Justice and Empowerment is presently organized as shown in the following chart. (7:1)

(d) Work Allocated to the Ministry of Social Justice and Empowerment, Under the allocation of Business Rules: Relevant Subjects :

(1) **Social Welfare** : Planning, Project formulation, research, evaluation, statistics and Training.

(2) Promotion of efforts including voluntary efforts for the well being Scheduled Castes.

(3) Education and Scholarships to students belonging to Scheduled Castes and OBCs.

(4) National Commission for the Scheduled Castes.

(5) Development of SCs and OBCs.

(6) Reports of the Commission to investigate into the conditions of Backward Classes.

(7) National Commission for Safai Karmacharis and all matters pertaining thereto.

(8) Implementation of the Protection of Civil - Rights Act, 1955 and the SC/ST (Prevention of Atrocities) Act, 1989.

(e) Organizational Setup of the Ministry of Tribal Affairs : (7:2)

(f) Work Allocated to the Ministry of Tribal Affairs Under the Govt. of India (Allocation of Business) Rules, 1961 : Relevant Subejcts :

(1) Social Security and Social Insurance to the Scheduled Tribes.

(2) Tribal Welfare : Planning, Project formulation, research, evaluation and training.

(3) Promotion and development of voluntary efforts on Tribal Welfare.

(4) Education and Scholarships to students belonging to Scheduled Tribes.

(5) Legislation relating to the rights of forest dwelling Scheduled Tribes on forest lands.

(6) Matters relating to Scheduled Areas and Tribal Areas specified in Part "A" of the table appended to paragraph 20 of the Sixth Schedule of the Constitution and report thereon.

Chart 7.2
Organizational Setup of the Ministry of Tribal Affairs

The Ministry of Tribal Affairs is presently organised as shown in the Following Chart :

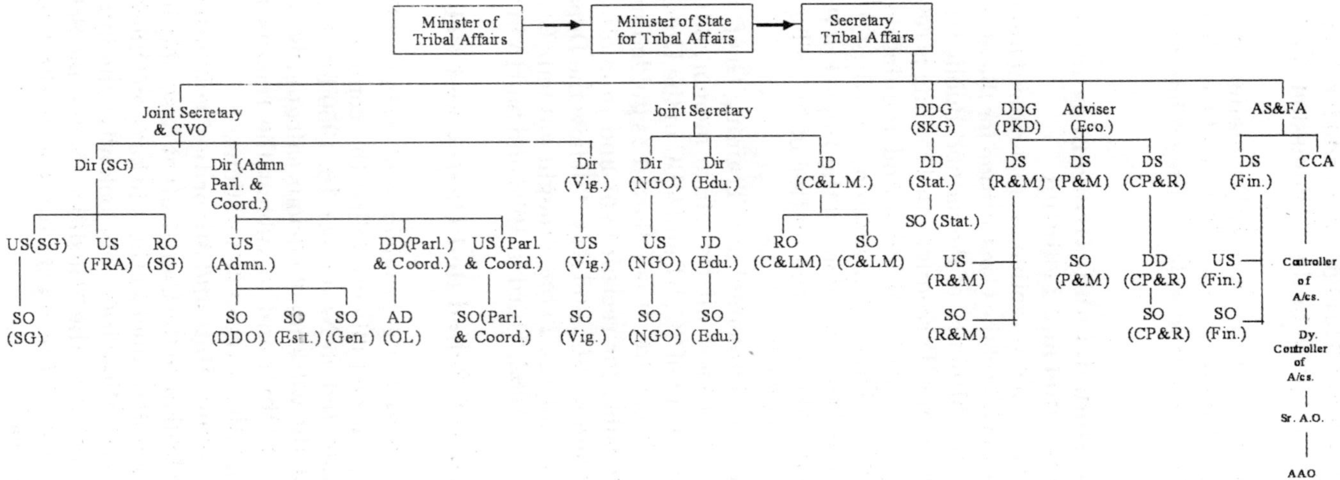

SG	: State Grants	Admn.	: Administration	AS&FA	: Addl. Secretary & Financial Adviser	Sr.AO	: Senior A/cs. Officer
Parl.& Coord.	: Parliament and Coordination	CP&R	: Cooperative Marketing and Regulation	CVO	: Chief Vigilance Officer	AAO	: Asst. Accounts Officer
NGO	: Non-Governmental Organisation	Edu.	: Education	DDG	: Deputy Director General	SO	: Section Officer
C&LM	: Constitutional & Legislative Matte-	FRA	: Forest Rights Act	CCA	: Chief Controller of Accounts	AD	: Asst. Director
P&M	: Plan & Miscellaneous	R&M	: Research & Media	Dir.	: Director		
Vig.	: Vigilance	Stat	: Statistics	DS	: Deputy Secretary		
Fin.	: Finance	Gen.	: General	JD	: Joint Director		
Estt.	: Establishment	OL	: Official Language	US	: Under Secretary		
				DD	: Dy. Director		

(7) Matters relating to autonomous districts of Assam excluding roads and bridge works and ferries thereon.
(8) The matter relating to the Commission for Scheduled Tribes.
(9) Implementation of the SC/ST (Prevention of Atrocities) Act,1989, excluding Administration of Criminal Justice, in regard to offences in so far as they relate to Scheduled Tribes.

7.2 Ministry of Personnel, Public Grievances and Pensions Department of Personnel and Training

So far as the matter of reservation in employment under Article 16(4) 16(4A), 16(4B) and 335 of the Constitution for the SCs, STs and OBCs is concerned, the Ministry of Personnel, Public Grievances and Pension, Department of Personnel and Training is responsible for providing suitable procedural rules and regulations to the appointing authorities. There is a section, called SCT Section (Scheduled Castes and Tribes Section) in the Depart of Personnel and Training, which looks after the matter of SC, ST and OBC reservation and recruitment.[2(a)]

The Department of Personnel and Training Govt. of India, makes compilation of al most all the office memorandums etc. relating to the appointment of SC, ST and OBC in the Union Public Services in a Special Brochure. It is followed as guide lines by all the authorities reponsible for recruitment and promotion of the backward classes including SCs and STs. Till now the Department of Personnel and Training (SCT) has brought out four Brochures, First in 1978, Second in 1982, Third in 1993 and fourth in 2011.

7.3 Commissioner for Scheduled Castes and Scheduled Tribes

(i) As per the then existing provisions of Article 338 of the Constitution, a special officer, called the commissioner for SC/ST was appointed on November 18, 1950 for monitoring and evaluating the working of various safeguards meant for the SC, ST and OBCs and to submit the reports there of annually alongwith his recommendations.[3]

In the memorandum "State and Minorities" submitted by Dr. Babasaheb Ambedkar to the Constitutent Assembly in March 1947, it was suggested, among others to have an Officer, called Superintendent of Minorities[3(a)] to look after the interests of the minorities including the Scheduled Castes and Scheduled Tribes and to submit the report thereon to the Union and State Legislatures.

The commissioner for SC/ST endevoured very hard and submitted his annual reports almost regularly alongwith his valuable recommendations to the President of India, through the concerned Ministry and the President laid those reports before the parliament for their consideration.

From 1951 to 1992 altogether 30 Reports were submitted to the President.

(ii) However, taking into account the magnitude of the task, the Parliament by its Resolution No.13013/9/77, SCT(1) dated July 21, 1978 Constituted a Commission consisting of the Chairman and four members in addiiton to the Commissioner for SC/STs w.e.f. 1.12.1978. The term of office of the commission was for three years. The powers and functions of the commission were broadly corresponding with the functions of the commissioner for SC/ST[4]. It worked till 1990.

(iii) Subsequently, the Parliament had passed the 65th Constitution Amendment Act, 1990, which provided for the National Commission for Scheduled Castes and Scheduled Tribes. This amendment came into operation on 12-3-1992. Accordingly the first National Commission consisting of seven members was appointed.

(iv) The National Commission for SC/STs however worked upto 2003. Later on, taking into account the complexity of the work, the Parliament has passed 89th Constitution Amendment Act, 2003 which came into operation on 19-2-2004. Accordingly, the National Commission for SC/ST was bifurcated into two – (1) National Commission for Scheduled Castes, (Under Article 338) of the Constitution and (2) National Commission for Scheduled Tribes, (Under Article 338 A) of the Constitution.

(a) National Commission for Scheduled Castes (Under Article 338 of the Constitution):

The National Commission for the Scheduled Castes consists of the Chairperson, Vice-Chairperson and three other members appointed by the President. The conditions of service and tenure of their office shall be such as the President may by rule decide.

The powers and functions of the National Commission are -

(1) to investigate and monitor all matters relating to the safeguards provided, under the Constitution or any other law for the time being in force, and to evaluate the working of such safeguards.

(2) to inquire into specific complaints of the Scheduled Castes.

(3) to participate and advise on the Planning Process of the socio-economic development of the Scheduled Castes.

(4) to present to the president annually reports upon the working of the safeguards.

(5) to make recommendations for the effective implementation of those safeguards to the Central and State Governments.

(6) the Commission for Scheduled Castes, while investigating any matter or any complaint shall have the Powers of the Civil Court.

(7) The Union and every State Government shall consult the Commission on all major Policy matters affecting Scheduled Castes.

(8) The President shall cause all such reports to be laid before each House of Parliament alongwith the memorandum explaining the action taken or proposed to be taken thereon.

(A-1) Regional Offices (NCSC) :

National Commission for SCs has 12 Regional Offices located at Agartala, Ahmedabad, Bangalore, Chandigarh, Chennai, Guwahati, Hyderabad, Kolkata, Lucknow, Patna, Pune and Thiruvananthapuram.

The duties of the State Offices of the Commission are :

(i) to act as the "eyes and ears" of the commission in the State(s) of their jurisidction.

(ii) to maintain effective interaction and liasion with State Government /UT Administration.

(iii) to conduct on the spot inquiries into cases of atrocities on Scheduled Castes.

(iv) to participate and advise in the planning process for socio-economic development as envisaged under clause 5 of Article 338 of the Constitution of India.

(v) to prepare and maintain a comprehensive and upto date data base of SC population, education, development in the State.

(B) National Commission for Scheduled Tribes :

The organization, powers and functions of the National Commission for Scheduled Tribes are laid down under Article 338(a) of the Constitution.

The Nation as Commission for Scheduled Tribes shall consist of a chairperson, Vice-Chairperson and three other members; and they shall be appointed by the President.

The powers and functions of the National Commissioner for ST are :

(1) to investigate and monitor all matters relating to the safeguards provided for the Scheduled Tribes under the

Constitution and any other law and evaluate the working of the safeguards.

(2) to inquire into specific complaints with respect to deprivation of rights and safeguards of the Scheduled Tribes.

(3) to participate and advise on the planning process of the socio-economic development of the Scheduled Tribes.

(4) to present to the President annually reports upon the working of the safeguards.

(5) to make recommendations for the effective implementation of those safeguards to the Central and State Governments.

(6) the commission for Scheduled Tribes, while investigating any matter or any complaint shall have the powers of the Civil-Court.

(7) the union and every State Government shall consult the commission on all major policy matters affecting the Scheduled Tribes.

(8) The Prsident shall cause all such reports to be laid before each house of Parliament alongwith the memorandum explaining the action taken or proposed to be taken thereon.

(B-1) Regional Offices (NCST) :

They are :

(1) Bhopal, M.P. Maharashtra, Karnataka, Kerala and Union Territories of Dadra Nagar Haveli, Lakshadweep.

(2) Bhubaneshwar, Andhra Pradesh, Tamil Nadu, West Bengal and Union Territories of Andaman, Nicobar and Pondicherry.

(3) Jaipur, Chandigarh, Gujarat, Haryana, Himachal Pradesh, J&K, Punjab Rajasthan, Uttaranchal, Daman and Diu.

(4) Raipur, Chhattisgarh.

(5) Ranchi, Bihar, Jharkhand, Uttar Pradesh.

(6) Shillong, Arunachal Pradesh, Manipur, Meghalaya, Mizoram, Nagaland, Sikkim and Tripura.

The duties of the Regional Offices of the Commission for ST are corresponding the duties of the Regional Offices of the Commission for SCs.

7.4 Liaison Officers and Special Cells

Officers of the rank of Deputy Secretary have been nominated by the Ministries and Departments to work as Liaison Officers who are in overall charge of the work relating to special representation in their respective Ministeries and attached and Sub-Ordinate Officers. They are responsible for ensuring that the instructions and guide lines in this behalf are strictly complied with.

It has also been made the special responsibility of Liaison Officers to conduct annual inspection of Rosters in the Offices under his charge. There is a small Special Cell within the Ministry / Department under the direct control of Liaison Officer. The duty of the Special Cell is to assist the liaison officer to discharge his duties effectively.

7.5 Nodal Officers

Under the Scheduled Castes and Scheduled Tribes (Prevention of atrocities) Rules, 1995, section 9, all the State Governments are required to appoint a Nodal Officer of the Level of Secretary to the State Government preferably belonging to SC/ST for co-ordinating the functioning of the District Magistrate, Superintendent of Police, Investigating Officers and other Officers responsible for implementation of the SC/ST Prevention of Atrocities Act, 1989. The Nodal Officer shall review (a) the reports received by the State Government under sub-rules (2) and (4) of rule 4 and Clause (XI) of rule 8. (b) the position of cases registered under the Act, (c) Law and order situation in the identified areas. (d) Relief to the victims (e) Reports from SC/ST Protection cell and NGOs. Moreover the Ministry of Justice has designated Divisional Heas as Nodal Officers for various States /UTs to inspect implementation of various Schemes of the Ministry and report, vide Office Order No.1-31/2008 dated 29-9-2009.[4(a)]

7.6 The Ministry of Housing and Urban Poverty Alleviation:

Safai Karamchari's are "engaged in or employed for, manually carrying human excreta or any Sanitational Work". Scavenging is an unclean traditional occupation exclusively of a section of untouchables.

With a view to studying the problem of the scavengers the Central Government appointed two committees, both under the Chairmanship of Mr. N.R. Malkani who studied the problem and recommended to convert dry latrines into water-borne latrines for liberating the scavengers from that ugly traditional occupation. The Commissioner for SC and ST has been harping upon this measure since a very long.

Consequently the Central Government had formed the National Commission for Safai Karmacharis for a certain period only. Presently the commission ceased to work as the matter of Sanitation is a state subject, but, in Pursuance of Clause (1) of Article 252 of the Constitution, the Parliament has passed "the Employment of Manual Scavengers and Construction of Dry Latrines (Prohibition)

Act, 1993, which came into force with effect from 26-1-1997 in 23 states and all union territories. Of remaining 5 states, Himachal Pradesh and Rajasthan have their own Acts, Manipur and Mizoram are scavenger free; only State of Jammu and Kashmir is yet to adopt it. It is noteworthy to state that the contravention of said Act is a criminal offence punishable with imprisonment upto one year or with fine upto Rs.2000/- or with both. The Act is being administered by the Ministry of Housing and Urban Poverty alleviation.[5]

7.7 National Commission for Backward Classes

The Parliament has passed the National Commission for Backward Classes Act, 1993 on 1-2-1993 on the background of acceptance of the Mandal Commission Report, in 1992. Accordingly the National Commission was appointed.

According to Section 3 of the Act, the Commission shall consist of five members, namely a Chairman who is or has been a Judge of the Supreme Court or of a High Court, a Social Scientist, two persons, who have special knowledge in matters relating to backward classes, and a member-secretary who is or has been an officer of the Central Government in the rank of a Secretary to the Government of India. Every member shall hold office for a term of three years from the date of he/she assumes office.

The powers and functions of the National Backward Class Commission are :

(1) to investigate the conditions of socially and educationally backward classes within the Territory of India. It is on the advice of the NCBC the Central Government makes changes in the central list of OBCs from time to time.

(2) to make recommendations as to the steps that should be taken by the Union or any State to improve their condition.

(3) to propose grants for improving their condition.

(4) the commission would submit the report to the president alongwith the recommendations.

(5) the president shall cause a copy of the report to be laid before each house of Parliament.[6]

7.8 National Planning Commission

At the national level Planning Commission was established in 1952 to formulate five year plans for achieving planned economic development. However, it is the extra constitutional and non-statutory body.[6(a)]

The Prime-Minister is the Chairman and other members include Union Ministers for finance and other experts in various fields relating to economics, finance, industry, social sciences etc. For looking after day to day work of the Planning Commission, there is Deputy Chairman at the Centre.

At the state level there is State Planning Board. The Chief-Minister is the Chairman and Ministers for finance and planning are members. Similarly a few Ministers and experts are members of the State Planning Board. At the Divisional Level, Divisional Commisioner and at the District Level the District Planning Committee are responsible to form Planning.

According to the guidelines of Government of India, certain proporation of the total Plan allocations is required to be earmarked and to be spent on the schemes of benefit of the Scheduled Castes and Scheduled Tribes through Scheduled Castes Sub-Plan and Tribal Sub-Plan.

7.9 Parliamentary Committee on Welfare of the SC and STs :

The motion regarding the formatiion of a Parliamentary Committee on the Welfare of the Scheduled Castes and Scheduled Tribes and the matter relating to them was passed in the Parliament in August 1968. Accordingly the Parliamentary Committee was formed with effect from December 18, 1968. The Committee consists of 31 members, 21 from the Lok Sabha and 10 from the Rajya Sabha.[7] The Committee has now been made a permanent standing committee of Parliament vide amended rules 331(a) and (b) of the Rules of proceedure and conduct of Business in Loksabha. The term of office of the Committee is of one year.

The functions of the Committee are :

(1) to consider reports submitted by the Commision for SC/STs.
(2) to report on the action taken by the Union Government on the measures proposed by the Commission and Committee.
(3) to examine the measures taken by the Union Government for secuirng due representation of the SC/Sts in service and posts.
(4) to study on the working of the Welfare Programmes for SC/STs; and
(5) to examine such other matter which is referred to it by the House or fit in the opinion of the Committee.

7.10 Comproller and Auditor General of India

According to Article 148 of the Constitution of India, the President makes the appointment of the Comptroller and Auditor General of India. He examines the annual accounts of the Union and the State Governments and ascertains whether the grants sanctioned for the particular purpose have been utilized according to rules and regulations.

It is his duty to submit to President, the reports relating to the accounts of the Union and the reports relating to the accounts of the states are submitted to the concerned Governor.

Thus, it is the duty of CAG to ensure that the funds alloted for a certain head are spent on that head of account only. If it is found contrary, he has to point out any inadequacy or irregularity in the accounts. Nobody has any authority to transfer certain amount from SCP or TSP head of account to any other account, otherwise this amounts to misappropriation of funds. Therefore, the CAG report assumes great importance.

7.11 Representatives of the Scheduled Castes and Scheduled Tribes :

In order the ensure a fair representation to the Scheduled Castes and the Scheduled Tribes in the decision making process of the Country the Constitution makes the provision of reservation of seats under Article 330 in respect of the House of people and under Article 332 in respect of the State Assemblies.

(1) So far as the reservation in the House of People is concerned, the Constitution provides under Article 330 as under -

(i) Seats shall be reserved in the House of the people for (a) the Scheduled Castes, (b) the Scheduled Tribes, except the Scheduled Tribes in the Tribal Area of Assam; and (c) the Scheduled Tribes in the autonomous districts of Assam.

(ii) The number of seats reserved in any state (or Union Territory) for the Scheduled Castes or the Scheduled Tribes under clause (1) shall bear, as nearly as may be, the same proportion to the total number of seas alloted to that state (or Union Territory) in the house of the people as the population of the Scheduled Castes in the State (or Union Territory) or of the Scheduled Tribes in the State (or Union Territory) or part of the State (or Union Territory), as the case may be, in respect of which seats are so reserved, bears to the total population of the state (or Union Territory). (3) Notwithstanding any thing contained in clause (2), the number of seats reserved in the House of the people for the Scheduled Tribes in the autonomous districts of Assam shall bear to the total number of seats alloted to that state a proportion not less than the proportion of the Scheduled Tribes in the said autonomous districts bears to the total population of the State."

TABLE 7.3
Reservation in Lok Sabha

S.No.	*State*	*Total*	*SC*	*ST*
1.	Andhra Pradesh	42	7	3
2.	Arunachal Pradesh	2	-	-
3.	Assam	14	1	2
4.	Bihar	40	6	-
5.	Chhattisgarh	11	1	4
6.	Goa	2	-	-
7.	Gujarat	26	2	4
8.	Haryana	10	2	-
9.	Himachal Pradesh	4	1	-
10.	Jammu & Kashmir	6	-	-
11.	Jharkhand	14	1	5
12.	Karnataka	28	5	2

(Table Contd.)

(Contd. Table 7.3)

S.No.	State	Total	SC	ST
13.	Kerala	20	2	-
14.	Madhya Pradesh	29	4	6
15.	Maharashtra	48	5	4
16.	Manipur	2	-	1
17.	Meghalaya	2	-	2
18.	Mizoram	1	-	1
19.	Nagaland	1	-	-
20.	Orissa	21	3	5
21.	Punjab	13	4	-
22.	Rajasthan	25	4	3
23.	Sikkim	1	-	-
24.	Tamil Nadu	39	7	-

(Table Contd.)

(Contd. Table 7.3)

S.No.	*State*	*Total*	*SC*	*ST*
25.	Tripura	2	-	1
26.	Uttarakhand	5	1	-
27.	Uttar Pradesh	80	17	-
28.	West Bengal	42	10	2
	Union Territories	**Total**	**SC**	**ST**
1.	Andaman Nicobar	1	-	-
2.	Chandigarh	1	-	-
3.	Dadra and Nagar Haveli	1	-	1
4.	Delhi	7	1	-
5.	Daman & Diu	1	-	-
6.	Lakshadweep	1	-	1
7.	Pondicherry	1	-	-
	Total : (+2 Anglo Indian)	**543**	**84**	**47**

Source :ECI.

TABLE 7.4
Reservation in Legislative Assemblies

S.No.	State	Total	SC	ST
1.	Andhra Pradesh	294	48	19
2.	Arunachal Pradesh	60	-	59
3.	Assam	126	8	16
4.	Bihar	243	38	2
5.	Chhattisgarh	90	10	29
6.	Goa	40	1	-
7.	Gujarat	182	13	27
8.	Haryana	90	17	-
9.	Himachal Pradesh	68	17	3
10.	Jammu & Kashmir	87	7	-
11.	Jharkhand	81	9	28

(Table Contd.)

(Contd. Table 7.4)

S.No.	*State*	*Total*	*SC*	*ST*
12.	Karnataka	224	36	15
13.	Kerala	140	14	2
14.	Madhya Pradesh	230	35	47
15.	Maharashtra	288	29	25
16.	Manipur	60	1	19
17.	Meghalaya	60	-	55
18.	Mizoram	40	-	39
19.	Nagaland	60	-	59
20.	Orissa	147	24	33*
21.	Punjab	117	34	-

(Table Contd.)

(Contd. Table 7.4)

S.No.	*State*	*Total*	*SC*	*ST*
22.	Rajasthan	200	34	25
23.	Sikkim	32	2	12
24.	Tamil Nadu	234	44	2
25.	Tripura	60	10	20
26.	Uttarakhand	70	13	2
27.	Uttar Pradesh	403	85	-
28.	West Bengal	294	68	16
	Union Territories	**Total**	**SC**	**ST**
1.	Delhi	70	12	-
2.	Pondicherry	30	5	-

Source : ECI.

The total number of SC/ST seats in the Lok Sabha (Under Article 330 of the Constitution) is as under -

(2) So far as the reservations in the state Assemblies are concerned, the Constitution under its Article 332 provides on the same line on which it provides in respect of the House of People.

Accordingly, the seats alloted to each State/Union Territory are as under. See Table 7:4 :

(3) There is provision of reservation of seats for the Scheduled Castes and Scheduled Tribes in the Panchayat and Municipalities in all the States. The Constitution under its Article 243(D) provides for reservation of seats in the membership as well as in the seats of Chairpersons at the Gram Panchayat, at the Block or Taluka level and at the District or Zilla Parishad Level. The number of seats are, however based on the proporation of SC/ST population in that particular unit of local panchayatiraj institutions to the total population of that area.

The Constitution under its Article 243T provides for reservation to the Scheduled Castes and Scheduled Tribes in the Nagar Panchayat, the Municipal Council and the Municipal Corporation at Membership level and even at Chairperson Level.

So far as the composition and the matters relating to the Panchayats and the Municipalities are concerned, the State Government would decide by Law.

(4) It should be borne in mind that there is a provision of Time Limit to the political reservations under Article 334 of the Constitution. Our Govt. is extending the original limit of ten years at its end for further ten years. The said Article has been further amended vide the Constitution 109th Amendment Act 2009. Accordingly, the amended Article provides reservation for SC/ST for a period of 70 years from the Commencement of the Constitution.

(5) There is provision of representation of the Scheduled Castes and Scheduled Tribes in the decision making process from local to national level bodies. It is, naturally their prime duty and responsibility to protect and promote the interests of the community which they are honourably representing. They are expected to be more active, more vocal and more assertive in protecting the interests of the more vulnerable community. They have that much strength and capacity to exert their influence very effectively and deter the men in Politics and administration by their knowledge, wisdom, strategy and intelligence. Presently, there are 84 SC + 47 ST = 131 seats

in the apex decision making body. They may bring about a miraculous change in the life of the most exploited classes in India, provided they come together on a common plotform, at least occasionally for the purpose of protecting the interests of their own brethren. They have, of course exemplified their courage and commitment to rise against their party discipline on several occasions for the cause of Dalits. They have to continue that spirit. They are expected to represent the interests of Dalits to the Government, and not the interests of Government to the Dalits.

7.12 The National Human Rights Commission : (NHRC)

The National Human Rights Commission has been Constituted under section 3(1) of the protection of Human Rights Act, 1993.

(a) The Commission consists of :

(i) a chairperson who has been the Chief Justice of the Supreme Court.
(ii) one member who is or has been, a Judge of the Supreme Court.
(iii) one member who is or has been the Chief Justice of a High Court.
(iv) two members to be appointed from amongst persons having experience in the matters relating to human rights.
(v) the chairperson of the National Commission for minorities.
(vi) the chairperson of the National Commission for the SC/ST.
(viii) the National Commission for Women.
(ix) the Secretary General.

(b) The Powers and Functions of the Commission are :

(i) to inquire, sue motu or on a petition presented to it by a victim or any person on his behalf, into complaint of (a) violation of human rights or abatement thereof; or (b) negligence in the prevention of such violation by a public servant.
(ii) to intervene in any proceeding involving allegation of violation of human rights pending before a court.
(iii) to visit any jail or institution to study the living conditions of the inmates and make recommendations thereon.
(iv) to review the safeguards for the protection of human rights.
(v) to review the factors or acts of Terrorism.

(vi) to study treaties and other international instruments and make recommendations for their effective implementation.
(vii) to promote research in the field of human rights.
(viii) to spread human rights literacy among various sections of society.
(ix) to encourage the efforts of non-governmental organization working in the field of human rights.
(x) the commision shall have all the powers of a civil court.
(xi) the commission shall submit an annual report to the Central Government.

The State Governments also may constitute the state human rights commissions to exercise the powers on the lines of the national level commission.

The distinguishing feature of National Commission for Human Rights is it has got "Suo Motu" power to inquire into any matter of human rights violation or intervene in any proceeding involving allegation of violation of human rights pending in any court in the country.

Another important thing is, according to Article 2(d) of the Protection of Human Rights Act, 1993, "Human Rights" means the rights relating to life, liberty, equality and dignity of the individual guaranteed by the Constitution or embodied in the International Covenants and enforceable by Courts in India." According to Article 2(f), "International Covenants" means the International Covenant on Civil and Political Rights and the International Covenant on Economic, Social and Cultural Rights adopted by the General Assembly of the United Nations on 16th December 1966." The Government of India has to respect those human rights and implement them.

7.13 United Nation's High Commissioner for Human Rights (UN HC HR) and Other Organs

On the background of Second World War (1939-1945) the United Nations Organization was founded by Nations of the World in 1945 for the promotion of international Peace and Security. India is a member state of the United Nations organization. The Constitution of India, under its Article 51(c) states that, "the state shall endeavour to foster respect for international law and treaty organizations in the dealings of organized people with one another." Accordingly, India had approved the Universal Declaration on Human Rights (1948); which has recognized the "inherent dignity and the equal and inalienable rights of the individuals."

(a) High Commissioner for Human Rights :

Economic and Social Council, one of the principal organ of the United Nations, empowered under Article 68 of the UN Charter appointed a Commissioner for Human Rights, which was approved by the General Assembly of the UNO on December 20, 1993. The High Commissioner is appointed by the Secretary General for a term of four years. He shall be a person of high moral standing, integrity and experience in the human righs field. His Office is at Geneva in Switzerland. Jose Ayala Lasso of Ecuader became the first High Commissioner in Feb.1994.[8]

The High Commissioner is responsible for promoting, co-ordinating and protecting human rights in the World. He advises the Secretary - General on the matter of human righs. The High Commissioner is assisted by the Deputy High Commissioner.

(b) The Human Rights Council :

Previously the Economic and Social Council appointed a Commission on Human Rights in 1947. However, the General Assembly, empowered under the Resolation passed on March 15, 2006, established the Human Rights Council in place of the Commission.[9] The Human rights Council shall consist of 47 members elected by the General Assembly. Their tenure is for three years. It performs the following functions :

(a) It shall serve as a forum for discussion on all human rights problems.
(b) It shall make recommendations to the General Assembly for necessary action.
(c) It shall undertake universal periodic review of the fulfilment by each state of its obligations.
(d) It shall work in close co-operation in the field of human rights with the respective Governments.
(e) The Council shall submit its annual reports to the General Assembly.

(c) Human Rights Committee :

In order to give a legal base to the Universal Declaration of Human Rights, the General Assembly adopted 'Inter national Covenant on Civil and Political Rights" in 1966. The covenant has declared certain important civil and political rights to all the world people.

The Human rights Committee was established in 1976 as per part IV of the International Covenant on Civil Political Rights. It consists of 18 members elected by states parties for a term of four years.

In order to achieve the purposes of the International Covennat on Civil and Political Rights the General Assembly of the UNO has adopted 'Optional Protocol to the International Covenant on Civil and Political Rights' on December 16, 1966. However, it came into operation on March 23, 1976.

Accordingly, the Human Rights Committee is authorised to receive and consider the communications from individuals against violation of his rights by the state party. However, "no communication shall be received by the Committee if it concerns a state party to the covenant which is not a party to the present Protocol."[10] Moreover, "individuals who claim that any of their rights enumerated in the Covenant have been violated and who have exhausted all available domestic remedies may submit a written communication to the committee for consideration."[11] The members of the Committee are appointed in their personal capacity.

India submitted its first report on July 4, 1984. The second report was submitted on July 12, 1989. The third report was submitted on November 29, 1995.[11(a)]

The Human Rights Committee studies the Reports submitted by states parties on measures adopted by them to give effect to the rights recognized under the covenant and makes suggestions to the states parties.

(d) **Economic, Social and Cultural Rights Committee :** This Committee on Economic, Social and Cultural Rights was established in 1985 to monitor, the implementation of the International Covenant on Economic, Social and Cultural Rights adopted by the General Assembly. The Committee consists of 18 experts elected by the Economic and Social Council. The members of the said committee serve in their personal capacity. It considers the reports submitted by states parties and submits its report to the Economic and Social Council.

(e) It should be borne in mind that, India has ratified both the covenants. They are (1) International Covenant on Economic, Social and Cultural Righs and (2) International Covenant on Civil and Political Rights on 10th April 1979; subject to 'declaration'.

(1) The Government of India declared that, the words "The right to self-determination" appearing in those covenants apply only to the peoples under foreign dominations and that these words do not apply to sovereign independent states.

(2) Article 9 of the International Covenant on civil and political rights should be applied so as to be in cosonance with the provisions of Clauses (3) to (7) of Article 22 of the Constitution of India. The Parliament may by law prescribe the circumstances under which a person may be detained.

(3) With respect to Article 13 of the International Covenant on Civil and Political Rights, the government of the Republic of India reserves its right to apply its law relating to foreigners.

(4) The provisions of individual liberty could be so applied to be in conformity with the provision of Article 19 of the Constitution of India.

(5) "With reference to Article 7(c) of the International Covenant on Economic, Social and Cultural Rights, the Government of the Republic of India declares that the provisions of the said Article shall be so applied as to be in Confority with the provisions of Article 16(4) of the Constitution of India."[12]

Thus, the individuals who are subject to the jurisdiction of the states parties who have ratified the protocol only may submit their complaints to the Human Rights Committee. The fact is India has not ratified the optional protocol to International Covenant on Civil and Political Rights so far. 'The reusult is,' as Justice A. Varadarajan observed that 'no individual can complain to the Human Rights Committee against any violation in India of any right protected by the Treaty of the United Nations."[13]

However, it should be noted that, India has ratified the Civil and Political Covenant as such it is under obligation to submit periodic reports to the Secretary General of the UNO, who shall transmit them to the committee for consideration on the measures taken for protecting those rights.[14] (Covenant Art. 40)

(f) The Committee on International Convention on the Elimination of All Forms of Racial Discrimination, 1965: (CERD)

According to Article 2 of the Universal Declaration of Human Rights (1948) "Every one is entitled to all the rights and freedom set forth in this Declaration, without distinction of any kind, such as race, colour, sex, language, religion, political or other opinion, national or social origin, property, birth or other status."

In pursuance of this priciple of the UNO, the General Assembly has adopted the International Convention on the

Elimination of All Forms of Racial Discrimination. The Convention came into force on January 4, 1969.

The Convention defines the term 'racial discrimination' under its Article 1. It is as under :

(1) In this convention, the terms, 'racial discrimination' shall mean any distinction, exclusion, restriction or preference based on race, colour, descent, or national or ethnic origin which has the purpose or effect of nullifying or impairing the recognition, enjoyment or exercise, on an equal footing of human rights and fundamental freedoms in the political, economic, social, cultural or any other field of public life.'

The International Convention on the Elimination of all forms of Racial Discrimination (CERD) had duly considered the Reports submitted by states party i.e. India in its meetings held on 23rd and 26th February 2007. The convention in its 1809 th meeting held on 6 March 2007, adopted the concluding observations in respect of India and reportedly conveyed to submit etc. periodic report on its implementation of the recommendations within one year of the adoption of committee's observations.

The observation of the committee contained in Para 8 of its Report dated 19th March 2007 is worth consideration.

"The Committee takes note of the State Party's position that discrimination based on caste falls outside the scope of article 1 of the convention. However, after an extensive exchange of views with the state party, the committee maintains its position expressed in General Recommendation No. 29" that discrimination based on 'descent' includes discrimination against members of communities based on forms of social stratification such as Caste and analongous systems of inherited status which nullify or impair their equal enjoyment of human rights (2002) Therefore, the Committee reaffirm that discrimination based on the ground of Caste is fully covered by article 1 of the Convention."[15]

The Committee further observed that, "the Committee invites it to include in its next periodic report detailed information on measures taken to implement anti-discrimination and affirmative action legislation, disaggregated by Caste, Tribe, gender, State/District and rural/urban population. The state party should also provide disaggregated data on the percentages of the union, state and district budgets allocated for that purpose and on the effects of such measures on the enjoyment by members of Scheduled Castes and Scheduled and other Tribes of the rights guaranteed by the Convention."[16]

This indicates that the committee on the Elimination of Racial Discrimination has taken due cognizance of the problem of the Scheduled Castes and the Scheduled Tribes, shown its concern over the matter and advised India to take necessary action to bring equality in the Society.[17]

Conclusion

Thus, there is a vast machinery involved in the administration, monitoring and evaluation of the measures undertaken for safeguarding the interests of the Scheduled Castes and Scheduled Tribes in India. However, they are not fully benefitted of the Law and the Law implementing machinery. Therefore, it is necessary to think as to why they are still vulnerable. The socially and nationally conscious people are expected to think over the matter seriously and find out the solution in the light of constitutional objective and relevant provisions.

References

1. Presently, Kumari Shelaja, Cabinet Minister and P. Balaram Naik, Minister of State are holding the charge of 'Ministry of Social Justice and Empowerment. The Ministry of Tribal Welfare is with V. Kishore Chandra Dev, Cabinet Minister and Rani Nara, Minister of State (28-10-2012).
2. Substituted by the Constitution 94th Amendment Act, 2006.

2a. V. Narayan Swamy, State Minister is holding the charge of the Ministry of Personnel, Pubic Grievances and Training (from 28-10-2012).

3. L.M. Shrikant was appointed first commissioner for SC/STs and Vimal Chandra was appointed Assistant Commissioner for SC/STs.

   There were five Regional Offices headed by the Assistant Commissioners : They were as under :

Sr. No.	*Region*	*HQ*	*Name of Officer*	*Date of Appt.*
1.	Bihar & Orissa	Ranchi	K.K. Leuva (SC)	1-7-1953
2.	W. Bengal, Manipur and Tripura, Assam	Calcutta	B.K. Bhandary	--
3.	Bombay, Rajasthan and Ajmer	Baroda	P.C. Dave	14-8-1953

(Table Contd.)

(Contd. Table)

Sr. No.	*Region*	*HQ*	*Name of Officer*	*Date of Appt.*
4.	Madhya Pradesh, Madhya Bharat, Bhopal and Vindhya Pradesh.	Nagpur	R.S. Chaudhari (S.C.)	15-9-1953
5.	Southern Region	Madras	O.K. Moorti	19-12-1953

(RCSCST (1953) p. 3)

3(a) DBAWS, Vol. 1, p. 398.

4. Chairman of the first SC/ST Commission was Shri Bhola Paswan Shastri (M.P. Rajya Sabha). Other members were Shri Shishirkumar, Shri A. Jayaraman, Shri T.S. Negi and Shri S.K. Mallick, Shri R.P. Khanna joined as Secretary.

4(a) Report 2009-10 p. 193, Ministry of Justice, Govt. of India.

5. For details see Annual Report (2009-2010) Published by the Ministry of Social Justice and Empowerment; Govt. of India. (Part 1, p. 47)

6. For details see Annual Report (2009-2010) by the Ministry of Social Justice and Empowerment, Govt. of India.Part 1, p. 89.

6(a) Basu D.D. Introduction to the Constitution of India. p. 329. Prentice-Hall of India. (1997).

7. Report of the Ministry of Social Justice (2009-2010, p. 215)

8. Agarwal H.O. International Law and Human Rights, p. 728. Central Law Publications, Allahabad (2008).

9. *Ibid*. p. 725, 726.

10. Article 1 of the Optional Protocol to the International Covenant on Civil and Political Rights (1966)

11. Article 2. (*Ibid*).

11(a) For details see A.G. Nooranis Article Human Rights : Indian Record. Frontline April 10, 2009.

12. Rao Rega Surya : Lecrtures on Human Rights and International Law. p. 367, 368. Asia Law House, Hyderabad (2006).

13. Justice Varadarajan A. in the forward to Dr. Y.N. Kly's International Law and the Dalits in India." Dalit Liberation Education Trust, Madras (1989).

14. Article 40 of the International Covenant on Civil and Political Rights. (1966).

15. CERD/C/IND/CO/19 March 2007.

16. *Ibid*.

17. For Previous CERD Observations dated 17-9-1996 and the Human Rights Committee Observations dated 04-08-1997, See the Homage, Published by Ambedkar Centre for Justice and Peace India, Tushar, 19 Rtd., Khar Mumbai (2006) Edited by Mr.Yogesh Varhade. (37)

8

Observations

It is, obviously true that the Constitution of India has pledged to Secure Justice, Social, economic and Political to all the Indian citizens, including the Scheduled Castes, Scheduled Tribes and Other Backward Classes of the society. So far as those weaker sections of the society are concerned, the Constitution has specifically endowed with a new identity as human beings which was hitherto unreasonably denied to them. In order to enable them to promote their socio-economic condition and to lead a life of self-respect, the Constitution has provided certain special safeguards to them. However, they could not achieve the expected results even after a long period of commencement of the Constitution.

What is the cause of their overall miserable condition is a question which has to be addressed. There is an adequate legal and institutional infrastructure at the Union and State Level. However, the Weaker Sections of the society are not availing justice. It could be reasonably inferred that it is only because of Lack of strong political and administrative will to implement the Constitutional and statutory provisions in letter and spirit, the weaker sections are not availing justice.

We have already discussed as to how the provision of reservation is a fundamental right and how it is mandatory to implement it. We have concluded that the illconceived theory of merit and efficiency is caste based and falacious. The Constitution of India is a supreme, value based and dynamic document. It is the personification of the will and wisdom of the people of India. Hence we have to put it into action in the benefit of the people as a whole. Everybody is fully entitled to avail of justice. We have concluded that denial of justice on any overt or covert clumsy ground is a perpetual harm to the body politic.

According to Justice V.R. Krishna Iyer "our Constitution has cognised the value of representative bureaucracy in its stress on reservation and other special facilities for the Scheduled Castes and Scheduled Tribes and, to an extent, the backward classes.

Confidence and contentment of the community in the Administration can not be secured unless the minorities and the weaker sigments - the real consumers of social justice - are represented in the Executive, Legislative and Judicative branches".[1]

Presently, the sword of uncertainty is hanging over the heads of Dalits. If the right of reservation is not construed in its real perspective as a fundamental right, there would not be any remedy in the event of its withdrawl from the statute. If on the ground of merit and efficiency, the backward classes are alleged to be unfit and deprived of their legitimate share in the administration, the young geenration of Dalits would be frustrated and demoralized to a great extent. If the Constitution is wrongly reviewed in such a way in which the special safeguards are no more provided for the Weaker Sections, how would they cope up with the adverse socio-economic situation and how would they be able to secure justice. If some of them are excluded form the Schedule or Sub-Categorised on some ulterior motive, their movement of liberation from the bondage of Brahmanism and Capitalism will lose its vigour. If on the pretext of globalization, liberalization and Privatization, Legitimate reservations are denied, the exploited classes would not be able to honourably survive. Therefore, a new approach has to be evolved and a new thought has to be given to this complicated and acute problem.

It is not a matter pertaining to a particular caste or community. This matter ought not to be viewed with a narrow parochial and communal point of view. The matter of upliftment of the weaker sections and bringing them to the main stream is a matter relating to the unity and integrity of the nation. No nation can be strong whose people are suffering from primary wants, who are deprived of education, emplyment, health care and due share in governance of their own country. We can not afford to keep them in their acute backwardness and ignorance. In the words of Justice Nasirullah Beg," just as the strength of a chain depends upon the strength of its weakest link so also the strength of a nation depends upon its weakest section."[2] Hence the weakest section has to be empowered for the overall empowerment of the nation. Thus, backwardness of a caste or community is not only their problem, but it is a national problem.

The policy of reservation or affirmative action is not a full proof solution on the problem of the weaker sections. Due to inherent apathetic attitude of the so called high caste officials the policy of reservation is not properly implemented. However, whatsoever may be its weaknesses, it is must, as there is no alternative to reservation. While making objective evaluation of the policy of reservation, Dr. B.D. Sharma, the ex-commissioner for SC/STs states that "some members of the Scheduled Castes and Scheduled Tribes are also able to acquire some positions particularly in the segment comprising Government Service, through the policy of positive discrimination. These successes, even though small, create a climate of hope, however faint it may be for every one. There is a feeling that sooner or later and if nothing else at least the next generation will make the grade. It is this combination of success and hope that which help in providing stability to the present system notwithstanding its intrinsic inequality."[3]

Although there is no alternative to the reservation policy, there is a dire need of additional measures for the overall improvement of the weaker sections of the society. We must bring in other supportive tools like implementation of the land reforms Act, anti-untouchability and anti-atrocities Act, encouragement to inter-caste and inter-sub-caste marriages, pre-matric and post-matric Scholarships and hostel facilities, proper provision and implementation of Scheduled Caste Sub-Plan (SCSP) and Scheduled Tribes Sub-Plan (TSP), legal aid and health care programme and Labour Laws etc. etc.

It is submitted that, taking into account the needs of the increasing population and the needs of the workforce for various purposes, the number of educational institutions including technical and management institutions of national importance ought to be increased. This, of course needs formulation of proper manpower planning on the part of the concerned authorities, so as to minimize mounting pressure on such institutions. In the field of employment also proper manpower planning has to be made. It is also necessary to see that no department, institution or industry would either indulge in reduction of its manpower capacity or keeping the posts vacant for no genuine reason.

It seems that there are numerous rules and regulations in respect of reservations. Besides, there are certain precedents, or judicial interpretations, some time contradictory and confusing. It is, therefore submitted that there ought to be a comprehensive legislation dealing with all the aspects of reservations in the educational institutions, public and private, aided and unaided. It is also submitted that there ought to be a comprehensive law relating to public and private services so as to avoid growing complexities of rules and regulations and judicial interpretations. It is true that some of the state Governments have made rules and regulations regarding reservations in educational institutions and public services. It is necessary to see whether they are based on some approved common policy and central laws. Some of the State Governments have not passed appropriate laws in respect of such an important matter. Hence, they are expected, in the interest of justice, to take necessary action expeditiously.

It has been observed that the so called high castes, feudal lords and elites in the society are deadly against the Constitutional safeguards being given to the socially and educationally backward classes. It seems, prima facie that the casteist people do not want their immediate lower classes or intermediatory classes should catch them up and come to their level.

It seems that the casteist people do not want entry of the backward classes and SC/STs in the super speciality courses and administrative and managerial positions. There seems to be much more litigation against reservations in promotion or consequential seniority. They probably think that a lower class employee should remain in lower cadre for ever.

The caste prejudices, especially against the backward classes are deeply rooted in the minds of the so called high caste people, caste is a blot on the society; which needs to be uprooted at the earliest possible.

While giving clarifications on the implementation of Mandal Commission Report in the Rajya Sabha on 9th August, 1990 the then Prime Minister Shri V.P. Singh said very rightly that, "Destinies of nations are not changed by enactments. Destinies of nations are changed when the social forces come forward, and demand a change in the system and that is the essence of change."[4] Thus, it is imperative on the part of the people to come forward and launch a strong movement for bringing about a just social order based on Justice in the real perspective.

The matter of welfare of the weaker sections of the society evidently comes under the jurisdiction of the Union Government. The Ministry of social justice and empowerment, Government of India deals inter-alia, with the socio-economic development of the Scheduled Castes and Other Backward Classes. The Ministry of Tribal Affairs, Govt. of India deals with the socio-economic development of the Scheduled Tribes. The matter of reservation in employment is dealt with by the Ministry of Personnel and training.

The Ministry of finance has to make necessary financial allocation for the SCSP and TSP. Thus all the departments are co-jointly responsible for the upliftment of the weaker sections.

There is a provision for evaluation of the working of various Constitutional Safeguards. The Constitution under its Article 338, Article 338(A) and Article 340 respectively provides for the appointment of the Commission for the Scheduled Castes, Scheduled Tribes and the Commission for the Backward Classes. They are expected, inter alia to investigate into all matters relating to the safeguards, to evaluate the working of such safeguards and to make recommendations for their effective implementation and to present the annual report to the President of India. It is however expected from them to be more active, efficient and effective in discharging their Constitutional duties.

It is submitted that the Denotified Tribes and Nomadic Tribes, being most vulnerable groups be considered to be Treated on par with the Scheduled Tribes so that they may be able to get benefit under the constitutional safeguards. However, there should not be any change in other beneficiary lists without genuine reason. No one should be allowed to usurp any undue benefit under the Constitution. We must avail of benefit under the Constitution only for bringing about social justice.

Undoubtedly our country suffers from acute social inequality and economic inequality. Some of the people suffer from a unique practice of untouchability. There is no 'endosmosis' among the castes and communities. In such a adverse situation we had adopted a sovereign socialist secular democratic Republic based on justice, liberty, equality and fraternity and it is in continuation with all hopes and ambitions, we are making this diversified country a nation and the process of nation making is going on with great zeal. Social inquality and economic inequality are the most formidable stumblic blocks in our way. We have accepted the planning process as a strategy to deal with socio-economic development in our country. We have been spending a huge amount on our planning process. However, we could not achieve the estimated success in it. Due to some of the dishonest and corrupt men in power and in post, we are not able to avail of the benefits of the five year plans as well as the political system that we have adopted. We are a great Republic, bu the unjust and corrupt feudal lords are on its helm. All these ills are deeply rooted in our traditional social system.

We must remember in the interest of the nation as a whole what Dr.Babasaheb Ambedkar, the Hon'ble Chairman of the Drafting committee of the Constitution of India has very categorically said while presenting the Constitution to the Constitudent Assembly on 25th Nov.1949. He said, "we must begin by acknowledging the fact that there is complete absence of two things in Indian society. One of these is equality. On the social plane we have in India a society based on the principle of graded inequality which means elevation for some and degradation for others. On the economic plane, we have a society in which there are some who have immense wealth as against many who live in abject poverty. On the 26th of January 1950, we are going to enter into a life of contradictions. In politics we will have equality and in social and economic life, we will have inequality. In politics we will be recognizing the principle of one man one vote and one vote one value. In our social and economic life, we shall by reason of our social and economic structure, continue to deny the principle of one man one value. How long shall we continue to live this life of contradictions ? How long shall we continue to deny equality in social and economic life ? If we continue to deny it for long, we will do so only by putting our political democracy in peril. We must remove this contradiction at the earliest possible moment or else those who suffer from inequality will blow up the structure of political democracy which this Assembly has so labouriously built up."[5]

References

1. Ayer V.R. Krishna (J) Some Half-Hidden Aspects of Indian Social Justice. p. 71. Eastern Book Co. Lucknow, (1980).
2. Beg Nasirullah J. Rights of Minorities under the Indian Constitution, p. 21.
3. RC SC ST (1987-89) p. 10.
4. Mandal Commission Report : Prime - Minister's Statement (1990) Govt of India Publication, New Delhi.
5. DBAWS (1994) 13 : p. 1210.

Bibliography

Agarwal H.O. International Law and Human Rights, Central Law Publications, Allahabad (2008).

Ahmad Aijaz : Nationalism and Globalization, Deptt. of Sociology, University of Pune, Pune (2000).

Ambedkar Prakash : Bahujan Chalwal, Kaushalya Pub., Aurangabad (2003).

Austin Granville : Indian Constitution, Oxford University Press, New Delhi (2006).

Awasthi & Kataria : The Protection of Human Rights, Orient Pub., New Delhi (2011).

Balkrishnan R. : Globalization and the changing Role for the State: An Indian View.

Beg Nasirullha J. : Rights of Minorities under the Indian Constitution. Buddha Vihar, Lucknow (1976).

Bhosale Narayan : Jat Panchayat : Taichi Prakashan, Pune (2008).

Biswas Swapan K. : Constitution Review : Tulsiram : C-39/Z-3, Block, Dilshad Garden, Delhi-95 (2000).

Bindra Ausu : Feminism and Womens Rights, Mangalam Pub. Delhi (2011).

Borkar V.V. - Kurulkar R.P. : Post-Graduate Employment Experience of Weaker Castes, Dr. Babasaheb Ambedkar Marathwada University, Aurangabad (1981).

Borale P.T. Segregation and Desegregations. Manak Tala & Sons, Bombay, 1968.

Bramhe Sulabha : Gatt Karar : Anupam Park, Pune (2000).

Chalam K.S. Globalization and the Future of Dalits : Mumbai (2004).

Choudhry and Naqui : Commentary on the SC and ST (Prevention of Atrocities Act, 1989, Orient Pub.Company, Allahabad (2011).

Chavan B.V. *Vodar Samaj. Sulochana Ramnath : Bhatakya Vimukanche Antarang*. Sugava Prakashan, Pune (1989)

Costa Benedict : India's Socialist Princes : (1973) Kalyani Publishers, Ludhiana (1973).

Das Bhagwan : Testimony. Bheem Patrika Pub. Jalandhar 1983.

Datt Ruddar and Sundaram : Indian Economy. S. Chand and Co.Ram Nagar, New Delhi (26th 1989).

Desai A.R. Social Background of Indian Nationalism. Popular Prakashan, Mumbai (1989).

Devare Shravan : *Maratha Samjache OBC Karan*, Sugava Pub; Pune (2008).

Chandra Bipan, Mukherjee Mridula and Mukherjee Aditya : Indian Since Independence, Penguin Books, New Delhi (2008).

Gail Omvedit (Ed) : Land Caste and Politics in Indian States, Deptt. of Pol. Sc., University of Delhi (1982).

Galanter Marc : Competing Equalities, Oxford University Press, Delhi (1984).

Gavai R.S. The Caste War over Reservations, Maharashtra State Republican Party, Untkhana Nagpur-1981.

IAN Brownlie/Guys : Goodwin Basic Documents on Human Rights Oxford University Press, New Delhi (2002).

Iyer V.R. Krishna : Sathe S.P. Review of the Constitution of India National Centre for Advocacy Studies, Pune (2000).

Jain M.P.O. Outlines of Indian Legal and Constitutional History, Wadhwa, Nagpur (2006).

Joshi Nayan : Law relating to Human Rights, Kamal Pub. New Delhi (2009).

Kagzi Mangal Chandra Jain : Segregation and Untouchability Abolition, Metropolitan Book Co., Netaji Subhash Marg, New Delhi (1976).

Kamble Narayan, Balande Vyankat and Shinde Sanjay (Ed.) : *Arakshan, Satye Viparyas* Chinmaya Prakashan, Jijamata Colony, Paithan Gate, Aurangabad (2008)

Kamble Uttam : *Jagatikaran Ani Dalitanche Prashna Sugava* Pub. Pune (2002).

Kamble N.D. Roots of Poverty in India, Social Research Institute, Aurangabad (1981).

Kamble Uttam : *OBC Rajkaran Lokvangmaya*, Mumbai (2008)

Khan Masood Ali : Violence and Minorities, Deptt. of Sociology, University of Pune, 1999.

Kharat Shankarro : *Asprushyancha, Muktisangram*, Indrayani Sahitye Prakashan, Shanivar Peth, Pune (2004).

Kly Y.N. International Law and the Dalits in India, Dalit Liberation Edu. Trust Madras (1989)

Kshirsagar R.K. Untouchability in India : Implementation the Law and Abolition, Deep and Deep Publications, Rajouri Garden, New Delhi (1986).

Kunhaman M : Economic Development and Social Change, University of Kerala, Trivandrum (1990).

Mungekar Bhalchandra : *Bharatatil Arthik Sudharana Ani Dalit,* Sugava Pub., Pune (2005).

Pande J.N. : Constitutional Law of India, Central Law Agency, Allahabad (2000).

Pande V.K.(Dr.) *Gatt Ani Bharat,* G.B. Shroff Samiti, Aurangabad, 1995.

Rao Rega Surya. Lect on Human Rights and International Law. Asia Law House, Hyderabad (2006).

Rao M.B. & Guru Manjula : WTO and International Trade, Vikash Publishing House Pvt. Ltd. : Masjid Rtd., Jangpura, New Delhi. (IInd: 1998-2007).

Ram Sita : Dr. B.R. Ambedkar as Constitution Maker, Current Pub., Agra (2010).

Roy Ajit : Political Power in India.

Rawls John : A Theory of Justice : Universal Law Pub. Company Delhi 2000.

Naya Prakash, 206, Bidhan Sarani, Culcatta (1981).

Shabbir Mohammad (Ed) : Human Rights in the 21st Century.

Sandanshiv D.N. : Reflections on the Counter Revolution in Marathwada (1978).

Sen Amartya : The Idea of Justice : Penguine Books, New Delhi 2010.

Shetty Rajshekhar V.T. : Dalit movement in Karnataka : The Christian Literature Society, Madras : (1978).

Sharma G.S. : Legislation and Cases on Untouchability and Scheduled Castes in India. Allied Publishers, 15 Graham Road, Ballard Estate, Bombay (1975).

Suman Manju : Dalit Mahilayen : Samyak Prakashan, New Delhi (2004).

Teltumbde Anand : Globalization and the Dalits, Sanket Prakashan, Shivaji Nagar, Nagpur (2001).

Teltumbde Anand : Ambedkar and Dalit Movement, Sugava Prakashan Pune (1997).

Thorat Sukhade : Reservation Policy for Private Sector : why and how, Sugava Pub.Pune (2004).

Thorat Sukhadeo, Aryama, Negi : Reservation and Private Sector. Indian Institute of Dalit Studies, New Delhi (2005).

Urade S.K. : Justice Vs. Injustice, Sanket Prakashan, Shivaji Nagar, Nagpur (1997).

Upare Hanumant : Mi OBC Boltoya. Bahujan Sahitye Prasar Kendra, Nagpur.

Veeramani K : The History of the struggle for social and communal justice in Tamil Nadu, The Dravidar Kazhazam Publications, Madras.

DBAWS Vol. 13, Govt. of Maharashtra, Statistical Outline of India (1999-2000).

Tata Services Ltd. 1999 Mumbai.

Supreme Court Cases : 2008 Vol. 6. Part I and II. Eastern Book Company, 34, Lalbagh, Lucknow : (2008).

The Protection of Human Rights Act, 1993.

The SC and ST Act, 1989 - the Ambedkarite Law Network : 2008, Mumbai.

Backward Class Commissions Report, Part I and II 1980. Govt. of India, New Delhi.

National Commission for SC and STs. Fourth Report. Govt. of India.

Wadhwa K.K. : Minority Safeguards in India; Constitutional Provisions and their Implementation, Thomson Press, India. (1975).

Long-suffering Brothers and Sisters, Unite! Buraku Liberation Research Institute, Osaka, Japan (1981).

Waghmare Janardan : The quest for Black Identity. Sugava Prakashan, Pune (2002).

Zelliot Eleanor : From Untouchable to Dalit, Manohar Publishers, Ansari Road, Daryaganj, New Delhi (1996).

Index

N

O

P

Q

R

S

T